One World or Many?

The impact of globalisation on mission

Edited by Richard Tiplady

William Carey Library
Pasadena, California

Technical editor: Susan Peterson
Cover: Jeff Northway

© 2003
World Evangelical Alliance
Missions Commission

Published by:
William Carey Library
P.O. Box 40129
Pasadena, CA 91114
626-720-8210

For information about other resources available from William Carey Library, visit our web site: www.WCLBooks.com.

ISBN 0-87808-451-7

Printed in the United States of America

Contents

Foreword

This book is a sign of hope and a promise of what a carefully planned experience of global dialogue may mean for the future of evangelical mission work and missiological reflection. Most of the authors are persons I have met around the world—women and men who represent a wide diversity of ethnic and cultural backgrounds and at the same time demonstrate a basic commitment to an evangelical stance. The authors are rooted in local churches, theological seminaries, universities, and mission projects in places as far apart as La Paz in Bolivia, Manchester in England, Manila in the Philippines, Uganda in Africa, and Seattle on the Pacific coast of the United States. This diversity explains the rich variety of styles, sources, and examples in their writing about globalization as the new context of mission in the world today. However, at the same time, you will find a common thread of commitment to biblical truth and a passion for its communication and application.

Under the Anglo-Saxon aegis, first of Great Britain and later of the United States, the last two centuries of evangelical missions have been characterized by a pragmatist approach to the understanding of the social and political context of their action. If empires and socio-economic systems allow us to "do our thing," then why should we care about analyzing our actions and finding out how our way of doing mission reflects more the values of those systems than those of the gospel? If they allow us to "do our thing" because we happen to be among those that benefit from them, why so much fuss about those that are their victims? This kind of blind pragmatism is not admissible anymore. One of the evangelical missiological trends after Lausanne 1974 posed forcefully the need for evangelists and missionaries to become aware of how their culture shaped not only their missionary methodologies, but also their versions of the gospel, in ways that were in open contrast with biblical teaching and theological conviction.

Pragmatists who champion the idea that mission is merely a matter of feeding our computers with data about needs and resources and then matching them through processes of management by objectives continue to refuse the self-analysis that would open their eyes to flagrant contradictions between their theology and their practice. They think that self-analysis is a sin of "armchair theoreticians."

The authors of this book show why a critical understanding of the context of mission, in both sending and receiving cultures, is indispensable for those practitioners who are engaged in missionary action and who at the same time want to be faithful to the Lord Jesus Christ as he is revealed in Scripture.

This book also shows that critical analysis may not fatally end fostering paralysis. One of the dangers of consultations and congresses that are committed to critical thinking is that they may become, in the end, just a periodic recitation of anti-system rhetoric. In theological language, their analysis may become simply a ritual exercise without redeeming consequences. In addition to their critique, these authors try to understand also the positive side of globalization from the perspective of Christian mission. I perceive in their contributions to this book, besides a critical approach to globalization, a willingness to work for reforms, to try new ways, and to find inspiration, ways of expression, and suggestions for different practices in cultural sources different from those of the evangelical canon. The dream of a uniform global evangelicalism that is a carbon copy of the mood, shape, and language of its Anglo-Saxon and European models has to be abandoned. As time goes on, nuances and variances will be apparent in the contextual expressions of evangelicalism around the globe. The continued dialogue and mutual encouragement of these forms of evangelicalism will be required for the challenges that postmodern globalization will present to the mission task in the years to come.

The Theological Commission and the Missions Commission of the World Evangelical Alliance are to be commended for their patient and persistent efforts to keep this dialogue going, in spite of all kinds of difficulties. Their work contributes to the credibility of evangelical mission at this point in history. It is my hope that this book will generate dialogue and debate that will carry on a theological agenda that an attentive reader may find outlined in these pages. For instance, it is necessary to continue probing into the depths of the New Testament teaching in its unity and variety, in order to develop through a global conversation a contemporary ecclesiology that will provide light and a language for the paradigm changes required at this point. Sociologists of religion such as Donald Miller in the United States are telling us that Protestantism has to be redefined in this new century because of the missional paradigm changes suggested by the development of post-denominational churches. Evangelicals must make a contribution to this redefinition on the basis of their global dialogue.

Besides analysis of social and economic processes in this book, there are also references to many people whose lives and experiences are vivid examples of how globalization affects individual persons. The frame for these stories is the fact that during 20 centuries, the gospel of Jesus Christ has continued to move on, according to God's design, by the power of the Holy Spirit. As we read the New Testament, we perceive how that frame of God's design is the most decisive factor, although the pages of Acts, the Gospels, and the Epistles provide us also with a vivid picture of what the Pax Romana was in the first century. This helpful analysis of the Pax Americana in the 21st century has a wider frame than the movement of globalization. That frame is the conviction that God's work will be accomplished through globalization and in spite of it. Soli Deo Gloria.

— *Samuel Escobar*
Valencia, Spain
March 2003

Listing the
usual suspects

Bill Taylor of World Evangelical Alliance Missions Commission provided more support and help than anyone could reasonably ask or expect. He's a true friend and an "older brother" who gave me an opportunity to contribute to the global missionary movement, and I hope that this book justifies his trust. Rose Dowsett leads the Missions Commission Global Missiology Task Force. Her advice and gentle guidance, as well as her sacrificial attendance for four days at our Chicago meetings in March 2002, at the end of a month-long trip away from home, have been of inestimable value. Much of the planning for this book was done while I worked as a director of Global Connections (UK), and Stanley Davies deserves thanks and appreciation for the financial contribution that made this possible, but much more for his friendship and guidance over six years of a working partnership that was second to none.

I knew some of the people who wrote for this book before we got together in the Globalisation Working Group. Others I got to know as we worked together. We began as colleagues but finished (I hope) as friends. Thanks to them for a stimulating and exciting time as we grappled with trying to define and understand one of the biggest issues of our time. Globalisation is in danger of being a theory of everything, a multiheaded hydra that won't lie down. I think we managed to chop off the main heads.

Most of all, my love and appreciation go to my wife, Irene, and son, Jamie, without whom life would be shallow and empty. They are the ones who do without their husband and father, while I swan off around the world, doing things like producing this book. Their contribution to this book is as important as anyone else's.

— Richard Tiplady

Introduction

RICHARD TIPLADY

> *"Globalisation has, with just reason, become a dirty word. Still, it's important to distinguish between the multinational might that force-feeds the world Kylie and Britney, and the healthy cross-pollination of the global village."*

In two short sentences, music journalist Neil Spencer (2002) sums up the different understandings of globalisation that underpin this book. On the one hand, globalisation is a dirty word. Memories of the protests and riots at the World Trade Organisation meetings in Seattle in 1999 and at the G8 summit in Genoa in 2001 conjure in our minds a sense that globalisation is just another word for empire. Western corporations are taking over the commercial and cultural spheres just as effectively as did the empires of previous centuries, and Western music and clothing styles are becoming a global norm. On the other hand, globalisation allows singers and musicians such as Colombia's Shakira, India's Midival Punditz, and Senegal's Labi Siffre to reach previously unreached Western audiences.

OK, so this is not a book about music. It is a book about globalisation and world mission. But we should nail a couple of myths right at the start:

1. Globalisation is not the same as Westernisation.
2. Globalisation is not just about economics.

True, it includes both of these things. But it also includes much more. So what do we mean by "globalisation"? It's a word that is thrown around easily, a code-word for the state of the world today, a cypher for contemporary trends. Those who have written chapters in this book were asked to think of globalisation in the following terms:

***Globalisation* refers to increasing global interconnectedness, so that events and developments in one part of the world are affected by, have to take account of, and also influence, in turn, other parts of the world. It also refers to an increasing sense of a single global whole.**

This global, interconnected whole manifests itself in many different areas of human life. We are probably most familiar with it in terms of economics. Global trading arrangements, negotiated through GATT and its successor the WTO, shape the financial destiny of every nation. It is not just mission that is "from everywhere to everywhere"— so is the distribution of products to the markets of the world. The financial capital markets move billions of dollars around the world each day, not because they are paying for anything that might be called "real" goods, but simply to take advantage of marginal differences in interest and currency exchange rates. National and regional governments court large foreign corporations, hoping through tax breaks and other incentives to attract their capital and their factories, along with the jobs and income that accompany them. We are also familiar with globalisation in political terms. The United Nations is (sometimes) seen as a suitable debating chamber for the world's nations to reach mutually acceptable decisions and to govern their actions. But the impact of globalisation is also evident in many other areas of human life—in the huge, unstoppable migrations of humanity around the globe; in the ubiquity of global brands such as Nike, McDonald's, and Coca-Cola; in the global reach of the media; and in the far-reaching impact of technological developments such as the Internet and mobile (cell) phones.

Right Here, Right Now

So globalisation includes a lot of things. But how has this single, interconnected world arisen?

The Beginnings of Globalisation

Estimates of when globalisation started vary. Some suggest it has been developing since the dawn of history, as human societies first learned to trade and exchange both goods and ideas. Others argue that it is closely tied to the emergence of capitalism and the modern era. A further contention is that it is much more recent than that, and that globalisation is a characteristic of a post-industrial era—a phenomenon of disorganised and highly mobile capital. But whichever may be the case, all arguments accept that there has been a sudden acceleration in globalisation in recent years.

continued on page 3

continued from page 2

Why the acceleration? Probably because of a variety of factors. Technological developments have created the opportunity. Travel is not quite instantaneous yet, but I can be anywhere in the world within 24 hours of writing these words. The words themselves can be anywhere in the world in seconds, thanks to email and the Internet. Economic factors have taken advantage of the possibilities provided by technology. Corporations have expanded into new and emerging markets and have shifted production around the world, in the cause of increased profits and a higher share price. Politically, the collapse of Communism in Eastern Europe and the Soviet Union in the late 1980s and early 1990s signalled the end of the bipolar worldview created by the Cold War and allowed the emerging multidirectional "new world order" to become more visible. Some have suggested that we have moved from the Berlin Wall to a No Walls world, although I'm not sure it is as simple as that. Overall, we can say that there is no one single driver of globalisation. Rather, it is the outcome of a combination of factors working together to produce this new sense of global interconnectedness.

Some would dispute whether it is that new. The so-called "world" religions of Christianity, Islam, Hinduism, and Buddhism linked together major regions of the world in the early Middle Ages and before, creating civilisations far larger than most of today's nation states. The European empires of the "high" colonial period of 1880–1920 oversaw a massive amount of global trade that declined considerably during the first half of the 20th century, the era of Depression and protectionism. But medieval civilisations like Christendom knew very little of what was going on elsewhere in the world, and the 19th century colonial empires were controlled and dominated by European nation-states. We should draw a distinction between "internationalisation," which includes mechanisms to facilitate communication and cooperation between nation-states (which remain dominant), and "globalisation," wherein the nation-states are but one group of "players" in the world, alongside transnational corporations, financial capital markets, free-trade areas and agreements, transnational political entities such as the United Nations and the European Union, and the many informal and less-visible networks of global connectedness that shape our lives.

— Richard Tiplady (in press)

One World or Many?

The book's title reflects a key question with regard to globalisation. As I have already noted, it is often assumed that globalisation is simply the latest form of Western or (even worse?) American domination by another name. This is held to be the case whether we are talking about economic or cultural domination.

Such domination is undoubtedly an aspect of globalisation. Several of the chapters in this book make this point very effectively. But what makes globalisation more than just a handy synonym for Westernisation is that it includes other things as well. Globalisation is about global interconnectedness, not global Americanness. It includes the global anti-capitalist protest movements that oppose economic globalisation, not just the transnational corporations and Western governments that are trying to take advantage of the economic ties.

The now-famous term "Jihad vs. McWorld" symbolises part of this reality. The spread of Western values and culture is not welcome in many parts of the world, and local cultural resources are drawn on to resist the perceived intrusion of foreign ways of thinking and behaviour. This can be manifested in religious fundamentalisms of various sorts (just as Christian fundamentalism attempted to resist an encroaching modernity in earlier generations). Ethnic identities can also be reinvigorated as suitable means of resistance.

But the situation is more complex than the simple "either/or" suggested by the term "Jihad vs. McWorld." Globalisation is not a one-way street, running from the West to the Rest. An interconnected world allows ideas and products from every part of the world to reach every other part of the world. And when they get to their new destination, ideas are not imbibed wholesale. They are adapted to fit the local situation. This phenomenon has been termed "glocalisation." The excerpt below expands on the concept further.

Baltis and Bollywood, Pokémon and Panasonic, Feng Shui and Falun Gong

As well as localising reactions, the idea that we are seeing the emergence of a bland, uniform, commercial culture based on Western ideas is further undermined by the observation that other cultures are also using the processes of globalisation to expand their reach. Non-Westernisation is as much a feature of globalisation as Westernisation is.

For example, the most popular meal ordered in restaurants in the UK is the Chicken Tikka Masala. Balti, a Pakistani curry, is also a favorite. The popularity of Indian food in the UK is shown by the existence of the "Curry Mile" in Manchester and similar large groups of restaurants in cities around the UK. The Chinese takeaway is ubiquitous. *continued on page 5*

continued from page 4

This movement and adaptation of food styles is not new. Consider that symbol of quintessential Englishness, the cup of tea. Tea, of course, is not grown in Britain but came from China and India (where the British began farming it in 1835 to break the Chinese monopoly, so it's not that Indian either). Maybe in the future a curry will be called an "English," not an "Indian"?

The Indian film industry, Bollywood, is not only bigger than Hollywood, but it has plans for global expansion, as shown by the success of recent films like "Monsoon Wedding" and the Oscar-nominated "Lagaan." Ang Lee's film "Crouching Tiger, Hidden Dragon" was a massive international hit, despite being a Chinese language film with subtitles. Chinese cultural influence on the West can be seen in the popularity of "feng shui"[1] in interior and garden design, and the interest shown in the persecuted Falun Gong religious movement. Even Hollywood itself, the ultimate visual purveyor of the American Dream, shows signs of sharing in this re-shuffle of cultural influence, as some of its biggest studios are now foreign-owned, such as Sony (Japanese) and Vivendi Universal (French).

Pokémon, a cartoon whose rise to global domination of children's imaginations in 1999–2001 was spearheaded by a yellow, electric-shock-inducing mouse called Pikachu, is Japanese in style and origin from start to finish. Movies, computer games, trading cards, and figurines tumbled over one another in a marketing blitzkrieg that swept children's allowances and parents' credit cards before it. Japanese goods also dominate the home-entertainment market, and their cars are produced and bought worldwide.

Glocalisation describes the way in which ideas and structures that circulate globally are adapted and changed by local realities. So while Wal-Mart sells Heinz and Del Monte products in its stores worldwide, it also pays close attention to local tastes. The Wal-Mart store in Shenzen, China, for example, sells chicken feet, Ma-Ling brand stewed pork ribs, and Gulong brand pickled lettuce. About 85% of the products come from 14,000 Chinese suppliers (Newsweek, 2002, p. 46).

McDonald's, that supposed pioneer of homogenised consumption, shows similar approaches to its local marketing. One finds numerous examples of adaptation to local tastes, such as the McBurrito in Mexico, McLlahua sauce in Bolivia (a local chili sauce found on every meal table), beer on sale in French McDonald's restaurants, and the Maharaja Mac in India (a vegetarian version of the Big Mac for a country where beef or pork consumption is risky to say the least). *continued on page 6*

---

[1] There is no truth in the claim that "feng shui" is Chinese for "Tidy your room!"

continued from page 5

McDonald's recognises that it is viewed by many as an example of American cultural and economic imperialism, and it asserts in response that it is instead a confederation of locally owned companies. It even ran adverts in France that poked fun at Americans and their food choices, emphasising that its food was made in France, by French suppliers, using French products (New York Times, 2001). Even when the American identity of McDonald's is undeniable, it produces reactions that reinforce local identities. When McDonald's first entered the Philippines, Filipino hamburger chains responded by marketing their products on the basis of local taste (whereas they had previously promoted them on the basis of their Americanness) (Waters, 2001, p. 226).

Now global corporations like Wal-Mart and McDonald's don't adapt to local preferences because of a philosophical commitment to global diversity. They do so because they have discovered that local tastes are not easily changed or homogenised, but instead show considerable resilience in the face of "global" flows of ideas and products. So it is possible to conclude that "neither global processes nor modernisation are expressions of a Westernisation that removes cultural differences.... localisation is an essential feature of global processes and modernisation" and that what we see are "multiple manifestations of global forces operating in local worlds" (Finnström, 1997).

— Richard Tiplady (in press)

Many Voices

This book aims to embody the principles of global missiology. Different writers from different parts of the world are included. If globalisation includes the whole world, then by definition any Christian response to globalisation has to include voices from different parts of that world. This book is not perfect in this regard. Too many still remain disenfranchised, without a voice. But it is offered as our best attempt. I hope that you will forgive any shortcomings.

There are not just different cultural perspectives on globalisation; there are different theological perspectives too. Different writers within this book have different opinions about the nature of globalisation and its ethical and missiological implications. We have not harmonised these views but include them within the book as testimony to these divergences. As the one who led the World Evangelical Alliance Missions Commission Working Group that looked at the issue of globalisation and mission and who edited the various chapters, I would say that my view of globalisation is probably more sanguine than some of those represented here. Both their voices and those that incline more to my own views need to be heard and understood.

This diversity of views might trouble some who believe that there must be a single "biblical" response to globalisation. Our discussions as a group showed us that there are different theological themes that can be applied to our subject. Perhaps our pre-existing theological perspectives have shaped our view of cultural and historical trends. Perhaps our pre-existing cultural preferences have shaped the theological themes we wish to emphasise. Perhaps both factors are involved. The outcome is that within this book you will find different views expressed. These views are passionately held, but they are motivated throughout by a desire to be true to the Bible and to honour God and his intention for his creation. You will probably find yourself nodding in agreement with those whose sentiments coincide with your own. Try to spend some time engaging with those whose views don't sit so easily with your own.

If you come from a tradition that is suspicious of or hostile to "the world," that sees all historical trends as manifestations of the "spirit of the age," or that views globalisation as neocolonialism (and all empires as "Babylon"), then you're going to have a hard time seeing anything good in globalisation. You will probably concentrate on the negative aspects of globalisation (of which there are many, as this book illustrates), and you will view globalisation as something to be resisted. This will be especially true for those who equate globalisation with Western domination. Likewise, those of you who see globalisation as something that God is doing to make world evangelisation easier probably need to curb your enthusiasm a bit. Globalisation is a complex set of phenomena that defy easy analysis.

My own theological understanding of culture has shaped how I have edited and produced this book. As human beings made in the image of God, we are capable of cultural innovations that are good. As fallen people, all our actions and thoughts are corrupted throughout by sin. But the image of God remains. We may be entirely in need of redemption, but we are not entirely evil. Human cultures are no different—as products of human thought and action, they are both good and evil, reflecting both God's image and also our sinfulness. And just as Jesus said that the weeds would be allowed to grow alongside the wheat until the harvest, so will good and evil co-exist until the end of history.

Some contributions within this book concentrate on the fallenness manifested in globalisation, identifying things to be resisted in the name of Jesus Christ. Other writers take a less judgemental view, simply observing the trends and considering how we should change in response. There is no easy answer to whether resistance or adaptation is correct. It probably depends on the context and the circumstances. Jesus is both Saviour and Judge of globalisation as much as of any other culture. Individual chapters may emphasise one aspect or another. It is hoped that the whole presents a more nuanced picture.

Navigating This Book

Globalisation impacts every part of human life, including our cultural and religious existences. Since we are whole human beings embedded in communities, globalisation has an effect on every aspect of our lives. This book aims to take account of this breadth of impact. Some chapters look at broad social trends that are affecting all people everywhere. Others consider the impact of globalisation on specific regions or issues, trying to embody or enflesh the big issues into specific sets of circumstances or situations. Still others consider the implications of globalisation on issues that we usually think of as "missiology" or "theology." Not that we want to reinforce this distinction unnecessarily. The whole of life is missiological, since the whole of life should be directed to the service of God. There is no part of human life over which Christ is not Lord. Every chapter in this book is missiological, even if not every topic addressed is usually considered as missiology "proper."

Following this introduction, Part 1 identifies the main features of globalisation. Ruth Valerio looks at the central economic aspects and discusses the concerns that economics should raise for anyone who cares about issues of poverty and justice. The "McWorld" and "Jihad" polarities are neatly repackaged by Sam George as "technoculture" and "terrorculture," which, as he notes, can both be seen as characteristic of youth culture around the world. The final chapter in this section, by David Lundy, explores the pluralisation that results from globalisation, neatly sidestepping the easy association of globalisation with increased Westernised homogeneity.

Part 2 looks at how globalisation is reflected in specific issues or areas of the world. Miriam Adeney makes a plea that concerns for ethnicity should not be seen simply as a reaction to the dominance of Western culture, but as a crucial element in the God-intended diversity of creation. Ruth Valerio provides a second chapter, this time looking at the impact of globalisation on the environment. Steve Fouch looks at health as a global issue and presents a strong case for a re-emphasis on the historical missionary commitment to health and medical work. Rose Dowsett looks at "those who hold up half the sky" and the ways that women, who are often marginalised in their societies, are especially affected by globalisation. Wanyeki Mahiaini provides a useful analysis of the impact of globalisation on one particular continent, Africa, showing how the macro-issues we have identified are working out in one particular region. To conclude this section, Fiona Wilson presents the results of a survey undertaken by Tearfund of its partners around the world, looking at grassroots perceptions of the impacts of globalisation.

Part 3 considers the implications of globalisation for areas usually included under the heading of "mission." Bulus Galadima reflects on the place of religion in a globalising world and the implications for Christian mission. Marcelo Vargas makes a strong plea for local contextual sensitivity in response to global homogenising pressures. Warren Beattie looks at the directions in which theology and globalisation are moving. We have two chapters on the implications of globalisation for the church. Alex Araujo asks the church to present itself as an alternative to the system offered by globalisation, and Ros Johnson looks at the opportunities that globalisation offers to local churches in terms of their own missionary activity.

The concluding chapter by Steve Moon and David Tai-Woong Lee asks us to consider God's own globalising intentions—a diverse world united in praise to him. This will only come about through world evangelisation and a strong commitment to global missiology. The ultimate aim of this book, and of all who worked to bring it into being, is that we might be privileged to play a small part in bringing God's intended world about.

References

Finnström, S. (1997). *Postcoloniality and the postcolony: Theories of the global and the local.* Working Papers in Cultural Anthropology #7. University of Uppsala, Sweden. Retrieved from http://65.107.211.206/post/poldiscourse/finnstrom/finnstrom2.html.

New York Times. (2001, October 14).

Newsweek. (2002, May 20).

Spencer, N. (2002, December 15). World round-up. *The Observer Review* (London), p. 13.

Tiplady, R. (in press). *World of difference: Global mission at the pic'n'mix counter.* Carlisle, UK: Paternoster Press.

Waters, M. (2001). *Globalization* (2nd ed.). London, UK: Routledge.

Richard Tiplady *works as an organisational development consultant for mission agencies, specialising in new projects and the future of world mission. He holds degrees from London University and Nottingham University, including a master's degree in the theology of mission. He was Associate Director of Global Connections (UK) from 1996 to 2002, editor of* **Postmission: World Mission by a Postmodern Generation***, and author of* **World of Difference: Global Mission at the Pic'n'Mix Counter***. He is married to Irene, and they have one son, Jamie. Both father and son are lifelong Manchester United supporters, and Richard is a qualified FA junior football coach. Website: www.tiplady.org.uk. Email: richard@tiplady.org.uk.*

Part 1
Main Features

1

Globalisation and economics: a world gone bananas

Ruth Valerio

Writing this chapter makes me reflect on the countries that I have touched today. My jeans come from Morocco and my T-shirt from Portugal. My coffee is from Costa Rica and my banana from the Windward Islands. My computer keyboard was made in Germany, whilst the screen is from China. We have a Japanese woman staying with us, taking a break from work to travel round the world, and I talked today to friends who are moving to Tanzania.

All of the above products have a story to tell: who made or produced them and how they travelled round the world to reach my house. Each one points to different aspects of the complicated world of economic globalisation, such as my society's move from producer to consumer, the benefits brought by that move, Export Processing Zones, the role of technology in economics, the flight of companies chasing the "bottom dollar," the mobile global elite, and the intensification of winners and losers. However, perhaps the product with the greatest story to tell is the humble banana.

Bananas are one of the basic foods of today; indeed, the banana is the world's most popular fruit.[1] Yet, my parents' generation almost never ate them, so what has happened in the world to make bananas such an ordinary part of life in the UK?[2]

Traditionally, Britain and the rest of the European Union bought their bananas from their former colonies, particularly the Windward Islands, which have become almost totally reliant on the industry. Britain invested into the original plantations, and Geest, the company that buys and sells most of the bananas, is a British company. The Lome Convention in 1975 formalised the EU's commitment to continue to import bananas from the Windward Islands.

However, 70% of the bananas involved in international trade are controlled by the big three American companies: Chiquita, Dole, and Del Monte. Not liking the EU protectionist policy on bananas, the US complained to the World Trade Organisation (WTO), which ruled in its favour. When the EU refused to back down, the US struck back and put import tariffs, in the end worth $191.4 million, on EU exports. The American complaint to the WTO came just days after Chiquita donated $500,000 to the Democratic Party. The tariffs were enforced by the Republican-controlled Congress after Chiquita donated $350,000 to them.

The situation today is one in which the overwhelming majority of the bananas produced for export are done so in appalling circumstances. The plantation workers live in poverty. In Ecuador, for example, the workers are paid just $1 a day, and some independent producers get only 3 pence per pound, which does not even cover costs. On average, the producer gets only 5% of the price of a banana.

Vast quantities of chemicals are used to treat the banana during production. Plantations in Central America apply 30 kg of active ingredients per hectare per year—more than 10 times the average for intensive farming in industrialised countries. In Costa Rica, 75% of banana workers suffer from skin lesions, and 20% of the male workers are sterile due to handling pesticides. Entire communities suffer from indiscriminate aerial crop spraying.

The impact on the environment need hardly be stated, let alone the fact that massive deforestation has taken place to provide the land for the plantations. The effect of all the chemicals on those of us who eat bananas is something that many worry about. It is interesting to note the response of a banana worker on a Chiquita plantation in Guatemala when asked if he ever ate the bananas he produced: "Good Lord, no!" he ejaculated. "People in places like this don't eat the fruit they cut. I guess we know better!"

---

[1] Worth £5 billion a year in the UK, bananas are the most valuable food product in supermarkets, outsold only by petrol and lottery tickets (Fairtrade Foundation). Globally, more bananas are sold than any other fruit.

[2] Much of the following information on bananas comes from *The New Internationalist* (NI) (1999, October).

The story of the banana sitting in my fruit bowl gives a helpful insight into the complex web of economic globalisation. Whilst leading to inevitable oversimplifications, the analysis that follows is useful at this juncture to outline the main facets of economic globalisation and to begin to explore some of the implications for mission.[3]

Facets of Globalisation

1. Economic globalisation is based on the principle of free trade and market capitalism.

This observation will hardly be news for most of us, but in case it is, let us explore the idea further. Economic globalisation works on the policies of trade liberalisation, privatisation, and financial market deregulation. It is believed that free trade between nations, with no protective barriers, is the most effective way of increasing global wealth and lifting poorer countries out of their poverty.

This global system only works where there is growth; thus, the economics of globalisation is profit-driven to the ex-

treme.[4] This drive towards continual growth has led to the emergence, and now dominance, of the transnational corporations (TNCs) so that, now, of the world's 100 largest economies, 50 are TNCs. Corporate mergers and acquisitions have thus become a familiar feature of the globalisation landscape. Indeed, the annual number of such mergers and acquisitions doubled between 1990 and 1997, when the total value reached $236 billion (NI, 2000, p. 24).

Another aspect of this growth-driven economy is currency speculation and foreign direct investment (FDI). Some say $1 billion, others say $2 trillion is turned over each day on the currency markets. Giddens (1999) notes, "In the new global electronic economy, fund managers, banks, corporations, as well as millions of individual investors, can transfer vast amounts of capital from one side of the world to another at the click of a mouse. As they do so, they can destabilise what might have seemed rock-solid economies—as happened in East Asia." Flows of foreign direct investment in 1995 reached $315 billion, almost a sixfold increase over the level

---

[3] The economic information that follows is taken from Valerio (2002a).

[4] As Bill Clinton (cited in Bruges, 2000, p. 81) observed, "I do not believe that a country with 4.5% of the world's people can maintain its standard of living if we don't have more customers." It is important to note that I am not against profit per se, and clearly businesses need to make a profit to survive. As I will explain later, the problem arises when excess profit is the goal, regardless of the consequences to people or planet. The same is true for the need for capital flows. It is important to point out the need for the foreign exchange market to operate smoothly and efficiently before talking about the recent inflation of capital flows and the instability such flows can bring about.

for 1981–1985. Over the same period, world trade increased by little more than a half.[5]

Before going any further, let us stop and ask ourselves how far the values of globalisation are impacting our churches and missions work. Chester (2000, p. 6) summarises the situation well:

It is tempting in the face of globalisation to suppose that the church requires corresponding global structures. It is tempting to suppose that the priority of the hour is to strengthen global institutions and create global networks. With globalisation concentrating power in transnational corporations and international institutions, surely we need powerful transnational Christian agencies. We need access to the national and global media. We need influence in the halls of power. We need national evangelistic campaigns, megachurches, and a powerful political voice. We want to think big.

How we judge success is a question we must all grapple with in the face of our society's tendency to judge everything numerically and financially. It can be all too easy to listen too much to the influential and disregard the views of those on the margins.

There is much discussion in mission circles about the increase in short-term work. Undoubtedly, this type of work can give rise to many opportunities. A friend commented to my husband recently, "I'm putting off coming with you to Africa, because I know that once I've seen it, my whole life will have to change." These "trips of perspective," as Mike Schut calls them, can be extremely valuable as Northerners travel to the South to engage in volunteer work, hear from local organisations, and stay with local people. Participants need to be ready to go with an attitude of learning and should be prepared, upon their return, to use their experiences to bring about policy or lifestyle changes in the North. However, those engaged in mission work must also resist globalisation's short-term values, which would have us believe that if we do not see instant "success," we should move on to the next exciting project (which will, of course, be bigger, brighter, and better).

Another point to consider is the way those of us in the wealthier countries see ourselves as customers and have grown used to thinking that we possess certain rights. What impact will this

---

[5] As with profit, I am not against a foreign exchange market per se. Where such a market operates smoothly and efficiently, I see the benefits that can bring. However, one of the results of currency speculation and the recent inflation of capital flows is that prices of commodities are at the mercy of market forces and are on a generally downward trend. For example, coffee is currently going through a crisis, with prices at their lowest since the 1930s. Despite this, the price of a cup of coffee in a coffee house is increasing, and the big coffee roasting houses, such as Sara Lee and Nestle, are reporting large profits (Nestle saw a 20% rise in profits in 2001). As we have seen with bananas, 90% of the price of a commodity stays in the North and is never seen by the producer. The problem of financial volatility caused by currency speculation could be solved by the introduction of the so-called "Tobin Tax"—a small worldwide tariff (less than 0.5%) that major countries would levy on foreign-exchange transactions.

mindset have on mission agencies, and how will we deal with people who exhibit a demanding attitude and who join a mission organisation?

2. The rules for how economic globalisation works are governed by the World Trade Organisation.

The WTO hit the headlines in 1999, when its meeting in Seattle was thrown into disarray by protestors, and its trade round was stopped by leaders from the South. Up until this time, the WTO was a little-known organisation that gained little attention.

The WTO has within its constitution the potential for working to benefit those who are poor. Its Generalised System of Preferences recognises, at least on paper, that the poorest and least developed nations need positive discrimination and that recognition alone is not enough.[6] WTO decision making is via consensus and so is potentially more democratic. However…

3. The WTO has problems.

The reality is that the WTO is dominated by the wealthy countries, particularly the US, Canada, Japan, and the EU. Its headquarters are in Geneva, Switzerland, which has one of the highest costs of living in the world. There are mountains of paperwork and legal documents attached to any negotiation, and a country needs a host of specialised experts and lawyers to be able to deal with these. The wealthy countries are able to have people in Geneva permanently, whilst poorer countries cannot afford anyone. For example, Japan has 25 representatives, while Bangladesh has only one, and over half of the least developed countries in the WTO have no representative at all (Christian Aid, n.d.). Discussions are thus weighted from the start.

Perhaps the WTO's most significant weakness is that free trade is its sacred cow (as with the IMF and World Bank) and is given priority above all else, at the expense of issues such as the environment and human rights.[7] Joseph Stiglitz (as cited in Oxfam, 2000), former Chief Economist at the World Bank, has said that they take "privatisation and trade liberalisation as ends in themselves, rather than means to more sustainable, equitable, and democratic growth." WTO rulings can even go against laws that are adopted to comply with international agreements.[8] Other examples include preventing legislation to ban cosmetics testing on animals, protecting companies trading with Myanmar, and preventing Thailand, which was concerned at the increase in young smokers, from banning cigarette imports (Bruges, 2000, p. 85).

---

[6] In contrast, the IMF and World Bank still very much reflect the political situation after World War II. For example, seven countries (the US, UK, Germany, France, Japan, Italy, and Canada) control nearly half the votes at the World Bank, and the US holds nearly 20% of the total votes in the IMF.

[7] Mofid (2002) puts the blame for this state of affairs on the way economics is taught, with its narrow focus on "self-interest" and "competition" as the sole motivating factors in economic activity.

[8] For example, the WTO ruled that American regulations to protect turtles were illegal, even though they were done in accordance with CITES, which was signed by 146 nations.

It is a sad fact that the WTO has only once upheld a ruling in favour of social or environmental issues.

The meaning given to "free trade" seems to change, chameleon-like, according to the interests of the wealthy. The Common Agricultural Policy (CAP) is a major example and the main reason that the WTO might yet collapse. CAP gives enormous subsidies to European farmers, whilst demonstrating great reluctance to open up markets to agricultural produce from the developing world. As the subsidies encourage over-production, excess produce is dumped on other, poorer countries, who then see the price of their national produce slump, which in turn affects the livelihoods of the farmers. UNCTAD predicts that the elimination of agricultural subsidies would result in developing countries being better off by around $19.8 billion (DFID, 2000, p. 2). So far as free trade is concerned, the wealthier countries fail to practice what they preach.

4. Economic globalisation is dominated by the TNCs.

Our case study of bananas gave us an obvious example of how this principle works, but this domination affects producers the world over. TNCs are often larger financially than the countries in which they operate and hence can control how things are done. This leads to the "race for the bottom dollar," which pushes aside human rights and environmental concerns.

This practice is demonstrated by Klein (2000, pp. 195-229), who exposes the free-trade zones in countries such as Indonesia, China, Mexico, Vietnam, and the Philippines. These Export Processing Zones (EPZs) are the areas in which consumer goods are made. They operate tariff-free, with no import or export duties and sometimes no income or property taxes either. It is thought that there are around 1,000 EPZs operating in 70 countries, employing roughly 27 million workers. The workday is long (up to 16 hours), and the workers are mostly young women working for contractors from Korea, Taiwan, or Hong Kong, who are usually filling orders for companies based in the US, UK, Japan, Germany, or Canada. The working conditions are very much below standard, with the minimum wage seldom reached, and trade unions are banned. The EPZs are designed to attract foreign investors, with the hope that they will contribute to lasting development in the chosen country. Thus, tax-free incentives are offered, as well as other things, such as, sometimes, the cooperation of the military to suppress any labour unrest. The reality, of course, is that foreign investment rarely touches the country, and the EPZs operate as offshore tax havens, benefiting only the companies involved—companies which fly off to another country as soon as conditions in the EPZs turn against them.

With the WTO interested only in free trade, there are no internationally respected laws to govern TNCs and ensure they are putting people and the environment before their profit-driven shareholders. Although not all TNCs are American, in the minds of many, globalisation equals Americanisation: the creation of a "one Disney McWorld."[9] This is certainly true of the church. As

---

[9] Giddens, Huntingdon, and Berger would agree with the argument stated in the book's introduction, that globalisation is more than just Americanisation.

Peter Harris (A Rocha International, personal communication) has observed, "When you go to a church in a major world city, chances are you could be in LA for all the cultural distinctiveness there is to the theology or forms of worship, whatever the language." The tools of the Internet have enabled Americans to disseminate their own literature and courses widely, often at the expense of people from other countries developing their own material that would reflect their individual cultures more adequately. Northern thinking thus dominates the church because, to put it crudely, Northerners have the money and resources to be able to do that.[10]

This domination inevitably affects mission thinking and practice. A South African friend living and working in a township told me of the frustrations he had with the AD 2000 and Beyond Movement. He saw the push from Northern mission centres as being of a globalising order, carrying the implication that the rest of the world had to accept the priority of AD 2000 missiology. The economics of the situation made it difficult to resist or ignore, and countries in the South tended to lose the theological space to frame their own questions and make their own contribution to global mission. My friend spoke of contending against the hegemony of AD 2000.

The mission scene as we have it today developed under the old system, under which the economically wealthier countries were the big mission senders. However, the church is now strongest in the predominantly poorer countries, and we need to provide a new economic system in the worldwide church that encourages missionaries from poorer countries whose churches cannot afford to send them. Perhaps one way would be to change from the colonial system, whereby missionaries were supported by the sending church, and adopt Paul's principle of being supported by the receiving church.[11]

The other side of the "trips of perspective" that were mentioned earlier is what Mike Schut calls "reverse missions," whereby Christians from poorer countries live and teach in the wealthier nations. It is imperative that those from poorer countries be heard and that those from more wealthy churches/mission agencies find the humility to sit at the feet of these others and let themselves be taught by them. This would enable us to discover the positive side to globalisation. David Smith (2000) expresses this well when he says, "Globalisation allows the opportunity for the wisdom of the whole church to be brought together. The contribution of the church from the South will bring great wisdom and insight to the global church. Various cultural perspectives will always add refreshing ways of looking at God and the gospel."

5. The shape of the workplace is changing.

After work today, my mother-in-law will come round to join us for dinner and help with bathing my daughter. I know how she will respond when I ask how her day has been: she's tired, her

---

[10] The WEA globalisation group from which this book emerged wrestled with this issue continually.

[11] This seems to have happened, for example, in Macedonia and Philippi.

work is piling up, she's doing the work of two people, and so on. For many, the workplace today has become a place of increasing pressure. Whereas before there would be periods of respite and stability ("pit stops"), now the pace is relentless, and uncertainty and turmoil are present continually. Pressure on productivity is increasing, but resources are decreasing. Decision making and problem solving are now often done on one's feet, with little time to think or reflect properly (Mike Perreau, personal communication).

Hence, it is not enough simply to bemoan those in the wealthy nations and assume that they suffer no ill effects from globalisation. Tom Sine (1999) has written extensively on the damage that globalisation does in that arena and the intense pressure that it brings, with people working longer and harder to keep up in the competitive global economy. A church leader told me recently of the problems of finding others in her congregation who would shoulder some of the responsibility of leadership with her. As people find themselves with less time and less money, our churches are suffering, because there are fewer people ready to take on the demands of being fully involved in a church.

Economic globalisation is thus changing the context in which families are raised, churches are operated, and mission is done in the wealthier countries (and increasingly elsewhere too). Mission agencies working in these contexts are finding that it is essential to counteract the culture of consumerism that is endemic in these societies. Sine (personal communication) observes, "As the marketers of McWorld redefine what is of importance and of value, those who are engaged in mission find themselves in a battle for the hearts and minds of those whom McWorld is targeting."

How mission agencies are involved with this changing context is another question. Too often, they have been perceived as poachers, taking people away from local churches. Instead, they must become partners, using their knowledge of gospel communication in other cultures to help its communication in their own culture.

It has long been recognised that people are often more open to the gospel when they are in another country. Global mobility is thus coming from two angles. Firstly, there is the mobility of the wealthy: those who can travel to the UK (for example) to study and just visit.[12] Secondly, there is the mobility brought by displaced peoples: economic refugees and asylum seekers. This mobility brought by economic globalisation, whether positive or negative, allows for many opportunities, and mission agencies are well placed to help local churches, through their knowledge of people's homelands.[13]

Finally, a clear feature of the global workplace is that English is becoming increasingly important, making it the key language to learn. This, again, provides opportunities upon which English-speaking mission organisations can capitalise, and strategies can be put

---

[12] So, Japan Christian Link gave us advice on how to talk about the gospel with the Japanese woman who is staying with us.

[13] A number of churches in the UK are working with asylum seekers and would benefit with cultural help from mission agencies.

in place for using English as a tool for mission.[14]

6. *Those who do not have the resources to participate are pushed into poverty.*

Consider the following statistics:

- 1.3 billion people have to live on less than $1 a day, and more than 800 million people do not have enough to eat (CAFOD, n.d.).

- A Nike quilted jacket costs £100 in a London shop, but only 51p of that goes to the Bangladeshi women who make it (CAFOD, n.d.).

- In 1976, Switzerland was 50 times richer than Mozambique. In 1997, it was 500 times richer.

- The top 1% of households in the US have more wealth than the entire bottom 95% (CAFOD, n.d.).

- Whilst financial transactions have been growing fast, two-thirds of them are between the few already-rich countries of the OECD (NI, 1997, pp. 18-19).

A key debate focuses on how far economic globalisation can be blamed for the appalling situation our world is in today.[15] It is inarguable that market capitalism has led to increasing global wealth, as the proportion of GDP traded internationally has risen from 5% in 1946 to 25% now (Bruges, 2000, p. 81). The Sachs/Warner study from Harvard University found that developing countries with open economies grew by 4.5% a year in the 1970s and 1980s, while those with closed economies grew by only 0.7% a year (Moore, 2001).

In light of such statistics, there are those who believe that markets are the way of creating wealth and that those who would stop markets from acting efficiently (by making a special case for poor countries) will in the end destroy the wealth of those nations. Take, for example, flower growers in Uganda. These workers produce flowers for export to Europe, which has now reduced its subsidies. Flower growing is hard work, but it pays better than subsistence farming. Not only do Europeans get flowers in winter, but the Ugandans eat better and are able to school their children (Celebrities, 2002). In other words, it may be a tough option, but in the long run, joining world markets is the only way to create wealth.[16] Such people also argue that many countries are held back not by unfair terms of trade, but by internal corruption or by the lack of an economic infrastructure which would allow them to deliver the goods in world markets (e.g., education, communication systems, trained labour force, etc.). This side of the debate wants markets to do all the work and wants to be free from government interference.[17]

However, there are also those who see poverty and increased inequality as endemic to globalisation. These people think in terms of power. They see the gap between rich and poor widening, and they blame the growth of global

---

[14] TESL (Teaching English as a Second Language) courses are an obvious example.

[15] My thanks to Roy McCloughry for clarifying the sides of the debate for me.

[16] The UK Department for International Development would be an excellent example of this view.

[17] For a very good defence of this position, see Micklethwaite and Wooldridge (2000).

capitalism for that gap. In the case of our Ugandan flower growers, they would question whether, overall, the workers are better off. Yes, they might have more money, but they now have to buy the basic goods they would have grown, which are now sold more expensively since demand is high. They are now at the mercy of market prices, and the chemicals being used to grow the flowers are threatening both their lands and their health. They might also ask why there was subsistence farming in the first place.

People on this side of the debate point out that the collapse of Communism has led to a much more ruthless kind of capitalism. They see that the way to change the operation of multinationals is by exposing their practices in the press and protesting publicly about their power. This side of the debate wants massive intervention to stop poverty caused by capitalism. They are pushing for partnerships between nation-states, NGOs, multinationals, and global agencies to bring about reform.[18]

The debate remains polarised, and the arguments are often highly complex and technical. However, one thing is clear: in our increasingly globalised world, the different issues involved in the problem must be seen as part of the wider whole, rather than as separate. As Heslam (2002, p. 25) points out, "The interests of the environment, economic growth, security, and democracy are diverse but also interconnected and therefore need to be treated together, rather than in isolation."

Technology has ensured that globalisation is here to stay, even if the economically wealthier countries become increasingly protectionist in outlook, as some future scenarios predict.[19] Capitalism seems to be the best way forward for generating wealth, and no viable alternatives are being proposed. The key seems to be in channelling globalisation, rather than demanding its demise, but channelling it so that the rights of local people and their environment come before the rights of shareholders to increase their profits. Two issues are paramount here. One is the reform of the WTO so that channelling globalisation as described above becomes its overriding principle.[20] Second, and interrelated, is the establishment of a system of accountability for corporations, whereby these organisations would adopt best practice in their work and would be accountable for any environmental and social damage.[21]

Implications for Mission

As we look at the positives brought by economic globalisation, it is good also to recognise the positives that globalisation can bring to mission. One

---

[18] One of the key voices on this side is Joseph Stiglitz (see Stiglitz, 2002).

[19] I am aware of the dangers of putting future scenarios in print. By the time this book gets published, the world scene may have changed again.

[20] This reform would include eliminating unequal voting rights, allowing flexibility in policies, and preventing the development of trade rules that stop national governments from pursuing the right policies for development.

[21] Underlying both of these ideals is the need to deal with corruption and bring in internationally recognised anti-corruption laws.

such benefit is the greater number of links with and knowledge of the world and the worldwide church. Whereas in previous centuries a person's life revolved round his or her small village, and travel outside that village was rare, now the world truly is our village, and people are familiar with many aspects of it. As it is easier to gain knowledge about other countries, so a church's awareness of Christians outside their own country can be stimulated, leading to a greater interest in mission and in being an outward-looking congregation.

This knowledge base has an impact on those engaged in mission too, as those "far-flung places" do not now seem quite so distant.[22] For many missionaries, email has revolutionised their lives and has made communication with friends, family, and their mission agency or home church much easier than previously, thus helping to reduce feelings of isolation and loneliness. Another factor in bringing distant places closer is that travel times have shrunk so remarkably.[23]

An interesting opportunity brought by economic globalisation is that mission agencies and their personnel now have a very marketable product to sell:

their cultural knowledge and know-how. For example, my father, who lectures in cross-cultural communication, has recently found doors opening up to him in secular disaster-response agencies. These organisations might have highly skilled medics or engineers, but they have little idea how actually to relate into the local culture where they are serving and hence how to be most effective. The same is true for businesses seeking to work on an international scale. Mission agencies carry a great deal of cultural awareness and international knowledge that can be most useful for such operations. Thus, mission agencies should not be afraid to look outside the traditional boxes. They may well find that interesting partnerships exist out there.[24]

The implications for mission of the link between economic globalisation and poverty seem obvious. Christians and churches reaping the benefits of globalisation are increasingly recognising the responsibility that is held for the sisters and brothers who have been left behind. Globalisation's effects on the poor mean that social concerns must be at the heart of mission and the church.[25] As Escobar (2000, p. 33) notes, "Christian compassion will be the only

---

[22] This does not, of course, mean that good cross-cultural communication skills are not essential. The reality of culture shock should never be underestimated. Those "far-flung places" can seem a lot further away than initially thought!

[23] When my great-great-grandfather went to India in 1846, the voyage took him four months by sea. By the time my parents sailed to Singapore in 1960, they were able to do it in only three weeks, and now my husband can fly to Ethiopia in 10 hours. This proximity to the rest of the world now can create its own problems, with missionaries never quite "leaving home" and hence never committing fully and settling into their new place.

[24] Another important opportunity is that brought by technology, but I shall leave that discussion to the chapter dedicated to that topic.

[25] There is, of course, nothing new about Christians in development, and many reading this will have been involved in social concerns for years.

hope of survival for victims of the global economic process." Araujo (2000, pp. 66-67) highlights the fact that "most of the still unreached peoples of the earth belong to countries that bring up the rear of globalisation." He makes the point that missionary preparation and training in this context may not differ much from the way pioneering missionaries were trained. Thus, sophisticated use of technology and mission models may hinder more than help.

How might mission engage with this state of affairs? Mike Perreau (personal communication) talks about moving from "job faking" (using a job as a disguise to enter a country) to "job taking" (i.e., "tentmaking") to "job making." Two of the greatest needs that people have in order to be able to survive in today's world are business skills and the finances to support those skills. Hence, micro-business and enterprise are a key factor in development. Mission agencies should be, and are, looking at how they can equip their personnel with enterprise-making skills.[26] English comes into play again here. Many missionary activities are focussed on the developing nations, where three needs predominate: health, education, and economics. Since English is a key factor in all three areas, teaching English can help a country access these areas.[27]

Implications for the Church and for Christian Lifestyle

Let us return to the story of the banana sitting in my fruit bowl. Whilst the picture I painted earlier was somewhat negative, there are also positive things taking place, with fair trade being the most obvious.[28] Alongside Fair Trade, many NGOs are campaigning to see a change in how bananas are produced. On a broader level, a Trade Justice Campaign is currently running in the UK. Virtually all the main NGOs involved in these issues have signed up and are campaigning to see the global trading rules changed.[29]

In October 2001, a well-respected opinion poll, the Mori poll, gave some surprising new findings as to people's

---

[26] However, mission agencies must ensure that their missionaries do not go in as "experts," placing themselves on a level above the local people. Another consideration is to work with local values and customs. In one North African country, an expatriate group started a woodworking factory for women, but they ran into problems when all the young women they trained married and then could not leave their home. When the group discovered that these women knitted whilst at home, they developed a knitting group to help improve the quality of the goods being produced and to allow the women to gain a small income. Gradually things started to change.

[27] As missionaries increasingly become involved in development work, great wisdom will need to be exercised by mission agencies as to how the resources of the wealthy are shared with the poor. The corrupting power of money must always be remembered—both for those who give and for those who receive. Even in my wealthy country, a speaker was heard to remark that he looked to Korean invitations because of the money he got from them.

[28] For more information on fair trade, see www.fairtradefoundation.org.

[29] See www.tradejusticecampaign.org.uk.

Paul Read and his family are involved in micro-enterprise development in south India and east Thailand. Their work aims at those living at or below the poverty line who then become their "clients": people with skills and ideas for self-employment who cannot get bank start-up funding because of lack of assets to offer as security. The Reads have seen many businesses start up, including tailoring, watchmaking, shoe repairing, food cultivating, and car paint spraying. The idea is to give a hand up, rather than a handout, to those in poverty, irrespective of their religion. This inclusiveness is deliberate and gives the project a community feel that is both more acceptable locally and useful for building relationships. After three years in India, the Reads have helped about 1,200 people in total (1% of the local population), from an investment of £16,000. The Reads see what they do as mission, even if it is not primarily evangelism. They see that **being** good news to those who are not Christians is just as valid as preaching **about** the good news. Their aim is to help the poor out of poverty, whatever their religion, and if someone accepts Christ through this involvement at some point, then praise God. In fact, two Muslim men have indeed become Christians through the work.[30]

Cred Trading Company Ltd was established out of the charity, Cred, in 1996. It retails sterling silver jewellery at the high street in the UK. The firm states: "Our core value is consistent with our foundation: 'to see justice for the poor.' We all realise that charity alone is never going to be the answer. The answer is lifestyle change, and we seek to offer the option of ethics in business in the jewellery sector, stocking our shop primarily from wholesalers, but also selling items from communities around the world. We are unashamedly profit-making and plough a proportion of that profit back into the Foundation. We require commercially successful companies to take up the mantle of social change with a 'for-profit social enterprise' agenda. This is what CTC Ltd seeks to do: impact the high street with excellence of product, excellence of service, and excellence of ethics."[31]

---

[30] For more information, contact reads@sify.com.

[31] For more information, see www.cred.org.uk.

opinions on globalisation. The results showed that people were suspicious of globalisation and sympathetic towards the anti-globalisation protestors. Bob Worcester, Mori Chairman, said that the survey was a timely indicator of people's underlying distrust of big companies when it comes to acting in people's interest. The fact that 41% of the British public believe the anti-globalisation protestors have a point should prompt a serious rethinking of the globalisation debate.

There are alternative ways of doing things, and there are people who are prepared to use their voices and purses in the push for change. The WTO meeting in Seattle not only brought the WTO into public focus, but also brought attention to the "anti-globalisation movement" mentioned above.[32] It should be noted that "anti-globalisation movement" is a name coined by the media. Those who belong to the movement are clear that, if they are against anything, then it is *economic* globalisation, not globalisation as a whole. The movement includes a huge array of pressure groups, individuals, charities, and NGOs, from all around the world, that are working to see a change in the way the global rules, and especially the TNCs, operate, in order to see more justice for the poor.[33] What is interesting about this movement is that there is no organisational centre, just a lot of individual groups and campaigns, all linked with each other like hotlinks on a website: "a chaotic network of hubs and spokes" (Klein, as cited in Roddick, 2001, p. 38).

In the UK, at least, single-issue campaigning has become one of the hallmarks of our day, with people increasingly perceiving that the real power lies with the TNCs, rather than with the political leaders. With our world so vast and complex, it seems easier to take one issue to campaign on than to get involved in the quagmire of the political corridors that can seem somewhat irrelevant. Nearly all of the major UK NGOs, therefore, are turning campaigning into a main focus.

Alongside campaigning is the growth of the concept of "ethical consumerism," as seen with Fair Trade bananas. There is a growing awareness of how my patterns of consumption here directly affect the lives of people in other countries and even the rest of creation. So, if I buy a banana with a label on it that says Dole, Chiquita, Fyffes, or Del Monte, then I am giving my consent to the way those companies treat their workers and the environment. However, if I buy a Fair Trade banana, then I am taking away that consent and giving my money to a system that will benefit the lives of that banana's producers. People are recognising that this selectivity in buying applies to all sorts of areas: clothes, pensions, toys, food, mortgages, electrical equipment, holi-

---

[32] It is also good to note that the World Bank changed its ways of working after the Seattle incident and has been taking strides to become more open and accessible.

[33] This is a phenomenon that is peculiar to our time. Never before have there been so many organisations working outside established political structures. Today, there are 26,000 international NGOs—four times as many as a decade ago. Some of these are specifically involved in the anti-globalisation movement. See, for example, www.adbusters.org; www.reclaimthestreets.net; www.directactionnetwork.org; www.ruckus.org.

days, investments, and so on. It also applies to the way I consume energy in the form of petrol, gas, and electricity and whether I throw things away rather than reusing or recycling them.[34]

> "If mission is about the growth of God's kingdom (rather than just about saving souls), then authentic Christian mission today must involve a radical critique of globalisation, together with teaching on discipleship that covers lifestyle and economic/political attitudes."
> — Dave Bookless, A Rocha UK

There is much here for the church and for individual Christians to try to grasp. We clearly have a responsibility to speak out on behalf of the poor. Coming from his American church context, Tom Sine (personal communication) lays down the gauntlet and challenges churches "to embrace a more politically radical faith that identifies with the powerless instead of sanctioning the politics of the powerful."

> "When I give food to the poor, they call me a saint. When I ask why the poor have no food, they call me a Communist."
> — Dom Helder Camara, a former Brazilian Bishop

We also have a responsibility to live our lives in ways that demonstrate that we follow and worship a God of justice and mercy. Many Christians around the world do not have a choice as to how they live their lives. However, for those who do have a choice, there is a need to rediscover the joy that comes from living more simply. Nearly 30 years ago, the Lausanne Covenant called Christians to develop a simple lifestyle (see Stott, 1996, pp. 142-149). It may well be said that this directive has not been heeded. In both affluent and poor contexts, we all too easily succumb to the temptations of greed and covetousness, seeing money and possessions as the basis for happiness and security. Simplicity, instead, is about discovering what it really means to be rich and realizing that wealth is found in our relationships with God, with one another, and with the rest of the created world (see Valerio, 2002b).

Relational Riches

Jim Wallis (as cited in Heslam, 2002, p. 14) maintains, "Economics is too important to be left to economists alone. It is high time to apply biblical theology to the crises of our global economy." To put it another way, "The realms of economics, culture, morality, and religion are not as separate as we sometimes think" (Cox, 1999, p. 387). If the church's mission is to be effective in a world dominated by economic globalisation, then we must be able to reflect theologically on the situations in which we find ourselves.

---

[34] Two excellent resources are World Development Movement (1998) and Ecologist (2001).

It is essential to understand personhood as "beings-in-relation," defined by being made "in the image of God" (Gen. 1:27). The most foundational aspect of God is that of the Trinity. The Godhead is composed of continually flowing relationships between the Father, Son, and Holy Spirit, so that each finds its identity through the others. For example, God's personhood as "Father" only comes into being in relation to God as "Son." Whilst the members of the Trinity have separate identities, yet there is absolute unity and harmony between them. The Father is the supreme author of all, yet there is equality between the Father, Son, and Spirit, and there is order in their separate roles, as they each exist to serve and glorify the others through those roles (Goldsmith, 2000, pp. 8-23).

It is this Trinitarian understanding that provides the foundation for what it means for humanity to be made in God's image, that is, in the personhood that is in God. In this understanding, personhood does not consist in being distinct and separate before relating together. Rather, personhood arises precisely through being together in relationship. It is this understanding of personhood that we image in our humanity. Instead of the static individuality of the Western worldview, the Genesis account leads to a view of humanity as social beings who become genuinely human only through relationships. These relationships are twofold: vertically, with God, and horizontally, with the created order, both human and nonhuman. Let us look at these two aspects.

1. As human beings, we relate to God, our Creator.

We have been created in order to be "for the praise of his glory" (Eph. 1:12), an expression of the unceasing love that exists between the persons of the Godhead. The picture of the Lord God walking in the garden of Eden in the cool of the day (Gen. 3:8) shows the perfect harmony that should have existed between God and humanity, but which was broken by the Fall.

It is no accident that the primary command in Exodus 20 is against idolatry: the worship of false gods in the place of the one true God. Having first reared its ugly head in the story of the Tower of Babel in Genesis 11, idolatry became Israel's perennial sin. For Israel, this was an issue of trust and security. Who would make their crops grow? Who would make the rains come? Who would protect them from outside attack? The command against idolatry is given its starkest expression in Jesus' bald statement, "You cannot serve both God and Mammon" (Matt. 6:24). There is no way round Jesus' words, and they speak straight to the heart of today's society. As with the Israelites, so with us, it is an issue of trust and security.[35] Do we dare trust the God we cannot see in the face of the images and values with which we are bombarded every day?[36]

---

[35] This concept is expressed wonderfully ironically in the American avowal, "In God we trust," printed on the dollar bill.

[36] This question leads appropriately to a consideration of consumerism and a biblical theology of money and possessions. Space does not permit elaboration here, so I refer you to my discussion elsewhere (Valerio, 2002b).

Jon Sobrino (as cited in Northcott, 1999, p. 66) summed up the situation this way: "The question of the poor … is fundamentally the question of God, and of what kind of God we worship." The basic question facing us is, "Whom are we worshipping?" There is no doubt that globalisation is an idolatrous culture, worshipping the God of Money, chasing futilely after the gods of happiness and success. Whereas Jesus comes to bring life (John 10:10), these gods can only bring death (similarly in the Old Testament, where idolatry led to death and imprisonment). For Sobrino, the idols of his country of El Salvador are those of wealth, militarisation, and private property: "divinities of death," as he calls them. He describes how they manifest themselves today through the economic structuring of society and the forces of international capitalism that "produce millions of innocent victims, whom they despatch to the slow death of hunger and the violent death of repression" (Sobrino, as cited in Northcott, 1999, p. 65).

The good news we carry is that, through the sacrifice of Jesus (the second Adam and true image of God, Col. 1:15), this harmony between God and humanity is restored again, as seen in the final chapters of Revelation. Here we are told, "The dwelling of God is with people, and he will live with them. They will be his people and God himself will be with them and be their God" (Rev. 21:3).

One aspect of the missionary's work, therefore, is to proclaim to the world this good news about Jesus. It is by new birth and faith in Jesus that people enter the Kingdom with its values and are given the Holy Spirit's power to live out these ideals. Evangelism, church planting, and teaching are hence central in all mission alongside the church, presenting the models of these values in the church's own life.

2. *The second area of our relationships is with one another.*[37]

Whilst in the Genesis creation narrative the marital relationship may be primary, it is not exclusively so. Cain's question to God, "Am I my brother's keeper?" (Gen. 4:9) carries a clear affirmative with it, and the Noachic covenant of Genesis 9 extends this charge still further. Because we have all been made in the image of God, we are each accountable for the life of our fellow humans. Basic to that accountability is the recognition that we find our true selves not as autonomous individuals but through our relationships with one another. As Colin Gunton (1992, p. 72) asserts, "Who we are is made known to us through the relationships in which we stand."

This view of our identity stands in direct contrast with that given to us by modern society. All around us we are told that we find our true selves in what we consume: the car we drive, the house we live in, the clothes we wear, etc.[38] Instead, we look again to the Trin-

---

[37] Our relationship with the rest of creation is considered in chapter 6 on globalisation and the environment.

[38] This is often described as *tesco ergo sum* ("I shop; therefore I am," using Tesco, the UK's largest supermarket), as opposed to Descartes' *cogito ergo sum*.

ity to see the model for our relationships. Whilst we each maintain our uniqueness, yet we should live in unity together, preferring the other and living lives of service.

Our relationships with one another are based on our understanding of each one being made in the image of God. Through faith in Jesus, the Son—in his incarnation, death, and resurrection—we have our image of God restored, and we also become sons (children) of God ourselves. Hence this description of prayer:

> A ceaseless interchange of mutual love unites the Father, Son, and Holy Spirit. Our prayer is not merely communion with God; it is coming to know God by participation in this divine life. In prayer we experience what it is to be made "participants of the divine nature"; we are caught up in the communion of the divine persons as they flow to one another in self-giving love and reciprocal joy (Society, 1997, p. 42).

Conclusion

The above understanding of humanity provides a sharp critique of globalisation. Globalisation reduces humanity merely to consumers and robs us of our ability to relate fully, whether to God, to one another, or to the world. A person who is viewed as just a human, devoid of all divine orientation, is in essence dehumanised. When we lose our true humanity, we must search for it elsewhere; hence, the rampant rise of materialism. When we lose our true

humanity, we lose our basis for compassion and concern; hence, the terrible injustices that happen in our world. Northcott (1999, p. 115) puts it succinctly: "The enslavement of whole societies to the dehumanising, but humanly generated, forces of globalisation is an extreme example of the cruelty and misery which issue from the denial of the spiritual origin and orientation of our humanness."

As we think through what mission means in our world of economic globalisation, we see that it is to image God in this world: to be living parables of the relational reconciliation that Jesus' life and death have brought. A powerful dynamic within this is that a biblical understanding of relationships rests on the firm basis of a giving away of oneself. Our role model for this is, of course, Jesus. Philippians 2:6-8 describes how Jesus "did not consider equality with God something to be grasped, but made himself nothing, taking the very nature of a servant," and, in doing this, "he humbled himself and became obedient to death, even death on a cross." Whilst Jesus' sacrifice is a once-for-all event, yet it still carries within it the principles for mission—for how we live our lives and conduct our relationships.

Jesus' death and resurrection are the means by which broken relationships are restored, reconciling God to humanity and humanity to one another (2 Cor. 5:18-21; Eph. 2:11-18). Our role is so to image God in this world that, by the power of the Holy Spirit, we might be the agents of that reconciliation.

References

Araujo, A. (2000). Globalization and world evangelism. In W. D. Taylor (Ed.), *Global missiology for the 21st century: The Iguassu dialogue* (pp. 57-70). Grand Rapids, MI: Baker Academic.

Bruges, J. (2000). *The little earth book.* Bristol, UK: Alistair Sawday Publishing.

CAFOD briefing. (n.d.). *The rough guide to globalisation.* Retrieved from http://www.cafod.org.uk/policy/policyroughguide.shtml.

Of celebrities, charities, and trade. (2002, June 1). *The Economist.*

Chester, T. (2000). *Christ's little flock: Towards an ecclesiology of the cross.* Tearfund discussion paper.

Christian Aid. (n.d.). *Trade for life* [Brochure].

Cox, H. (1999). In M. Dempster, B. Klaus, & D. Petersen (Eds.), *The globalisation of Pentecostalism: A religion made to travel.* Oxford, UK: Regnum.

Department for International Development (DFID). (2000). Making trade work for poor people. In DFID report on globalisation, *Eliminating poverty: Making globalisation work for the poor.* London, UK: Author.

The Ecologist. (2001). *Go M.A.D.! 365 daily ways to save the planet.* London, UK: Think Publishing.

Escobar, S. (2000). The global scenario at the turn of the century. In W. D. Taylor (Ed.), *Global missiology for the 21st century: The Iguassu dialogue* (pp. 25-46). Grand Rapids, MI: Baker Academic.

Foust, T., Hunsberger, G., Kirk, J., & Ustorf, W. (Eds.). (2002). *A scandalous prophet: The way of mission after Newbigin.* Grand Rapids, MI: William B. Eerdmans Publishing.

Giddens, A. (1999). *A runaway world: Reith lecture on globalisation.* New Delhi, India. Retrieved from http://news.bbc.co.uk/hi/english/events/reith_99/week3/lecture3.htm.

Goldsmith, M. (2000). *Jesus and his relationships.* Carlisle, UK: Paternoster Press.

Gorringe, T. (1999). *Fair shares: Ethics and the global economy.* London, UK: Thames & Hudson.

Gunton, C. (1992). *Christ and creation.* Carlisle, UK: Paternoster Press.

Heslam, P. (2002). *Globalisation: Unravelling the new capitalism.* Cambridge, UK: Grove Books Ltd.

Hutchinson, M. (1999). *What's wrong with globalisation, anyway?* Cambridge, UK: Currents in World Christianity Project.

Institute of Directors. (2002). *Globalisation: The real nature and impact.*

Klein, N. (2000). *No logo.* London, UK: Flamingo.

Micklethwaite, J., & Wooldridge, A. (2000). *A future perfect.* London, UK: Heinemann.

Mofid, K. (2002). *Globalisation for the common good.* London, UK: Shepheard Walwyn Ltd.

Moore, M. (2001, First Quarter). Trade rules for global commerce. *Global Future*, p. 2.

The New Internationalist. (1997, November).

———. (1999, October).

———. (2000, January/February).

Northcott, M. (1999). *Life after debt: Christianity and global justice.* London, UK: SPCK.

Oxfam. (2000, May). *Globalisation.* Oxfam GB Policy Paper 5/00. Retrieved from http://www.oxfam.org.uk/policy/papers/global/global1a.htm.

Roddick A. (Ed.). (2001). *Take it personally: How globalisation affects you and powerful ways to challenge it.* London, UK: Thorsons.

Sine, T. (1999). *Mustard seed vs. McWorld: Reinventing Christian life and mission for a new millennium.* Crowborough, UK: Monarch Books.

Smith, D. (2000). Paper presented at Global Connections conference, *The emerging paradigm: Mission thinking for the third millennium*. Doncaster, UK.

The Society of St. John the Evangelist. (1997). *Living in hope: A rule of life for today*. Canterbury, UK: Canterbury Press.

Stiglitz, J. (2002). *Globalisation and its discontents*. London, UK: Allen Lane, Penguin Press.

Stott, J. (Ed.). (1996). *Making Christ known: Historic mission documents from the Lausanne Movement 1974–1989*. Carlisle, UK: Paternoster Press.

Valerio, R. (2002a). *Globalisation and poverty*. Cred Papers. [Provides further bibliography on globalisation] (Available from ruth@cred.org.uk)

———. (2002b). *Simplicity: Living life to the full*. Cred Papers. (Available from ruth@cred.org.uk)

World Development Movement. (1998). *The good life: Your guide to everyday actions which ensure a fairer deal for the world's poor*. London, UK: Author.

Ruth Valerio *works with the organisation Cred, teaching and resourcing the church on globalisation, justice and poverty, environment, and lifestyle issues. She is on the Council of the World Development Movement and on the Tearfund Theological Resources Team. Ruth is based in Chichester, UK, with two preschool children, and is chair of her local Community Association. Email: ruth.valerio@virgin.net.*

2

Emerging youth cultures in the era of globalization: TechnoCulture and TerrorCulture

Sam George

Globalization and culture mean different things to different people. Their relationship to youth and religion is even more ambiguous. Globalization and the emerging culture are deeply intertwined subjects and have a reciprocal relationship. The emerging generation will shape the future of both.

Globalization is commonly seen through the lens of economics or politics, but culture is another important lens to consider. Globalization lies at the heart of contemporary culture, and cultural elements lie at the heart of globalization. Some view culture as the "intrinsic aspect of the whole process" of globalization (Tomlinson, 1999, p. 22), while others assert the priority of culture by saying, "Material exchanges localize; political exchanges internationalize; and symbolic exchanges globalize" (Waters, 1995). The conventional approach confounds an explanation of the multidimensionality of globalization, and we must avoid giving casual priority to one dimension over another.

Nevertheless, cultural implications are central to understanding the human side of globalization, and youth culture will have a significant bearing on globalization's future. Globalization isn't about Western culture anymore, but it is a new form of culture that knows no boundaries and is spreading globally. In this chapter, use of the term "emerging culture" is not restricted to popular culture or any subculture, but it is a common cultural expression of the coming generation and that generation's underlying philosophical moorings. Youth culture simultaneously shapes globalization and is shaped by it. Young people have a symbiotic relationship with globalization that accelerates its influence in their lives. Some have called youth culture the "vehicle for globalization" (Dean, 2000), while others deny the existence of any homogenous global culture.[1] It is widely agreed that while there is no such thing as a global culture, yet there is a globalization of culture (Featherstone, 1990, p. 1). *National Geographic*, in its cover article on global culture, claimed, "Cultures are in a constant state of flux" (Global, 1999, p. 12). Culture must be understood as a dynamic entity and not as a static one anymore. New cultures emerge constantly, existing ones take new forms, some are preserved forcefully, and some even die.

> Money moves.
> Goods move.
> People move.
> Ideas move.
> And cultures change.

Although the emerging culture of the global youth is complex and defies reasoning, it is a vital element in understanding the future of globalization and religion. Youth is often viewed as the emerging market the world over (half the world is below the age of 25), and winning the loyalty of youth is key to any business. In political circles, the youth vote bank has turned the tides on leadership in many parts of the world. In religious circles, most people make their life commitment to a faith during their formative years of adolescence. For these and other reasons, it is critical to navigate through the emerging cultures in order to bring the unchanging truth of the gospel to them.

Two Perspectives: From Above and Below

In this chapter and the next, I want to map two emerging cultures among the youth of the world from two distinct perspectives—globalization from above and globalization from below. The cultures could also be viewed as McWorld and Jihad, or top-down and bottom-up, or the high and low cultures of globalization, respectively. The emerging culture defining globalization from above would be technology or **TechnoCulture**. Tech savvy-ness is a chief characteristic of the emerging generation around the world. The form of technology may vary, and its knowledge and use may vary too. But the inclination of youth toward technology and their capacity to acquire techno-skills and knowledge are universal. The common ground of the TechnoCulture of the global youth consists of computers, the Internet, and wireless devices.

---

[1] John Tomlinson, Richard Barnet and John Cavanagh, and Tom Friedman are among those who hold this view.

```
. . . . . . . . . . . . . . . . . . . . . . .
:                                           :
:        T e c h n o C u l t u r e          :
:                                           :
:                   ⇩                       :
:                                           :
:           globalization                   :
:                                           :
:                   ⇧                       :
:                                           :
:        T e r r o r C u l t u r e          :
:                                           :
. . . . . . . . . . . . . . . . . . . . . . .
```

In the next chapter, I want to make a case about an uncommon theme in the discussion of youth culture—a culture of terrorism, or **TerrorCulture**, as "globalization from below." Since the events of September 11, 2001, the culture of terrorism has been etched in the minds of people worldwide. The ongoing war on terrorism and the growing militancy around the world have a youthful face. Young people comprise the army of terrorist networks globally, and there is a growing propensity toward violence.

Both TechnoCulture and Terror-Culture are representative of the global youth. They are not "either/or" features but a **concurrent** reality of the global youth populace. Young people can be seen as swinging between these extremities, with each culture driving the debate in its own direction. Although TechnoCulture is more predominant in advanced countries and TerrorCulture in poorer parts of the world, streaks of both cultures can be located throughout the globe. Both continue to cast considerable influence on the global society.

Both cultures have a **subversive** nature at their core, and they are very attractive to the young. The emerging generations are easily drawn to the claims and rewards of these cultures. They are easy "converts" to the cultural ideologies. They see the potential for fulfillment of their deeper longings, and they view the cultures as a way to make their lives matter in this world. In these fluid/turbulent cultures, young people find a purpose for their lives and a cause worth pursuing.

The serious spiritual **quest** of the emerging generation and their sense of spirituality often astound those who have taken a serious look into emerging cultures. Today's youth are sick of conventional religious institutions and prepackaged pieties. They are quick to

```
. . . . . . . . . . . . . . . . . . . . . . .
:                                           :
:        "Our hearts are restless           :
:             until they find               :
:           their rest in Thee."            :
:              — St. Augustine              :
:                                           :
. . . . . . . . . . . . . . . . . . . . . . .
```

decipher false religiosity and shallow spirituality. As Christ-followers, we have much to learn from the cultures of technology and terrorism and much to contribute to them. These cultures reveal a God-shaped vacuum. We must engage TechnoCulture decisively and bring these new realities to bear upon Kingdom purposes. We must change with the continually changing culture, yet preserve the truth of the gospel of Jesus Christ and the historic Christian faith.

The cultures of terrorism and technology also **intersect**. Modern technology is used by terrorist groups these days, and there are terrorizing effects of modern technology on society and on the world as well. Recent terrorist networks have exhibited advanced knowledge and proficiency in using modern tools such as the Internet, mobile communication, airplanes, explosives, etc. The major components of defense expenditures of many advanced nations are set apart for building advanced technological infrastructure. Use of the latest tools is a scary experience for many people, especially for adults. They are often left behind in the ever-expanding wealth of knowledge and talent. For those who never had an opportunity to acquire the physical and mental dexterity that are needed, technology tools can be overwhelming.

A cross-cultural missiological paradigm to engage these emerging cultures is key to doing **ministry** in the 21st century. Understanding these cultures of technology and terrorism and every subculture between these extremes is absolutely essential for every youth worker, missionary, or church leader. Then comes the need to make Jesus Christ relevant in these cultures—calling the emerging generation to radical discipleship, building Christ-centered communities of faith, and bearing witness to the coming generations and cultures. If we fail to take these emerging cultures seriously, the Christian faith is only a generation away from extinction!

C@tch the W@ve: TechnoCulture

Few people have as much faith in technology as Nicolas Negroponte, the founding director of the Media Labs at the Massachusetts Institute of Technology (MIT). Along with his son Dimtri, he set up a mission to provide laptops with Internet access for every one of the world's 1 billion children through a foundation they formed called 2B1 (To Be One). They believed that universal Internet access is tantamount to creating world peace, securing the fate of humanity, and ensuring the health of the planet and the global economy. Electronic game maker Sega Enterprises was the first major donor to the foundation.

As the saying goes, we do not know who discovered water, but surely it was not a fish! When we are entrenched with technology so deeply, will we ever find what we really are in? In this technological world, what is it to be human? Does this culture nurture our soul and fulfill its yearning? Where does God fit into all this? What are the tenets of the "religion" or god espoused by the high-tech generation? Are we aware of the new spirituality of the cyber generation? What can the church learn from the cyber generation? How could we shape our future mission efforts to impact the emerging generations and cultures?

TechnoCulture: Whatever?

Throughout human history, some form of technology[2] has always been the root cause of economic and social change in the world. We first shape our tools, and they in turn shape us. Some types of technological innovation have been the catalyst for revolutionary changes in the culture of their time. The invention of the wheel in ancient civilization transformed transportation and

---

[2] I use "technology" in a generic sense of human activity that has elements of improvement, innovation, efficiency, etc. Technology here should not be understood as this machine or that gadget or any branch of science, such as computers, medicine, etc., but as the entire organized and interdependent ensemble dictating the technization of everyday life, work, and play. Technology is methodical, it is purposive and has material outcome, it generates knowledge, and it uses resources.

travel; the invention of currency transformed trade and spread capital around the world; and the invention of the printing press transformed learning, media, communication, and knowledge dissemination all over the world. Additionally, consider the far-reaching impacts of electricity, the steam engine, the telephone, airplanes, nuclear power, genetics, etc., on the cultures of the world. Each had its own set of critics and proponents. However, **large-scale adoption** of these technologies by the coming generations established them as a normative part of life from then on.

So, what is TechnoCulture? Scholars are divided. Jacques Ellul, the French philosopher, dealt with this question in a chapter titled, "Is there a technical culture?" He concluded, "A technical culture is impossible" (Ellul, 1990, p. 141). One of his critiques asserts, "Technique is universal, but culture cannot be, for human beings are not universal. We all have a place, a race, a formation, and a specific time" (Ellul, 1990, p. 144). Yet dominant characteristics of the contemporary society are such that the rest of the world constantly influences us, even when we are deeply rooted in our locality. The term "glocal" has come to define the duality of contemporary life as both global and local. This trend has challenged the conceptual frameworks by which we have traditionally grasped the social order.

The contemporary culture is inundated with technological **sophistication**. John Naisbitt called it the "Technologically Intoxicated Zone," where we both fear and worship technology (Naisbitt, Naisbitt, and Philips, 1999). Today we are fascinated by technology's gadgetry, reliant on its constant companionship, addicted to its steady delivery of entertainment, seduced by its promises, and awed by its power and speed. Technology has squeezed out the human spirit and intensified our search for meaning. We either love it or hate it. There's no middle ground. We are either afraid of the daily dose of breaking technology news, or we are inspired by it. For most of us, technology is far from neutral. It shapes our choices and directs our actions, whether we are ready or not! Who could deny that TechnoCulture is the chief distinctiveness of contemporary life? Arjun Appadurai (1996, p. 32) named "technoscape" as one of the five cultural flows in explaining the fundamental disjunctures between economy, culture, and politics in his globalization theory.

There is more to global TechnoCulture than what seems obvious—the convergence of tastes, consumption patterns, and sophisticated gadgetry. It is too simplistic to view TechnoCulture as the use of common brand wear, media preferences, or the spread of the Internet across the world. There is a more profound cultural and generation cleavage that is occurring in societies worldwide. For example, there are "Nintendo kids" in Japanese society (Japanese teenagers of the 1990s), the Digital Generation (computer whizkids) from India, and MTV band (young people with multimedia and multisensory abilities).

What lies at the core of this TechnoCulture is the **reprogramming** of perceptions, social values, and meaning by the emerging generation, which stands in contradiction to that of their parents or grandparents. TechnoCulture is giving rise to a "cross-border civilization" or a new "global community." Japanese business strategist Kenichi Ohame includes a cultural discourse on globalization in relation to the capitalist market economy and nation-state. He argues, "The new generation of youngsters is much less accepting of traditional Japanese notions of authority and conformity, much more culturally open, questioning, and creative: everything can be explored, rearranged, reprogrammed.... Everything, finally, is open to considered choice, initiative, creativity, and daring" (Ohame, 1995, p. 36).

We are so steeped in this technological culture that even while lamenting its consequences, we unconsciously use the tech jargon and imagery, for life without them is almost unimaginable. Every new technology generates novel forms of human activity and has the potential to reshape our lives dramatically. Every new technology has social, cultural, moral, financial, intellectual, and emotional implications. In this chapter, I intend to limit myself to the cultural implications of recent technological phenomena, such as computers, the Internet, and wireless technology in relation to globalization and youth.

Generation Y-erless: Hey, where are you?

For the first time in human history, younger generations access, acquire, process, and control more information than their predecessors. They possess knowledge that their parents do not (Alch, 2000), such as how to reset the radio on the car, why the VCR is not blinking 12:00, and how to install more memory in a computer. The younger generation is also capable of doing

harm that only the military could do in the past (see Adams, 1998). For example, a German teenager breaks into the NASA computer network to steal space shuttle designs, and a Filipino college student sends a virus, the Love Bug.[3]

One of the main characteristics of the emerging generation is the technology orientation of its members. Technology is almost second nature to young people, if not first. They learn to use computers before language, mathematics, or science. In fact, they learn everything else through computers and the Internet. TechnoCulture is the **amniotic fluid** that makes this generation thrive. Technology is defining them and owning them, sometimes even manipulating them. Technological tools shape their identity, form virtual communities, and even offer intimacy. Virtuality is more real than reality to many youngsters. Wireless technology has finally broken the **umbilical cord** and birthed this generation into the New World.

Mobile phones have suddenly become an "omnipresent" and absolutely essential accessory for this generation. One's sense of **belonging** to the world (the world is in one's address book)

---

[3] The Love Bug shut down government agencies, and large portals came to a grinding halt, damaging corporate information, etc. The official CIA estimate of the damage amounted to $4 billion, with some unofficial estimates going as high as $60 billion.

and one's status are tightly interwoven with the gadgets that one carries. With this technology, one has the choice to take a call or avoid it without missing much. Convergence of technologies has brought the Internet, games, music, video, etc., into mobile telephony. The vision of 4G (fourth generation) mobile telephony is to make computing ubiquitous by going wireless, allowing it to be working all the time with limitless bandwidth. There is also a plethora of other wireless devices and hand-held accessories that this generation takes for granted. Life without them is almost inconceivable.

For the first time ever, a generation of teens and tweens is growing up with an information network. Some call these young people "Children of Revolution" (Digital, 2002). Others call them the "Net Generation" (N-Gen) (Tapscott, 1998). They are early adopters, hyper-connected, mobile, and always on. Teens live in a world where "religious chat rooms and websites act like spiritual supermarkets, offering an assortment of belief systems all within one click" (*Newsweek*, 2000, May 8). It takes a generation to unlock the potential of a transformative technology, and today it is the N-Gen. IM, P2P, and MP3[4] are all a regular part of their lives. While others marvel at the digital future, they take it for granted. Think of technology as the difference between one's second language and the first, and imagine the impact when full fluency hits the workplace, the shopping mall, and the living room. In the past, you put away childish things when you grew up. But these tools are taking over the adult world. The technology is **trickling up!**

Technology has become a critical factor in forming a common culture of the emerging people globally. Today's young people are generally more technology-savvy than their predecessors. The information explosion, competency, and usage of the latest technology have become distinctive features between generations. Young people even wonder how the world could ever exist without some of the technology gadgets. Computer skills and knowledge become essential to life, not just to making a living.

Youth culture: real-time, real cool!

The tidal waves have crashed over every corner of the culture (Sweet, 1999b). The latest movies, books, websites, and game software have enormous attraction to youths, not only for their entertainment value, but also to allow participation in the buzz of social and work life. In most cases, cultural value ranks higher than utilitarian value. Technology is more than a product or information for youth; it is an obsession. Young people are hardcore believers in what technology can do, and they become the earliest consumers of all new innovations. Youth buy a new product to **define** themselves, not just because it looks interesting or feels right. TechnoCulture is ingrained in the emerging generation—both fueling it and producing it at the same time.

The ubiquitous aspect of teenhood is the relentless need to **communicate**.

---

[4] These acronyms stand for instant messaging, peer-to-peer, and a popular media format, respectively.

Some messages are too urgent for email—especially for teenagers. Using instant messaging in the US, text messaging via SMS in Europe, and i-mode and other services in Japan, kids worldwide are asking the pressing questions:  "What are you doing after school?" "Will you go out with me?" "Isn't s/he cool?" The same was true when telephones first appeared early last century.[5] Some scholars view young people's attraction to wireless devices as more of a fascination with technology. They believe these devices have become a "conduit to community and communication. Without these gadgets, they are out of the social loop, which could have devastating effects" (Easton, 2002, p. 213).

Instant messaging and SMS features have also redefined **language** and spelling. Computer lingo is replacing some conventional use of language and meaning, e.g., boot up (= wake up), shutdown (= sleep), cut and paste, mouse, web, virus, spam, etc. New rituals, such as networking, instant messaging, and surfing, and new hieroglyphics, such as ":)" and ";)", have swept into mainstream communication. Also, the youth culture has switched from words to images as the primary means to communicate. It thrives on imagery, whether conveyed through visual communication, metaphorical usage, narrative preaching, or other means.

The nature of more recent technological innovation promotes the idea of cultural **immersion** and an experiential dimension. One doesn't *watch* MTV; instead, one enters into the world of image-rich overflow of 24-hour programming in the mesmerizing medium of hyper-quick cuts and ever-varied camera angles. Interactivity is an important feature that includes a mass-scale participation of the audience. Music in digital formats aids the flow of content and expresses a spirit of sharing (through peer-to-peer networks such as Napster and Gnutella). Longing for a community, members of this generation share their tastes and aspirations. They often grope in the darkness of the Internet world, firmly convinced that there is more to life than what is obvious or what they have discovered. Often their "wired" sense of existence transcends every barrier.

The comfort and anonymity of the **virtual** world distinguish this generation. This attachment could be interpreted as a sign of the Net Generation's inability to confront the real world or as an attempt to emulate the reality of the world in more discrete forms. Video games and reality shows are largely a matter of reality imitation. Some of the youth show extreme dexterity of hands and minds, emerging from indulgences in video games after spending hours with a joystick and TV console. Whereas adults used television merely to watch the programs, lying on the couch to catch the game scores or a movie, N-Gen members have found more exciting and participatory use of the same equipment.

There is an accelerated nature to TechnoCulture. **Speed** is everything, not just a movie name. Time is measured in megahertz and nanoseconds.

---

[5] For more detailed history of information revolutions, see Lubar (1993, pp. 119-164).

Life is lived out in real-time. The Net Generation is plugged in, online, image-driven, and media-saturated—continually and obsessively. Just-in-time inventory and instant communication are not just buzzwords, but a philosophy. All these changes have not come without a cost, however. Lower attention span, depression, anger, and frustration are part of the package. As a generation, these young people have lost their social and relational center.

Although some theorists believe that Americanization has created the global culture, most scholars agree that there is no such thing as a global culture. But there is indeed globalization of culture, meaning the simultaneous "cultural integration and disintegration process which takes place on only the interstate level but ... which transcends the state-society level and can therefore be held to occur on a trans-national or trans-societal level" (Featherstone, 1990, p. 1). Geographical borderlessness is causing cultural borders to become more porous, due to cultural exchanges and the development of new cultural norms. The melting pot is no longer an apt metaphor for global culture. Instead, global culture is the **"morphing"** of various cultural images into a new entity with multiple nodes of dissemination aimed at a global audience. Another image comes from the title of British artist Damien Hirst's (1997) book: *I want to spend the rest of my life everywhere, with everyone, one to one, always, forever, now*. Some other interesting titles describing this culture include *The death of distance* (Cairncross, 1997), *Brave new unwired world: The digital big bang* (Lightman, 2002), and *Male, female, email: The struggle of relatedness in a paranoid society* (Civin, 2000).

The cellular phone is another good metaphor of the emerging generation. It is a new wireless form of a technological innovation of the previous era. Such a phone is not merely something I use, but it is something that has become part of me. It defines me—mobility without losing connectivity. A generation ago, it was only connectivity that mattered, but now it is mobility with connectivity and everything else that comes with it. The phone stays with me, moves with me, and always connects me to the rest of world. Without it, I feel powerless and disconnected. It is not something I use, but an essential wearable accessory. Recently a young man told me, "I have never worn a watch and never will. I get the time from my cell phone." This is a radical redefinition of how I get what I need. And the time is always local time, regardless of where I go. We will see more of such global tools that help define locality and vice versa.

TechnoTrends: The future just happened!

Many agree with Douglas Robertson (1998, p. 180), who asserted, "The invention of the computer is the most important event in the history of technology, if not in history, period." Others have drawn parallels to the printing press as a delivery mechanism during the Protestant Reformation (see, for example, Sweet, 1999a, 2000a, 2000b). But computers are merely part of a greater revolution that technology is paving all around us. Jack Welch, the high-profile corporate chief of General Electric, identifies the Internet as the greatest technological innovation of our times. The slogan of Sun Microsystems, "The network is the computer," re-

defines what a computer really is. The socio-cultural revolution that the Internet has caused is unprecedented and is greater than the technological revolution itself. The "wire the world" project of some telecom giants is not only knitting the world together through high-speed bandwidth lines (planning to bring the Internet within the reach of every human being on the planet), but also creating a new socio-cultural consciousness (see Gilder, 2000).

In the last decade or so, there has been a complete shift from analog to digital technology, including telephone switching, transmission, and content creation. The results of digitalization include (1) the convergence of various technologies, such as radio, television, and Internet; (2) miniaturization of products; (3) "wi-fication," or the development of a wide range of wireless devices; (4) cost-effective alternatives; and (5) an information and service based economy.

Convergence is not just about interoperability, but it is an ideology of our times. The seductive lure of wireless Internet is that it combines the best of the worlds of computing, Internet, and mobile communication. It holds the power to deliver to users personalized, location-sensitive content and applications that previously were either impossible or impractical. Consumer brands such as McDonald's and Reebok view mobile communication as their main competition for leisure spending. Peer-to-peer (P2P) computing[6] shifted the power from commercial interest to the individual and will become normative for wearable computing.

Another pertinent dimension of TechnoCulture is the issue of **obsolescence**. Every innovation buries the previous ones. The old cliché "creative destruction" is at the heart of the business models of the microprocessor and the software industry. Quantum leaps constantly occur in innovation. After analyzing various tangible ingredients that made Silicon Valley of California a success in the information economy, many believe the greatest contributing cause is the intangible factor called clusters. It is said, "Culture is more important to Silicon Valley's success than economies or technologies" (Micklethwaite and Wooldridge, 2000, p. 210). Elizabeth Weil (1997), a youth culture

"The information highway is going to break down boundaries and may promote a world culture, or at least a sharing of activities and values. The highway will also make it easy for patriots, even expatriates, deeply involved in their own ethnic communities, to reach out to others with similar interests no matter where they may be located. This may strengthen cultural diversity and counter the tendency toward a single world culture."

— Bill Gates (1995)

---

[6] Marc Andreessen, founder of Netscape, called P2P the most important development on the Internet.

writer, said it well: "Prepare to feel obsolete. It's the first step to moving ahead." The foremost quality of highly successful clusters in Silicon Valley is a "distinctive bias for youth." Other characteristics that are extremely valuable to the technology culture include high tolerance for failure, risk-taking ability, and enthusiasm for change. All of these come naturally to the emerging generation. Thus, inexperience is the experience needed in this culture.

Four centuries ago, the English statesman-philosopher Francis Bacon wrote that information is **power**. Joseph Nye compared this power with military and economic powers and calls the power of information "soft power" from a foreign policy and international politics perspective. But it is basically a culture power—Western nations engaged in the export of culture or cultural imperialism. Information technology has given enormous amounts of power to individuals and small enterprises—power that was once available only to giant corporations. The enormous amount of wealth creation, through the spread of popular culture, means a power shift is happening in favour of the younger generation.

CyberSpirituality: always on

The quest of this generation is more evident than that of any other culture because of its technological nature. Today's youth exhibit strong spiritual intuitions. They are turning products of this culture for their **inner longing**. Naomi Klein (cited in Sittenfeld, 2000, p. 244) captured the idea well in *No Logo*: "We are looking to brands for poetry and for spirituality, because we're not getting those things from our communities or from each other. When Nike says, 'Just do it,' that's a message of empowerment. Why aren't the rest of us speaking to young people in a voice of inspiration?"

Different kinds of technology have had significant influence in shaping spirituality throughout the centuries. Tidal waves of change in Christian history can be traced back to innovations in road construction. In Rome, Paul took the gospel to the then-known world using the newly laid roads. Other innovations include architecture, music, printing, transportation, and currency. "The technology of the book [referring to the Protestant Reformation and the printing press] altered Christian spirituality in momentous ways. Spirituality is **shaped** by technology. Always has been. Always will be" (Sweet, 2000a, p. 35). Emory University anthropologist Charles Nuckolls poignantly captured the search of today's uprooted person when he wrote, "People feel they want something they've lost, and they don't remember what it is they've lost. But it has left a gaping hole." His observation appeared in a major cover story in *Newsweek* magazine entitled, "In search of the sacred: America's quest for spiritual meaning" (In search, 1994).

Spirituality is alive and thriving on the Internet. The emerging generation is strangely aware that material things will not fill that "gaping hole" in them. Youth can be seen everywhere on the Net, searching to find answers to their nagging questions about life— its origin, destiny, meaning, and purpose. There is a growing tendency

> People are interested in spirituality, but not necessarily in religion, including Christianity.

to look for religious and spiritual information online, and a recent study (*Wired*, 2002) arrived at a figure of more than 2 million American Internet users on any given day. Cyber shrines are offering virtual "puja" to their devotees. The Internet is inundated with spiritual practices, and browsing has even turned ritualistic. Simply going online gives a sense of connectedness to something bigger than oneself. Young people prefer to stay connected all the time, and yet they know that there is more to life than what they have discovered.

In the contemporary culture, we have come to fear as well as worship technology. We see technologies as toys and quick-fixes. Technology has become a great equalizer by creating a level playing field, including the religious field. Talking of electronically leveled institutions, Tom Beaudoin (1999, p. 56) notes, "The sense of 'no one is in control' makes cyberspace hostile to the hegemony of religious institutions." Cyberspace also threatens the stability of religious institutions because it is radically pluralistic. Every opinion is regarded, every voice heard among those who are on the Net. None is superior to any other; we must give sincere hearing to every viewpoint.

Thomas Friedman (1999, pp. 7-8) predicts that in the 21st century, globalization will go "farther, faster, cheaper, and deeper." This will be true of the new spirituality as well. We would use all that is at our disposal in our quest for that "gaping hole." This new cyber-spirituality is quickly spreading all over the world. Pollster George Gallup (cited in Myers, 2000, p. 96) confirmed it: "Surveys document the movement of people who are searching for meaning in life with a new intensity and want their religious faith to grow." If George Barna's research projections hold true, more than 100 million people will soon be looking to the Internet for spiritual nourishment (Barna, 2001).

Beliefs of TechnoCulture: Utopianism?

TechnoCulture has its own unique set of beliefs. Some are obvious: "Technology has solutions to all human problems," "The market is the true test of everything," "Whatever can be done, will be done," "Everything gets better over time," "Money is the highest good," "All government and regulations are bad," etc. There is an over-reliance on the spreadsheet way of knowledge, which says that if something cannot be quantified, then it has no value. If you cannot count it, it does not exist. How do you quantify social services, art, or poetry? Do these things have no value because they are non-quantifiable?

Paradox is common in TechnoCulture. Two seemingly contradictory views are embraced at the same time. TechnoCulture holds a "both/and" view of the world, rather than an "either/or" view. Fuzzy logic comes naturally to

> "It is good to hold on to the one thing and not lose hold of the other; for someone who fears God will succeed both ways."
> — Ecclesiastes 7:18 REB

the emerging generation. Among older folks, paradox creates paralysis, and contradictions are unacceptable even in their wildest imagination. Today's youth have arrived at the realization that everything around them cannot be clearly explained away. They are pushing the envelope of current understanding. They possess a near-fatal attraction for paradoxes and have discovered that fuzzy thinking is woven into the tapestry of the universe—a world in which matter is both particle and wave, a world comprised of both matter and antimatter. They celebrate mystery more than explanation.

TechnoCulture is all about **personalization**. The old paradigm of standardization and mass production does not work anymore. For the first time, technology has developed to cater to an individual's whims and fancies, leading to extreme individualism. Levi creates special-order jeans designed by the customers, and Dell makes a computer according to user specifications—not to mention "My AOL," "My Citibank," etc. Like the Internet, ministry to this generation needs to be highly personal, interactive, and highly relevant. Instead of broadcasting to the masses, it must focus on **"narrowcasting"** to the individual. A TechnoCulture ministry must meet real needs of real people, where they live and when they need it. It will not happen at the convenience or the availability of the leader.

The other incredibly toxic aspect of this culture is the narcissism of the high-tech community. Young people have bought into the idea that they are part of the best, the most important, the most innovative thing that has ever happened, and anyone who is outside doesn't add any value. They believe they carry the mantle of a perfect world, and they hope to see the technological utopia in their lifetime. The contemporary sense of **utopianism** in TechnoCulture isn't anything new. Every innovation before the present time also possessed the same idealism. The dream of utopia derives from our dis-

satisfaction with the present and our hope to create a blissful future for the human race. The popular works on this theme are Aldous Huxley's (1948) *Brave New World* and George Orwell's (1949) *Nineteen Eighty-Four*, both of which contain an anti-technology bias. In the later version, *Brave New World Revisited*, Huxley (1965) accurately indicted technology.

"Modern technology has led to the concentration of economic and political power and to the development of society controlled (ruthlessly in the totalitarian states, politely and inconspicuously in the democracies) by big businesses and big government. But societies are composed of individuals and are good only insofar as they help individuals to release their potentialities and to lead a happy and creative life."
— Aldous Huxley

Orwell's book was a despairing prediction that totalitarianism would inevitably be victorious and would submerge humanity. 1984 came and went. Some of Orwell's forecasts were accurate, while many others were wide of the mark. The human spirit and values triumphed over the despair about the future of man as portrayed by Orwell. We have not surrendered our human qualities and become soulless automata. Instead, newer technologies have only augmented our deeper longing for God and others.

One could paraphrase Cassius from a Shakespearean play: "The fault, dear

Brutus, is not in our technology, but in ourselves, that we are the underlings." Since we are fallen creatures, the best of our inventions cannot achieve a state better than our own. It takes humility to admit that all of our technological creations are only a reflection of our imperfections. A perfect world cannot be made out of imperfections. We must let the perfection of God invade our imperfect world. The story of the **redemption** of the world and the utopian order Jesus promised is the only hope in the TechnoCulture and every culture.

Search for meaning: Why is common sense so uncommon?

TechnoCulture has given rise to the Information Age or vice versa. We are blinded by endless bit-level data, but we lack the technique to infuse knowledge laden with values into the equation, or else we lack the vantage point to make sense of it all. One of the leading critics of technology culture,

> Today we are overfed
> with information
> and malnourished for meaning.

Theodore Roszak (1969), objects to the basic method of scientific thinking, calling it the "myth of objective consciousness." His "counter culture" consists of "the *young*,[7] who oppose the technological society and seek alternative living patterns." We must recognize how the young are the first ones to adopt technological innovation. At the same time, they are the first ones to discover technology's fallacy. Today, technology is used both to create and to oppose the prevailing culture. The countercultural tendencies push the limits of our inquisitive minds that fuel further exploration for newer tools. Roszak believes that man wants to find the meaning of his existence and a clue to his true identity. Without meaning, work is not worth doing, and technology has no value. Though technologists mean well, they produce soulless works, which lack the gift of love. "The information culture is killing the soul of the world," as Tom Mahon (1997) observed. There is a new type of ignorance amid the accumulation of knowledge.

Jacques Ellul's (1964) *The Technological Society* is one of the most voluminous and frequently quoted criticisms of technology. According to Ellul, our society is characterized by "technique"—defined as "the organized ensemble of all individual techniques which have been used to secure any end whatsoever." Ellul feels that, "Man has become so concerned with technique, perfection of technique now overrides the end desired, and technique itself becomes an end rather than a means." He even thinks technique and humanism are incompatible. Like a tidal wave, technique inexorably advances, with humanity helpless before it. But Ellul offers no solution. According to him, utopian society might be static, as it was in the Middle Ages.

Common among all critics of technology is the fact that they glamorize

---

[7] Emphasis mine. Roszak locates the young as the counter-cultural.

the past while decrying the present. Some favor simplicity and uncomplicated periods of history; others come down hard on evils of the present. Since the future is unknown and the present is overwhelming, these critics take refuge in the "good old times." C. P. Snow (1993, p. 31) pointed out, "The Industrial Revolution looked very differently according to whether one saw it from above or below." So will it be with every technological revolution to come. People will fall into the category of either the "haves" or the "have-nots," privileged or exploited. This classification has nothing to do with technology, but instead reflects the people who are behind the technology. Likewise, the problem is not with TechnoCulture, but it is with our failure to incarnate Jesus Christ and his values into the emerging cultures.

Just as critics accompanied every technological innovation of the past, there were also strong advocates of TechnoCulture. Faith in technology has been vigorously defended in the last century, and the TechnoCulture continues to evolve. Some leading thinkers were J. Bronowski, Melvin Kranzberg, Harrison Brown, R. B. Fuller, Marshall McLuhan, and Carl Mitcham.[8] The optimism of defenders of technology continues to see the future of mankind in a technologically sophisticated world, with quantum gains in new innovations using current innovations. The benefits of technology are too obvious. So TechnoCulture is here to stay, in spite of its critics, and it will gain greater momentum. We must be careful not to deify technology, yet we should give praise to what merits praise. We must intelligently and compassionately order technology for the future, while recognizing its limits and harmful effects.

Ministry in TechnoCulture: faith that works

The tools of TechnoCulture are just tools, and they can be used for good or evil. Their use should be maximized for Christian ministry. These tools can never replace real ministry, but they can extend existing ministries and can create new ones. We must go beyond the hype and explore TechnoCulture's real potential for ministry. The newer tools and the culture they form should never intimidate us. Instead, we must **redeem** the TechnoCulture with the Spirit of Christ for the glory of God.

> "Do not go where the path may be. Go instead where there is no path, and leave a trail."
> — Ralph W. Emerson

The emerging generation defies old identities. These young people do not fit into the usual categories. They are difficult to classify, tough to label, and downright unpredictable, thus making it difficult to know exactly who is being reached in our missionary enterprise. If we continue to emulate old models of church and mission work, we're going to miss the emerging generation. The "one size fits all" approach will definitely not be the most effective model of the 21st century.

---

[8] For a detailed evaluation of these advocates of technology, see Watkins and Meader (1987) and Mitcham (1994).

Is This a Christian Ministry?

A project called "Unwiring the World" (Schwartz, 2001, p. 48) was founded in 1998 by Alex "Sandy" Pentland, academic head of the MIT Media Lab, and Jose Maria Figueres, former president of Costa Rica. Unwiring the World is creating portable digital town centers in the Central American jungle: recycled shipping containers furnished with telemedicine units, cash machines, microcomputer schools, soil-and-environment testing labs, FM radio stations, wireless satellite links, and big-screen TVs. Seven of the units, dubbed LINCOS, or little intelligent communities, have been installed in off-the-grid areas in Costa Rica and the Dominican Republic, where they are being used by residents to help form agricultural cooperatives, launch e-commerce initiatives, and access education and employment information online.

Is Bridging the Digital Divide a new mission strategy? Isn't "bridge" an incarnational metaphor? Could missionaries be the agents of taking the benefits of technology to the ends of the world, instead of waiting for it to trickle down? Or resist the digitalization so that there is no divide in the first place?

Just as Jesus broke into human history through his birth, we must **incarnate** Christ into the TechnoCulture. The incarnational Christian realizes that the gospel travels through time not in some ideal form, but from one inculturated form to another. Max Stackhouse (1988, p. 6) makes a distinction between the "textuality" of the church (its faithfulness to the gospel) and its "contextuality" (its faithfulness to the world in which it finds itself). Lesslie Newbigin (1988, p. 50) rightly insists that the gospel only retains "its proper strangeness, its power to question us … when we are faithful to its universal suprarational, supranational, supracultural nature." So it should be with TechnoCulture.

Christian leaders ministering in the TechnoCulture do not operate by mission. Rather, they focus on **relationships** and on the gifts they see in people. They follow their intuition and celebrate creativity, spontaneity, and diversity. They develop a healthy appetite for constant **learning** (also unlearning!) and operate in **teams**. They focus on a central **person** (Jesus Christ), rather than on a central doctrine. When they live out the gospel in the real world, they make it unquestionably attractive in this culture.

The most common rhetoric about technology falls into two extremes: unconditional acceptance or blanket rejection. Many see the emerging generation falling into the former, yet young people are quick to reject any innovation that fails to meet their inner longing. Just as they are quick to experiment with new tools, they are also quick to abandon new tools for still newer tools. Without knowledge, they are pursuing their inner yearnings. The **cyberlibertarian** worldview amounts to a wholehearted embrace of technological determinism. Other theories (such as social constructionism or the social shaping of technology) believe that all outcomes are negotiated among a variety of actors in a complex setting of the market or the world. Another ideology that is evident in technological culture is radical individualism. Members of the techno-savvy generation revel in the prospect of ecstatic self-fulfillment in cyberspace, and they emphasize the need for individuals to disburden themselves of the encumbrances that might hinder the pursuit of rational self-interest.

The obsessions of the cyber-libertarians are counterbalanced by the **cyber-communitarian** philosophy. This philosophy tends to stifle innovation and progress through excessive concern over the social impact of technological marvels. Adherents are quick to discern some of the evils of our creation, which the cyber-libertarians fail to see.

Although there are new problems to tackle with every new technology, these problems must not dissuade our creative spirit. What we need to do is to develop a larger framework to evaluate the use of technology. A divine reference point becomes key in the debate and elevates the discussion to a higher plane. It leads to the recognition that technology in itself has no salvific value, and also that not all uses of technology

are sin. The TechnoCulture, like every other culture, is in need of a Saviour. Thus, all technology creators and users are in need of a God-initiated plan of salvation. In order to make the eternal message of the gospel of Jesus Christ relevant in TechnoCulture, we must understand the following three basic developmental concepts: identity, intimacy, and community.

Identity

Anonymity and a multiplicity of identities on the Internet have further complicated the process of identity formation. The imperative to self-knowledge has always been at the heart of philosophical inquiry of adolescent development. Our need for a practical philosophy of self-knowledge has never been greater as we struggle to make meaning from our lives in the Techno-Culture. New epistemology recognizes that identity is not unified entity, but multiple subjectivities. The coming generation is more comfortable with a diffused sense of self and teaches us about handling multiple identities.

Intimacy

We crave intimacy, and we fear it as well. Computers, the Internet, and wireless gadgetry can give us a marvelous feeling of pseudo-intimacy. It is easy to bare our soul to someone in the TechnoCulture, just as it is easy to hide or pretend. Particularly in high tech, where work is the only thing in one's life, the online avenue may be the only way to have a connection that is human. But although technology has value, it's not a replacement for the real thing. It is good for some things, but it is not the same as having neighbours and friends. This generation has also learned that the pain of broken relationships on the Internet is for real, not virtual.

E-community

Sometimes, discussions among Net enthusiasts on the subject of "community" are delinked from traditions of usage and meaning in the wider community. Technological ability does not create community automatically, yet the coming generation will push the limits of our understanding about community. Whether we go by the shallowness of the cyber-libertarians or the hype of techno enthusiasts, this generation has proven our innate need for community. We are wired internally for community and cannot live by ourselves. This generation aims to establish community through tools that they know and have lived with. Surely TechnoCulture has come in aid of forming and promoting community like nothing else in the near past. But there is more to Christian community than virtuality and a wired sense with someone across the world.

Applications

1. Observe and learn technocultural expressions from young people that you know.

2. Develop a cross-cultural missiology for TechnoCulture.

3. Think about how you could incarnate Christ in TechnoCulture.

4. Handle fears of using technology and think of how to overcome them.

5. Explore how you could use technology for the purpose of telling stories and connecting people to an experience of God, authentic community, and life-mission.

6. Bridge some gaps in digitalization in your neighbourhood.

7. Be an embodied apologetic (live out the gospel) in TechnoCulture.

Conclusion

The church and mission leaders have been largely naïve about the effects of globalization and the emerging cultures. The dramatic changes in our mission context call for serious study of the contemporary cultures and the development of a mindset to adapt to the changing cultural landscape. Christendom is turning more technophobic and could be described as "offline" (in some cases, not even wired!). It is not in touch (not just tomorrow, but even today) with the changing culture around it. The young people of the world (who comprise half of the world's population) are in the forefront of the TechnoCulture revolution.

It is also time to break the rules about culture, mission, and leadership in order to penetrate emerging cultures with God's purposes. It is time to renounce past baggage and sit afresh at the Lord's feet to learn what the Spirit of God is doing in our times. The challenge before us is to hear and obey God with a sense of abandonment and to discover new ways of ministering to emerging generations, using resources God has placed in and around us. It is time to go beyond knowing and believing God's truth to experiencing and demonstrating God's presence and power. It is time to incarnate Jesus into the TechnoCulture.

As with the past technological revolution (particularly printing), we should be ahead of the curve, rather than lagging behind or playing catch-up. So as followers of Jesus Christ, let us BOOT UP and GO ONLINE!

Questions for Reflection

1. What technological characteristics do you see in young people you know?
2. What features of TechnoCulture can we celebrate, and what ones need critical evaluation?
3. In what way is it fair or not fair to blame technology for contemporary ills in the world?
4. What lessons from cross-cultural missions could be translated into TechnoCulture?
5. What could we learn from the techno-savvy generation about missions?
6. What does leadership to mission in TechnoCulture look like?
7. How would you keep TechnoCulture tools from becoming "gods"?
8. How has your mission organization been impacted by TechnoCulture?

References

Adams, J. (1998). *The next world war: Computers are weapons and the front line is everywhere*. New York, NY: Simon & Schuster.

Alch, M. L. (2000, July). Get ready for the Net generation. *USA Today*, pp. 26-27.

Appadurai, A. (1996). *Modernity at large: Cultural dimensions of globalization*. Minneapolis, MN: University of Minnesota.

Barna, G. (2001, May 21). More Americans are seeking net-based faith experiences. *Barna Research Online*. Retrieved from http://www.barna.org.

Beaudoin, T. (1999). *Virtual faith: The irreverent spiritual quest of Generation X*. San Francisco, CA: Jossey Bass Publishers.

Cairncross, F. (1997). *The death of distance: How the communications revolution will change our lives*. Boston, MA: Harvard Business School Press.

Civin, M. A. (2000). *Male, female, email: The struggle of relatedness in a paranoid society*. New York, NY: Other Press.

Dean, K. C. (2000, July). *We aren't the world*. Princeton project on globalization, youth, and religion. Retrieved from http://www.ptsem.edu/iym/globalization.

Digital generation. (2002, September). *Wired* Magazine.

Easton, J. (2002). *Going wireless: Transform your business with mobile technology*. New York, NY: Harper Collins.

Ellul, J. (1964). *The technological society*. New York, NY: Alfred Knopf.

———. (1990). *The technological bluff.* Grand Rapids, MI: William B. Eerdmans Publishing.

Featherstone, M. (1990). Global culture: An introduction. In M. Featherstone (Ed.), *Global culture: Nationalism, globalization and modernity.* London, UK: Sage Publications.

Friedman, T. L. (1999). *The Lexus and the olive tree: Understanding globalization.* New York, NY: Farrar, Straus & Giroux.

Gates, B. (1995, November 27). The road ahead. *Newsweek.*

Gilder, G. F. (2000). *Telecosm: How infinite bandwidth will revolutionize our world.* New York, NY: Free Press.

Global culture. (1999, August). *National Geographic.*

Hirst, D. (1997). *I want to spend the rest of my life everywhere, with everyone, one to one, always, forever, now.* New York, NY: Monacelli Press.

Huxley, A. (1948). *Brave new world.* New York, NY: Harper & Row.

———. (1965). *Brave new world revisited.* New York, NY: Harper & Row.

In search of the sacred: America's quest for spiritual meaning. (1994, November 11). *Newsweek*, p. 55.

Lightman, A. (2002). *Brave new unwired world: The digital big bang.* New York, NY: John Wiley & Sons.

Lubar, S. (1993). *InfoCulture: The Smithsonian book of Information Age inventions.* Boston, MA: Houghton Mifflin Co.

Mahon, T. (1997, February 14). *National Catholic Reporter.*

Micklethwaite, J., & Wooldridge, A. (2000). *A future perfect.* New York, NY: Random House.

Mitcham, C. (1994). *Thinking through technology.* Chicago, IL: University of Chicago Press.

Myers, D. G. (2000, April 24). Wanting more in an age of plenty: Our wallets are fat, but our souls are empty. *Christianity Today, 44*(5), pp. 94-99.

Naisbitt, J., Naisbitt, N., & Philips, D. (1999). *High tech, high touch: Technology and our search for meaning.* New York, NY: Broadway Books.

Newbigin, L. (1988, April). The enduring validity of cross-cultural mission. *International Bulletin of Missionary Research, 12*, pp. 50-53.

Ohame, K. (1995). *The end of the nation-state: The rise and fall of regional economies.* London, UK: Harper Collins.

Orwell, G. (1949). *Nineteen eighty-four.* New York, NY: Brace & Co.

Robertson, D. S. (1998). *The new Renaissance: Computers and the next level of civilization.* New York, NY: Oxford University Press.

Roszak, T. (1969). *The making of the counter culture.* New York, NY: Doubleday & Co.

Schwartz, B. (2001, February). Unwiring the world. *Fast Company.* Retrieved from http://www.fastcompany.com/online/43/lookfeel.html.

Sittenfeld, C. (2000, September). No brandsland. *Fast Company.* Retrieved from http://www.fastcompany.com/online/38/nklein.html.

Snow, C. P. (1993). *The two cultures.* New York, NY: Cambridge University Press.

Stackhouse, M. (1988). Contextualization, contextuality and contextualism. In R. O. Costa (Ed.), *One faith, many cultures: Inculturation, indigenization and contextualization.* Maryknoll, NY: Orbis Books.

Sweet, L. I. (1999a). *AquaChurch.* Loveland, CO: Group Publishing.

———. (1999b). *Soul tsunami: Sink or swim in new millennium culture.* Grand Rapids, MI: Zondervan.

———. (2000a). *Carpe manana: Is your church ready to seize tomorrow?* Grand Rapids, MI: Zondervan.

———. (2000b). *The postmodern pilgrims: First century passion for the 21st century world.* Nashville, TN: Broadman & Holman.

Tapscott, D. (1998). *Growing up digital: The rise of the Net generation*. New York, NY: McGraw-Hill. Also retrieved from http://www.growingupdigital.com.

Tomlinson, J. (1999). *Globalization and culture*. Chicago, IL: University of Chicago Press.

Waters, M. (1995). *Globalization*. London, UK: Routledge.

Watkins, B., & Meader, R. (1987). *Technology and human values: Collision and solution*. Ann Arbor, MI: Ann Arbor Publishers.

Weil, E. (1997, April). The future is younger than you think. *Fast Company*. Retrieved from http://www.fastcompany.com/online/08/kids.html.

Wired churches, wired temples: Taking congregations and missions into Cyberspace. (2002, January). A project of Pew Internet and American Life. Retrieved from http://www.pewInternet.org.

***Sam George** serves with a non-profit Christian foundation in Chicago, Illinois. He graduated in mechanical engineering and holds a master's degree in business management from India. He worked in the software industry in India, Singapore, and the US for eight years before stepping into Christian ministry in 1996. Sam studied at Fuller and Princeton Seminary, focusing on youth ministry and leadership. He is active in many youth ministry initiatives in India and other parts of Asia. His research interests are in the emerging generation, culture, and the church. He is married to Mary George, Ph.D., and is active in a local Indian community church. Email: snmg99@hotmail.com.*

3

TerrorCulture: worth living for or worth dying for

SAM GEORGE

In my second chapter on youth and globalization, I want to look at another emerging culture among the global youth. Just as TechnoCulture shapes "globalization from above," there is another significant culture when we view "globalization from below," which I will call TerrorCulture. In both cultures, there are strands of a much deeper reality of being young and searching for God and meaning.

TerrorCulture is a culture of violent aggression that is on the rise among youths everywhere. There seems to be a growing tendency toward violence in the emerging generation. This proclivity is not limited to any geographical territory, religious group, or socio-economic class. Although militancy and terrorism are obvious expressions of TerrorCulture,[1] there are other manifestations, including violent rebellion at home, gun culture, media violence, school shootings, youth gangs,

---

[1] In this chapter, we might look primarily at religiously motivated violent opposition to modernity, but TerrorCulture is not limited to this focus. Benjamin Barber has called TerrorCulture "Jihad" (implying that it contains an Islamic overtone), while Samuel Huntington has called it "Clash."

Portrait of a Suicide Bomber

Ahmed Shah, at 17, was shy and introverted, preferring the solace of his room to the chatter of his friends. His father, Yusuf Shah, a schoolteacher, says Ahmed usually spent his time studying so he could become a doctor. He even got himself photographed wearing a doctor's coat and a stethoscope and kept the framed picture in his room.

Since Ahmed was the youngest of three brothers, none in the family thought his behaviour had changed when he started spending nights in the local mosque next door. It was good, his parents thought, that he was taking an interest in religion. They were somewhat troubled, however, when on some evenings Ahmed would read the Quran by candlelight when there was no power. It soon became a routine—the flickering flame and the Quran, with Ahmed suddenly reading aloud and crying.

Then one day, Ahmed just left home. Three weeks later, he called his father and said, "*Abbu, mein jaa raha hoon*" ("Dad, I'm leaving"). A few hours from then, the Shahs heard security vehicles screech to a halt outside their door. Their son, they were told, had exploded himself at the Army headquarters in Srinagar (Kashmir). His neighbours in downtown Srinagar locality were shocked that the shy, Class XII dropout could have been a suicide bomber. He had driven a stolen red Maruti laden with explosives to the high-security barrier. All that remained of him were several pieces, his body having been blown over a distance of 100 metres.

— Story adapted from Portrait (2001)

and underground movements in different parts of the world. This is the culture of the marginalized and disadvantaged youths of the world. Both globalization and religion have a **reciprocal** relationship with Terror-Culture, shaping it and being shaped by it.

The Kashmir Valley has seen some 45 suicide attacks (29 in 2001 alone) since the Kargil conflict came to an end in July 1999. The two strikes in New Delhi were highly symbolic: the Red Fort in December 2000 and the Parliament Complex in December 2001. One of the fascinating common denominators in the worldwide terrorist or separatist movements is that youth are at the forefront of these movements. Countless numbers of young people lay down their lives every year and become "martyrs" for various ideological causes. This phenomenon is not limited to the "fault lines" of the world such as

Afghanistan, Kashmir, Palestine, Sri Lanka, or Yemen; rather, it is rapidly **spreading** all over the world.

The resurgence and global expanse of terrorist activities are evident from the September 11, 2001 attacks on the World Trade Center and the Pentagon. The symbol of global mobility, the airplane, has been turned into a weapon against globalization itself, knocking down the symbols of capitalism. Yet the September 11 attacks were not just attacks on globalization; they were also an **expression** of globalization. Anti-globalization protests are among the most globalized events in the world today. However, they have had little effect on globalization overall, while TerrorCulture is changing the equation of globalization entirely. Just as in TechnoCulture, youth are on the cutting edge (bleeding edge, actually) of TerrorCulture. The nexus of globalization and religion lies at the heart of TerrorCulture. The products of globalization have found a perfect match for the intentions of terrorist groups, and the tug of war for the New World Order continues.

Modern terrorism, it is said, originated in the bleak ghettos of Beirut and Belfast. Since then, the phenomenon has come a long way and has spread its tentacles to all corners of the world: the farm crisis fueling a violent Sikh nationalism, with unemployed and angry youth taking up arms, or Tamil Tigers equipped with cyanide capsules in Sri Lanka, or a Bible-flaunting Timothy McVeigh in Oklahoma City. Terror has become the **shortcut** to fame for anyone with a cause and a grievance. It has been greeted with instant indignation but has also served its purpose. What makes the definition of terrorism more difficult is that one man's terror-

ist is another man's freedom fighter. TerrorCulture is not restricted to any region and has no religion; instead, it has embraced the values of hatred and violence. It has earned publicity for the perpetrators, has created martyrs for the cause, and has generated emotive mythologies.

The expression of TerrorCulture made during the terrorist attacks on America distinguishes itself from traditional crime and violence in the sense that these acts do more harm to the **living than the dead**. Terrorist acts are now performed for a television audience around the world. Their target is never the innocent victims, but the larger audience whose lives will be gripped in fear. TerrorCulture aims to destabilize the economy, the society, and the geo-  political clout of nations, not simply kill a few people. The acts are strategically conceived, funded, and executed by global networks.

Anthony Giddens (1999) called **fundamentalism** "a child of globalization." Benjamin Barber (1996) observed that "interdependence makes boundaries permeable not just for the good but for the bad, for Jihad no less than for McWorld." *Time* magazine's cover page article on the Al-Qaeda network (Inside Al-Qaeda, 2001, p. 67) admitted, "As they [intelligence experts] dig deeper, it is becoming clearer how effectively globalization has spread terrorism around the planet." Another shocking revelation of the network has been the way young people around the world are being recruited, trained, and entrusted to carry out sophisticated terrorist activities. TerrorCulture has become the new fad of many youngsters. In fact, they are finding it worth enough that they are willing to lay down their lives for it.

TerrorCulture: Why Youths?

Youths are in the forefront of Terror-Culture. As a group, terrorists are young and daring, they possess professional skills, they are global citizens, and they are fun-loving and determined. The new recruits of extremist groups around the globe tend to be young, single males. News headlines confirm the involvement of youth: "What makes youths volunteer?" (2001), "Young and ruthless" (Why, 2001), "Youth driven into extremism" (2001), "Youth terrorists" (2001), "Child soldiers" (2001), etc. The youths include both poor school dropouts and university students, both idealists and devout seekers with a sense of something missing in their lives. They tend to be members of financially and socially marginalized sections of society. A tabulation of the ages of Sikh extremists killed by police indicated that most of the victims were in their early twenties (Juergensmeyer, 2000).[2] Emmanuel Sivan (as cited in Juergensmeyer, 2000, p. 191), a leading scholar of modern Islamic history, observed that Hamas consists largely of "urban males in their late teens," while the age requirement to join the Tamil Liberation Movement in Sri Lanka is only 10! (Catch, 2001). The Northern Alliance in Afghanistan claimed that it never inducted anyone below the age of 18, but the rule was never enforced.

Our world is astonishingly young. More than half of the world's population falls below the age of 25. The United Nations reports that 85% of the global youth population lives in Third World countries. This figure is expected to rise to 89% by 2020.[3] Teenagers in China alone exceed the total population of America. Islam is the second largest faith in the world, with over 1.2 billion adherents; it is also the fastest growing religion. With a high fertility rate among Muslims and the death of older men due to war, the Islamic population is mostly young. Close to 55% of them fall under the age of 30. In Iran, about two-thirds of the population are age 30 or under. The *New York Times* (2001, December 7) called these young people "the angry generation longing for jobs, more freedom, and power." Demography is changing not only our society, but also economic and political systems.

The US teen population is expected to rise from 29 million to 36 million in the next decade. Regarding this trend, *Rolling Stone* (as cited in Dean, Clark, and Rahn, 2001, p. 18) concluded, "Resistance is futile. Teenagers are **driving** our culture—and they won't be giving the keys back anytime soon." Youth are discerning and fickle, but their loyalty is easily won. Both Techno-Culture and TerrorCulture have found it easier to win the loyalty of the emerging generation than of any other seg-

---

[2] Juergensmeyer quoted figures based on obituaries printed in *World Sikh News* during 1988.

[3] See www.un.org/esa/socdev/unyin/q-and-a.htm. The United Nations defines youth as people between the ages of 15 and 24.

ment in the society. Young people make ideal recruits because they are easy to indoctrinate as well as to intimidate.

Within the first six months of the outbreak of war in Afghanistan in September 2001, it is believed that more youngsters **joined** the cause of Jihad than at any other time in history, much like Jewish youth going to Tel Aviv in 1967 to fight the Arab-Israeli war. Among the radical youths, many want "the clash of civilizations to happen" (What, 2001, p. 74). In 2002, hundreds of children were known to have been forced into the ranks of terrorist outfits in the Kashmir Valley. Hundreds were arrested and returned to their homes by the Indian Army, but many more have died (Catch, 2001).

The demographic explosion in Islamic societies and the availability of a large number of often-unemployed males between the ages of 15 and 30 form a natural source of instability and violence. Samuel Huntington considers this milieu to be the major reason for the propensities of violence in the Islamic world. He also points out that the **youth bulge**, meaning the years when the 15- to 24-year-olds exceed 20% of the total population, has a significant impact on violence. In Sri Lanka, for example, the peaking of the Sinhalese nationalist insurgency in 1970 and of the Tamil insurgency in the late 1980s coincided with the youth bulge in that country. This correlation was present in the Tiananmen generation in China and in the conflicts in Chechnya as well. The high birth rates among the Islamic and Asian countries, coupled with a lack of educational and vocational opportunities, not only result in widespread poverty, but also produce migrants and fighters. Both factors drive globalization in the differing forms of multiculturalism and terrorism. A United Nations projection indicates that in the future the Muslim population will be disproportionately young and will have significant political influence.

More than the statistics of the youthfulness of the emerging generation, there is another important reason that young people worldwide are more inclined towards the emerging Terror-Culture and TechnoCulture. It's not just that young people see things differently; they have a **different** way of looking at things. They have a very unique perspective, and that is their strength. They are deeply spiritual and fervent in their quest for the ultimate truth. We might call them by different names across the globe, but the teens and tweens of the 1990s and beyond are a different breed altogether. They hold a new worldview and a new consciousness shaped both by their inner spiritual longing and by the prevailing culture around them.

Culture Wars and a Culture of Wars

Globalization and culture are deeply intertwined. Globalization lies at the heart of contemporary culture, and cultural practices are at the heart of globalization. Immanuel Wallerstein (1990) called culture the "ideological battleground of the modern world system." Other scholars on culture have referred to a global culture in terms of cultural homogenization, assimilation, integration, distinction, etc. Arjun Appadurai (1990) summed the matter up well:

> The new global cultural economy has to be understood as a complex, overlapping, disjunctive order, which cannot any longer be understood in terms of existing center-periphery models

(even those that might account for multiple centers and peripheries). Nor is it susceptible to simple models of push and pull (migration theory) or surpluses and deficits (balance-of-trade model) or consumers and producers (neo-Marxist developmental theory).

Often the debate regarding youth culture in the context of globalization has focused on the popular culture. The discussions are generally confined to changing cultural patterns and their impact on adolescent development. Global cultural studies have compared the aspects of traditional culture with Western culture, assimilation, the evolution of hybrid cultures, etc. In many parts of the world, the globalizing of the popular culture is regarded as cultural imperialism. The popular culture has for the most part been so preoccupied with its own profitability and market dominance that it has ignored or failed to take seriously the culture of war. As Western society has battled over its ideological differences and partisan politics, the culture of death and destruction, or TerrorCulture, has been **brewing** around the world. This culture holds the potential to steer the globalizing powers in an entirely different direction.

Human history is punctuated by wars, and wars will continue to define our future. "Organized crime," predicted Professor Louise Shelly of Washington American University (as cited in Juergensmeyer, 2000), "will be a defining issue of the 21st century, as the Cold War was for the 20th century and colonization was for the 19th century. Transnational crime groups are the major beneficiary of globalization." Most of the organized crime and terrorist networks have engaged in these extreme measures. The irreconcilable **paradox** of a sense of justice among youth, coupled with incidents in their own lives or being witnesses of atrocities against humanity, drive them to extremism. As they grow up, they are willing to take any measures to establish fairness in the world around them. As Huntington (1996, p. 265) noted, "The fundamental source of conflict in this New World will not be primarily ideological or economic. The great divisions among humankind and the dominating source of conflict will be cultural."

Another important feature of Terror-Culture is that the globalizing forces of economy, technology, and culture do not appear to change people's sense of who they are or where they belong. Barnet and Cavanagh (1994, p. 138) cited the example of how "Serbs and Croats, Sinhalese and Tamils, listen to the same Michael Jackson songs while they take up arms against each other." Violence becomes the ultimate form of **identification**—the acute necessity for self-definition amidst radical cultural flux, in which artificial distinctions between neighbors are ruthlessly upheld (Appadurai, 1999).

While in the past ethnicity, nationality, and cultural and faith heritage helped shape the identity and sense of belonging in the community, now these areas are all being redefined. We live now in a multi-ethnic, multicultural, multinational, and multi-whatever world. This reality is borne out clearly in the testimony of a British lawyer, Anjem Choudary, age 40, who is a British passport holder and an extremist in an Islamic group. Choudary asserted, "For a Muslim, a passport is no more than a travel document.... Our allegiance is solely to Allah and his messenger, not to the Queen or any country. Nationality means nothing" (What, 2001, p. 74). Nationality, citizenship, oath, pledges, etc., are getting a major twist in their understanding. But in these kinds of cultures, matters of faith continue to provide the philosophical **foundations** and much-needed motivation to carry out such horrendous acts.

Faith Matters: Where Is God?

Traditionally, religious violence attacked the houses of worship of other faiths. Examples abound, such as the destruction of the Jerusalem Temple in Israel, the demolition of the Babri Mosque in India, the destruction of churches in Indonesia, etc. But the recent attacks, although religiously motivated and although branded by many as religious fundamentalism, have been turned against economic and military targets. This change in focus is the result of the marriage of globalization and religion, whereby the products and services of globalization are used to carry out attacks against globalization itself for religious motives. This new war does not target the leaders of any faith anymore, but it destroys innocent followers in order to engage in a psychological warfare between the leaders, ideologies, and worldviews. It aims to shake the **foundation**, expecting the superstructure to collapse. It engages suicide bombers in aerial attacks on institutions that are standing tall in the landscape of modernity. Also, the counterattack is not targeted at any nation or faith, but at individuals and networks of terrorists. But the religious undercurrents are obvious in all these encounters.

Mark Juergensmeyer analyzed the global rise of religious **violence**, including Christians attacking abortion clinics, strife between Catholics and Protestants in Northern Ireland, Hamas attacks in the Middle East, Jews who supported the assassination of the Israeli Prime Minister, Sikhs who killed the Indian Prime Minister, and Japanese Buddhists who released nerve gas in Tokyo subways. Juergensmeyer concluded that the rise of globalism and the end of the Cold War have led to a crisis in moral leadership. Religion not only gives people a sense of origin, meaning, and destiny in life, but also is increasingly used to control and manipulate people. The diverse nature of interpretation and understanding of scriptures, conflicting divine revelations, and the challenge of engaging in "cosmic war" have made faith matters more vital than ever, in spite of the attempt of modernity to replace faith with reason.

For religious terrorists, violence first and foremost is a **sacramental** act or divine duty. Terrorist acts are executed in direct response to some theological demand or imperative and are justified by sacred scriptures. There is also the visible emergence of radical clerical leaders, who merge intentional activism and militant ideologies with theological justifications. Religion thus provides the legitimacy for acts of terrorism. By engagement, one becomes a divine agent to carry out God's order in the world. Another reason behind religiously violent activity is the aim to resist secularization. Violence provides defensive aggression and hostility against neo-colonial evil forces and against falling prey to a Western imperialistic agenda.

According to Erik Erikson (1980, p. 65), "Religion, through the centuries, has provided this bedrock of confidence. In times of crisis, it has served to restore a sense of trust." In between the stages of life of childhood and adulthood, youth experience acute marginality in traditional societies built around families, where there aren't any highly developed youth cultures as in Western industrialized societies. There are not many alternatives that are contending for the allegiance of the youth, except the terrorist groups. The religious groups provide much-needed home and extended kinship. Youth are developmentally predisposed toward what Erikson called "totalism"—the vulnerability of an unformed self to fusion with an **ideal**. Instead of possessing the ideal, the ideal possesses them, and they are drawn to movements that capitalize on their affective spiritual awareness and on their idealistic desire to "go the distance" for something worthy of their fidelity (Dean, 2000).

Many Muslim leaders hate the West, because the decadent pleasures of Western culture are luring the faithful away from Islam. Of course, many Christians share this abhorrence for Western culture's indulgence in immorality, pornography, sexual perversion, and divorce. The best thing that the West could do for Christianity is to make itself attractive, reclaim moral leadership, and establish a society based on moral values. The notion of the current war on terrorism as the West vs. Islam facilitated the reduction of antagonism within the Islamic nations. They not only distanced themselves from the Western Christian ideology, but also began to come together in their opposition to the West, leading to the theory of civilizational clash.

Many believe that the war on terrorism is a clash of civilizations. More aptly, it is the clash of worldviews, in which a progressive and scientific worldview is coming against the traditional and tribal worldview. It is easy to export the products and services of globalization, such as communication and technology tools, across the world, but it is harder to develop people who can build such tools. The concepts of the free market, accountability in political systems, and the rule of law are based on the Christian worldview, which does not fit well in various other religious worldviews. A *New York Times* (2001, November 2) editorial stated that if terrorism is to be defeated, the world of Islam must take on board the secularist-humanist principles on which the modern world is based and without which Muslim countries' freedom will remain a distant dream. But there is another **religion** of violence and a value system of hatred that is quickly spreading across the world, and youth are promptly responding to this culture—the culture of guns.

Rite of Passage: Guns 'n' Roses

The 2001 terrorist acts in America have caused much reflection on why terrorists perpetrate such horrendous deeds. Why do they hate the West so intensely? Many reasons have been set forth by the experts, including lack of educational and economic opportunities, limited freedom and power, unemployment, corruption, religious sanctions, fanaticism, etc.

Without prospects for higher education or better economic avenues, many young people drop out of educational pursuits. With skyrocketing unemployment rates due to weak economic development or corrupt leaders, the youth look for other avenues for their youthfulness. The recent crackdown on terrorist networks has revealed that many young, educated professionals have also gone over the edge into fanaticism and fundamentalism. They are searching for a nobler cause in life. Unfortunately, religious fanaticism appears to be providing them with what they see as a "noble exit." They are seeking a more definite cultural identity and sense of belonging. Many bright young Muslim immigrants in Europe and America find in religious fundamentalism an outlet for their energy and talents (Battle, 2001). The young are drawn to extreme Islamic politics, which eventually lead them to terrorism.

 Guns have become a literal **metaphor** of the rite of passage into the TerrorCulture. The challenge of terrorist leaders to the young can be summed up as, "Deny yourself, take up your guns, and follow," much like Jesus' challenge to his disciples (Luke 9:23). On completion of strenuous preparation at the terrorist training camps, young people are rewarded with automatic assault weapons. The scenes of 12-year-olds skipping along with AK-47s slung over their shoulders seem almost normal in Afghanistan.

TerrorCulture provides ample avenues for the young to enter adulthood. It adds value, purpose, and **significance** to an otherwise completely marginalized life. The sheer profusion of humanity in many parts of the world means that life is regarded as cheap. The population explosion in China, India, and Islamic nations, together with limited economic empowerment in those areas, has caused the worth of individuals to dwindle. For a meagre amount of money, hit men (actually youths) are available for hire, and even life-threatening "assignments" require very little compensation. Ministry in TerrorCulture will have to restore worth and dignity to every individual life.

Young people in every era are **claimed** by their cultures during puberty; if this does not happen, both the youths and their offspring become a threat to the tribe of origin (Esman, 1990). Young boys are being lured by the machismo and romance of guns and fatigues. Afghanistan's youth have never known peace; they have lived through wars all their lives. Hollywood war films are used in terrorist training camps in Afghanistan. For two decades, the country has been at war, first with the Soviets and then among homegrown factions. If Afghanistan is ever to settle into peace, its children will have a very difficult time adjusting to a place where people don't resolve political squabbles with the pull of a trigger.

Young boys long for affection and crave male **role models** to emulate. When their fathers or other men around them fail to provide role models, they look elsewhere. When they are empty on the inside and hungry for love that was denied during childhood, they will risk anything to grab just a little fleeting affection or attention from those who will take them "under their wings." The popular culture has provided enough models from the fields of art, music, sports, media, technology gizmos, etc., to keep large numbers of youth preoccupied with them. But in the absence of positive role models, young people often turn to extremist leaders.

Final Act: When Death Means More Than Life

The young people of TechnoCulture and TerrorCulture (McWorld and Jihad) have a strange fascination with death. They are not afraid of dying and are only looking for a reason to make the final exit. Their language is filled with metaphors of death. Most of the young terrorists die a cruel death. Gen-X suicides are as common as fleas on dogs. Self-destruction is the ultimate **rebellion** and a way out of a life made more cruel by the world around them.

In the popular culture, the destructive themes are evident from the recent acts of violence in public schools, the prevalence of gangs in urban areas, and the high suicide rates. Writing about Gen-Xers, Kevin Ford (1995, p. 104)  affirms, "We think a lot about death. And it leads to despair and depression. Our preoccupation with death is displayed on our skins: we avoid the sun, we cherish our pallor, we look like ghosts or corpses. Xer women often favor makeup in shades of white, black, blue, and purple—the colors of death and lividity and corpsehood." The obsession with **death** causes young people to take risks and dare death to come and get them. Suicide rates are three times higher among Xers than among the Boomers; three-quarters of all teenagers have contemplated suicide, and one-quarter have attempted it (Arterburn and Burns, 1992).

Martyrdom is a popular idea among all terrorist outfits. Martyrdom attacks (i.e., suicide bombers) against Israeli targets have become the most dramatic and bloody weapon in the armory of the Palestinian militant groups. The cyanide capsule tied around the necks of Tamil Tigers is a literal reminder of having renounced their right to life. To many young men who have lived their entire lives under humiliating conditions, commitment to martyrdom is a final act of power, stemming from desperation. They act in the belief that they will go straight to paradise, where they will get places of honour next to God. According to Islamic tradition, he who gives his life for an Islamic cause will have his sins forgiven and a place reserved in paradise. The promises of an eternal life of pleasure with plenty of comfort, food, alcoholic beverages, and sex are very attractive to single young men. The reward of a Jihad martyr recently increased from 70 to 100 black-eyed, beautiful, and willing virgins, in an attempt to recruit more youth. These young people are also assured that their families will be looked after well. A martyr is revered and gives his family the highest status ever. His name becomes immortal. The **legacy** left by a martyr provides an irresistible appeal for other young people and is a powerful recruitment strategy.

When robbed of broader, transcendent meaning, many turn inward and easily fall victim to the extremist idea as a form of **salvation**. Referring to youth, Eckersley (1995), who claims he is not a Christian, stated, "There is no expectation of an afterlife—no fear of hell, and no hope of heaven, and it does not matter if you die." Some heroes gain their reputation by the life they live; others, by the death they die. The call of martyrdom gives young people a sense of mission and a noble cause big enough for their lives.

Ministry in TerrorCulture: Battle for Souls

The terrorist networks and global capitalism are doing a better job of winning the **allegiance** of young people around the world than the church is. The pull of TechnoCulture and TerrorCulture on the emerging generation is so intense that young people cannot see anything else. So what must the church do? What message does it have for the emerging generation? Who will eventually win the battle for souls in the coming world? What can the church learn from emerging cultures?

> "If a man has not discovered something that he will die for, he isn't fit to live."
> — Dr. Martin Luther King, Jr.

All religious terrorist groups aim at nothing less than the souls of their adherents, not only with regard to beliefs, but also with regard to various interpretations of those beliefs. The moderate and fanatic Muslim groups are gunning for the hearts and minds of youths throughout the Muslim world. Clerics in many Middle Eastern nations have turned back to religious rule, and governance by Islamic law is the norm. Moderates are trying hard to offer youths a compelling role model other than radical Islam. The souls of the Muslim youth are being **pulled** in opposite directions.

Beneath the veneer of hatred and violence of young terrorists, we see fragile young men struggling to find a cause worthy enough to live for in a world that cares too little for its young. Like all other marginalized youths in our society and church, terrorist youths are created in God's image, and we must celebrate their worth and value unconditionally. The **idealism** of youth is the face of divine order, and their relentless quest for divine knowing can only be met in Jesus Christ, not in a religious system, not even the church. Young people challenge us to shed the mediocrity that we as the church have settled into and to incarnate God's hope for the whole of humanity.

The business world is quick to recognize the large emerging market of youth populace and is positioning its products and services so as to win their loyalty. Referring to the global teenage market, an article in *Fortune* (Tully, 1994) reported, "No marketing challenge is more basic than capturing the heart and mind of teens. There are billions to be earned." The Western corporate world is awash with stories of how corporations are betting their fu-

> "The mind of sinful man is death, but the mind controlled by the Spirit is life and peace."
> — Romans 8:6 NIV

ture on younger generations. A new executive position on culture watch is found not only in the MTV and fashion business, but also among automakers, software, and consumer products. An article titled, "The future is younger than you think" (Weil, 1997) chronicles the stories of how future product development is being done by teenagers in Silicon Valley in California. Not only has the TechnoCulture set its eyes on the future, but it is also using the future to capture and control the future. It is winning the very hearts and souls of the emerging generation every day.

Both TechnoCulture and Terror-Culture are making radical claims and are holding out challenges to the emerging generations, and both are winning more converts to their ideology. They extensively use battlefield language, like conquer, dominate, destroy, reject, kill, overpower, etc. TerrorCulture sees the conquest territorially, while Techno-Culture sees it economically. The former is motivated by religious beliefs; the latter, by profits. But the bottom line in both cases is converts. Ministry in TerrorCulture will call for radical discipleship.

At present, the church pales in comparison to TerrorCulture in the power of its rites and rituals for young people. However, the church has the potential to compete with and even outpace both TechnoCulture and TerrorCulture in meeting youth's quest for significance, security, and community. Sadly, groups such as Occults and New Age are aggressively pursuing the emerging generations, not to mention that the Mormons have sent youth missionaries to most cities of the world specifically to reach youth (Livermore, 2001, p. 332). Will the church wake up to its challenge of the emerging generation?

The contemporary church faces the challenge of **reclaiming** a mission to its own future and not just some marginalized youths out there. The church should not reduce its ministry to youth merely to some programs, recreational activities, or worship nights. The typical Western, middle class conception of youth ministry, with youth pastors and a youth department within a denominational structure or a youth organization, may not be transferable or effective around the world. A ministry that is rich in resources and based on curriculum and entertainment might not be the most appropriate youth ministry model for the rest of the world. We must develop new models of ministry in order to win the emerging generations to Christ.

Followers of Jesus Christ around the world have a daunting task of **showing** to the emerging generations a Christ who is worth dying for and also worth living for. In the history of humanity, Jesus alone stands tall, beckoning us to make our lives really count for his greater purposes. Jesus died that we may live. He defeated death on the cross. We do not have to pay with our own blood, because someone else has done it already. And in dying to ourselves and letting him live through us, we can really have a life in the first place. Jesus alone deserves our total allegiance, both in life and in death. Jesus' followers must share and show a life of meaning and hope. We have a

> "I (Jesus) came so they can have real and eternal life, more and better life than they have ever dreamed of."
> — John 10:10 Message

story of love, affirmation, and self-worth. Amidst a culture of death, we can breathe life; in a culture of war, we can be agents of peace; in a culture of hopelessness, we can bring a ray of hope and purpose. A complete allegiance to the person of Jesus Christ alone can give the young people of the world a coherent sense of their being, establish profound connections to the world around them, and give them a purpose worth living for. In total obedience to one who died in their place, can they die to their own self and live unto the eternal purposes of God?

As followers of Christ, we must **recognize** the power of TerrorCulture and capture afresh the life-giving power of the gospel. We must celebrate life and richness of life in Jesus Christ. We must affirm the spiritual longing of the emerging generation and must lead young people to the person of Jesus Christ, rather than to any doctrine or church. We must create a safe haven for these marginalized youths to discover their God-given potential and purpose in life. Ministry in TerrorCulture calls us to go beyond the "feel good" Sunday morning Christianity. We must count the cost of a **radical discipleship** and be willing to pay the price.

Applications

1. Identify marginalized youths and the shades of TerrorCulture prevalent among them.

2. Research about young people involved in terrorism and their religiosity.

3. Think about how you could relate to youths deeply entrenched in TerrorCulture and share the gospel of Jesus Christ.

4. Develop a cross-cultural missiology for TerrorCulture.

5. Evaluate violence in the media, schools, and the neighbourhood and its influence on youths in the community.

6. Explore Scripture regarding the radical nature of God's call (counting the cost of discipleship).

Conclusion

Today's youth will look for the right things in the wrong places, just like their predecessors. Their most basic pursuit remains the same throughout generations. What they really need is a **radical** reordering of the self in light of their relationship with God. Young people will continue to look for a God who is big enough for them, and they will make a life commitment to such a God who is capable of turning their lives inside out and the world upside down. Youth need a life worth living and a cause truly worth dying for. They need a purpose larger than life itself, which will add profound meaning to their global existence.

We must enable youths to discern the allure of both TerrorCulture and TechnoCulture and must help keep them from being victims of destructive forces. Yet we must redeem the currents of the times for God's eternal purposes. We must challenge young people to establish the redemptive purposes of God for their times and for the generations to come. Jesus alone is one **worth living** and **dying for!**

Questions for Reflection

1. What are the shapes of TerrorCulture?

2. Explain how and why youths get marginalized.

3. What similarities and differences do you find between gangs and terrorists?

4. How could lessons from cross-cultural mission be translated into TerrorCulture?

5. What does the leadership in TerrorCulture mission look like?

6. Why do you think TerrorCulture appeals to young people?

7. How could you present the gospel to youths in TerrorCulture?

8. Why do you think the Christian message lost its radicality? How would you restore it?

References

Appadurai, A. (1990). Differences in global cultural economy. In M. Featherstone (Ed.), *Global culture: Nationalism, globalization and modernity*. London, UK: Sage Publications.

———. (1999). Dead certainty: Ethnic violence in the era of globalization. In B. Meyer & P. Geschiere (Eds.), *Globalization and identity: Dialectics of flow and closure*, pp. 305-329. Oxford, UK: Blackwell Publishers.

Arterburn, S., & Burns, J. (1992). *When love is not enough*. Colorado Springs, CO: Focus on the Family.

Barber, B. R. (1996). *Jihad vs. McWorld*. New York, NY: Ballantine Books.

Barnet, R. J., & Cavanagh, J. (1994). *Global dreams: Imperial corporations and the New World Order*. New York, NY: Simon & Schuster.

The battle for hearts and minds. (2001, October 22). *Time, 158*(18), pp. 45-54.

Catch them young. (2001, November 24). *Frontline, 18*(24), p. 58. Chennai, India. Retrieved from http://www.flonnet.com/fl1824/18240680.htm.

Child soldiers. (2001, November 19). *India Today*.

Dean, K. C. (2000, August). *We aren't the world*. Princeton project on youth, globalization, and the church. Unpublished manuscript.

Dean, K. C., Clark, C., & Rahn, D. (Eds.). (2001). *Starting right: Thinking theologically about youth ministry*. Grand Rapids, MI: Youth Specialties Academic/Zondervan Publishing.

Eckersley, R. (1995, Autumn). Values and visions. *Youth Studies Australia*, pp. 15-16.

Erikson, E. H. (1980). *Identity and the life cycle*. New York, NY: Norton.

Esman, A. (1990). *Adolescence and culture*. New York, NY: Columbia University Press.

Ford, K. G. (1995). *Jesus for a new generation: Putting the gospel in the language of Xers*. Downers Grove, IL: InterVarsity Press.

Giddens, A. (1999). *A runaway world: Reith lecture on globalisation*. New Delhi, India. Retrieved from http://news.bbc.co.uk/hi/english/events/reith_99/week3/lecture3.htm.

Huntington, S. P. (1996). *The clash of civilizations and the remaking of world order*. New York, NY: Simon & Schuster.

Inside Al-Qaeda: Bin Laden's web of terror. (2001, November 12). *Time, 158*(21), pp. 65-71.

Juergensmeyer, M. (2000). *Terror in the mind of God: The global rise of religious violence*. Berkeley, CA: University of California Press.

Livermore, D. (2001, July). Billions to be won: Going after the largest mission field in the world—youth. *Evangelical Missions Quarterly, 37*(3), pp. 330-335.

New York Times. (2001, November 2). Vol. 152, No. 52,290, p. A26.

———. (2001, December 7). Vol. 152, No. 52,325, pp. A21, A23.

Portrait of a suicide bomber. (2001, December 24). *The Week*, p. 14. Published by Malayala Manorama Group, Kochi, Kerala, India.

Tully, S. (1994, May). Teens: The most global market of all. *Fortune*, pp. 90-97.

Wallerstein, I. (1990). In M. Featherstone (Ed.), *Global culture: Nationalism, globalization and modernity*, pp. 31-55. London, UK: Sage Publications.

Weil, E. (1997, April/May). The future is younger than you think. *Fast Company*, Issue 8, p. 93. Retrieved from www.fastcompany.com/online/08/index.html.

What makes youths volunteer? (2001, November 12). *Time, 158*(21), p. 34.

Why they hate us. (2001, October 22). *Newsweek, 138*(16), p. 31.

Youth driven into extremism. (2001, October 15). *Outlook*, p. 16. Mumbai, India.

Youth terrorists. (2001, October 28). *New Strait Times*. Singapore.

Sam George *serves with a non-profit Christian foundation in Chicago, Illinois. He graduated in mechanical engineering and holds a master's degree in business management from India. He worked in the software industry in India, Singapore, and the US for eight years before stepping into Christian ministry in 1996. Sam studied at Fuller and Princeton Seminary, focusing on youth ministry and leadership. He is active in many youth ministry initiatives in India and other parts of Asia. His research interests are in the emerging generation, culture, and the church. He is married to Mary George, Ph.D., and is active in a local Indian community church. Email: snmg99@hotmail.com.*

4

Multiculturalism and pluralization: kissing cousins of globalization

DAVID LUNDY

In relating globalization to multiculturalism and pluralization, it can be argued that, paradoxically, opposing phenomena are represented, yet they also feed off each other. That is to say, an observation of postmodern society leads us to conclude that globalization is both a cause and a result of multiculturalism and pluralization. Just as many societies do not encourage close relatives to intermarry, even though an attraction may be present (as the colloquialism "kissing cousins" suggests), there is a lot about these three societal realities that Christians might be uncomfortable in encouraging. In this chapter, then, we will seek to delineate the close relationship of globalization vis-à-vis multiculturalism and pluralization, but we will also critique their dynamic interfacing Christianly and especially missiologically.

Before proceeding, let me define the following terms as they will be used in this chapter. ***Multiculturalism*** can be understood as "a deliberate fashioning of society so as to make it culturally/ethnically heterogeneous." Thus, for instance, the Canadian Multiculturalism Act of 1971 enshrined in legislation a policy of multiculturalism, whereby Canada agreed to facilitate wide-scale immigration and to encourage each ethnic and religious minority group to retain its own distinctive customs and norms, while fitting into Canadian society in a broad sense. Instead of a "melting pot" society being envisaged, in which the individual entities all merge together, a "salad bowl" population would be created. In a salad, each ingredient retains its own texture, color, and taste while blending into the whole.[1] At the heart of moving to a more heterogeneous society—now similarly promoted in countries such as the USA and Australia—is the celebrating of the diversity that multiculturalism engenders, as reflected in a statement by then-Prime Minister Trudeau (as cited in Seim, 1999, p. 65): "The more secure we feel in [our own] particular social context, the more free we are to explore our identity beyond it."

Pluralization, if we are going to distinguish it from multiculturalism, can be defined as Os Guiness does (as cited in Carson, 1996, p. 18):

> … the process by which the number of options in the private sphere of modern society rapidly multiplies at all levels, especially at the level of worldview, faiths, and ideologies [so that] … choice becomes a value in itself, even a priority … [as] change becomes the very essence of life.

In a narrower sense, ***religious pluralism*** relativizes all truth claims so that it "suggests that world religions are all culturally bound expressions of genuine contact with the divine" (Clark, 1991, p. 37).

Multiculturalism Giving Rise to Globalization

While migration has always occurred—such as the Israelites moving en masse from Egypt to Palestine—the rate of crossing borders in the last century has been unprecedented in human history. Demetrios Papademetriou of the International Migration Policy Program at the Carnegie Endowment for World Peace in Washington, DC, indicates that 200 million people, or 3% of the world's population, live in a country in which they were not born. This demographic shift has in turn altered monocultural societies into multicultural ones.

Here are some samples of how migration patterns have reconfigured the demographic landscape, especially of Western world nations.

■ According to the 1996 census, 17.7% of Canada's population was made up of visible minorities, compared to about 6% three decades earlier. In other words, whereas prior to 1961, two-thirds of immigrants arrived from Western Europe, a trend that was slowly reversed, since 1991, one-third of all immigrants came from Hong Kong, China,

---

[1] This analogy is developed with respect to racial pluralism by Grace Sangok Kim (1996, p. 252).

Spreading the Gospel Multiculturally

My wife Linda and I lived in downtown Toronto in a condominium for three years. One of Linda's first concerns was to find a hairdresser with whom she felt comfortable, whose shop was within walking distance, and whose price was right! She started going to a hair salon run by a Filipino lady. As they started talking, Linda discovered that this vivacious woman was a genuine Christian. A few months later, Linda ended up getting her hair done by a Chinese lady at the shop. Never failing to take advantage of a God-given witnessing opportunity, Linda mentioned that her husband was pastoring the English-speaking congregation of a Chinese church in the city. The woman exclaimed, "That's great! I'm a Christian too. My boss led me to faith in Christ."

In subsequent months, Linda returned to having her hair done by the manager of the salon, the Filipino woman. But one day, a new hairdresser was at work, and since all the other operators were busy, Linda ended up with the new lady. Linda knew enough about features to discern that this beautiful woman was Somali. She asked, "Are you Somali?" Surprised, the woman blurted out, "Yes!" Knowing that Somalians are, for the most part, Muslim, Linda was well into a friendly conversation that would lead to an opportunity to share her faith. But the Somali lady declared, "Don't worry. I believe in Jesus too. That lady introduced me to the Saviour," pointing to her Chinese colleague.

India, Sri Lanka, and the Philippines (Couto, 2001). Thus, Canada now has 860,000 Chinese (27% of the visible minority population), 671,000 South Asians (21%), and 574,000 African-Caribbean Canadians (18%), among 31 million people (Thomas, 1998, p. 2).

■ New York City has more than 350,000 Dominicans—more than the Dominican Republic's capital city of Santo Domingo, with 225,000 (Greenway and Monsma, 1989, p. 63). Similar concentrations can be seen in other world class cities, such as Vancouver, British Columbia, which has more Sikhs than any other city outside the Punjab. Paris has more North Africans than most of the cities of North Africa. London has vast Arab, Caribbean, and Bangla-deshi communities. Amsterdam is full of Indonesians.

■ Due to the increased presence of visible minorities, such as Chicanos and African Americans, it is estimated that the USA will have a population that is more than 50% non-white by 2050 (Muck, 1990, p. 13).

■ Most of the major languages of the earth are now spoken in certain Western world megalopolises. Los Angeles is home to over 100 spoken languages (Ripley, 1994). Toronto has been designated by the United Nations as the world's most cosmopolitan city, with almost 200 languages spoken on its streets and in its homes (Thomas, 1998, p. 3).

■ With this diverse ethnic mix has come a plethora of religions. In Canada, a decade ago there were 253,000 Muslims; in 2001, there were 650,000 (according to the Canadian Muslim Congress). There were 161,000 Sikhs in Canada in 1991, compared to 400,000 today (according to the World Sikh Organization), and there were 157,000 Hindus in 1991, compared to 300,000 now (Csillag, 2001). On a similar note, while there are an estimated 4-6 million Muslims in the USA today, the majority of whom are African-American, by 2015 Islam could bypass Judaism to become the second largest religion in the USA (Zoba, 2000).

With the internationalizing of our Western world cities come globalizing tendencies. That is to say, everyone's culture becomes everyone else's culture. There is a global village sense to living in major urban centers of Europe and North America, let alone in many cities of the Two-Thirds World. The reality of multiculturalism has meant, in turn, a gradual shift in attitudes and values toward relativizing everything. Each culture or religion, we are told, is to be respected as equally legitimate and valid. What comes to dominate is what has been called "politically correct" thinking that has as its absolute the concept that there are no absolutes. This mindset is captured amusingly by Jewish talk show host Dennis Prager (as cited in Carson, 1996, p. 43), who on one of his shows made this telling comment about how religious tolerance is not modeled in the American public school system:

Liberals are always talking about pluralism, but that is not what we mean.... In public schools, Jews don't meet Christians. Christians don't meet Hin-

dus. Everybody meets nobody. That is, as I explain to Jews all the time, why their children so easily intermarry. Jews don't marry Christians. Non-Jewish Jews marry non-Christian Christians. Jews-for-nothing marry Christians-for-nothing. They get along great because they affirm nothing. They have everything in common—nothing. That's not pluralism.

Pluralization

What is pluralism or pluralization then? Before we tackle any Christian understanding of it, we must understand that the ease of travel and the accessibility of information about what is happening in every part of the world, wrought by the Internet, satellite TV, and the microchip revolution, have, in part, given rise to this migration from South to North. And insofar as the physical dislocation has been in one direction, the same effect of multiculturalism through mass communication technologies—technologies that enable Berber tribes in the Sahara to watch "Baywatch" reruns, or Chinese villages to want CNN-style democratic principles to run their local governments—begins to take hold in traditional Two-Thirds World cultures.

We thus end up with pluralization one way or the other. In the North, it is seen visually, through diversity of ethnicity and consumer choice, as one walks the streets. In the South, it is cultivated through satellite TV and the Internet. Therefore, it is a pluralization that is influencing billions, and so, ironically, it is also becoming a kind of globalizing phenomenon. The globe increasingly is familiar with pluralization, and transnational corporations exploit it to peddle their products universally, but in such a way as to take local tastes into account. Documenting this globalizing dynamic and how we got there, Thomas Friedman (2000, pp. xviii, xix), in *The Lexus and the Olive Tree*, summarizes the process well in this observation:

> Today's era of globalization is built around the falling telecommunication costs—thanks to microchips, satellites, fiber optics, and the Internet. These new information technologies are able to weave the world together even tighter. These technologies mean that developing countries do not just have to trade their raw materials to the West and get finished products in return; they mean that developing countries can become big-time producers as well.... If the first era of globalization shrank the world from a size "large" to a size "medium," this era of globalization is shrinking the world from a size "medium" to a size "small."

Technologies such as the Internet that were utilized first of all economically to open up markets internationally in turn became channels of the democratization of information. Again we listen to Friedman (2000, p. 67) attempting to fathom the meaning of this globalizing development:

> Put all of this democratization of information together, and what it means is that the days when governments could isolate their people from understanding what life was like beyond their borders or even beyond their villages are over. Life outside can't be trashed or made to look worse than it is.

And life inside can't be propagandized and made to look better than it is. Thanks to the democratization of information, we all increasingly know each other's lives—no matter how isolated you think a country might be.

The hallmark of pluralization philosophically, then, is tolerance to points of view other than one's own. Dogmatism is out, and inclusivism is in. Pluralization further means to celebrate diversity, or differences, in their own right, whether they are cultural or moral. Hence, we should not be surprised, for example, that postmodern artists juxtapose seemingly contradictory styles from different sources (Grenz, 1996, p. 20). Pluralization means integration of a diverse and eclectic society, or as Friedman (2000, p. 9) puts it: "The globalization system ... has one overarching feature—integration." When push comes to shove, economic-driven homogenizing pressures of globalization win out over a resolute commitment to keep things the same (tradition) or to retain local values as having ultimate significance (Friedman, 2000, p. 32). Economically, then, pluralization becomes subsumed to the goals of transnational corporations that seek a worldwide market for a narrow range of products.

The unforgivable sin philosophically, however, becomes dogmatism about one belief system. As Donald Carson (1996, p. 35) puts it:

> Open-mindedness ... no longer means that you may or may not have strong views yet remain committed to listening honestly to countervailing arguments. Rather, it means you are dogmatically committed to the view that all convictions that any

view whatsoever is wrong are improper and narrow-minded. In other words, open-mindedness has come to be identified with not the means of rational discourse, but with certain conclusions.

Given this mindset, it should not surprise us to find that even among evangelicals there is an apparent ambivalence to biblical absolutes, as evidenced by a Gallup poll that found that 20% of American born-again Christians believe in reincarnation, and 26% believe in astrology (Colson, 2000). This clash between the traditional (meaning allowing for local differences and tolerating diversity) and the new (meaning the leveling of differences and the globalization of culture), according to Friedman, finds symbols in the tension in the Middle East over which is more important—the preservation of olive trees (symbolizing the local values) or the ability to drive a Lexus automobile (symbolizing that which the global Westernization of culture promotes). For the Christian, which is meant to win out—the fruits of globalization (the Lexus) or pluralization (the celebration and preservation of local values)?

Or is "glocalization," the striving for a healthy balance between universals (globalization) and particulars (pluralization), the way forward? In terms of understanding ultimate reality, of course, the Christian is not in favor of pluralism; only the truth can make one free! We are not in favor of pluralism, except in the sense of not removing the right to choose between competing truth claims, or except in the case of things, as determined by Scripture, that are morally neutral. Pluralism calls for openness to diversity, but it mistakenly insists that relativism (the belief

that no truth is final truth) is necessary for there to be authentic openness. Someone has labeled **relativism** as "having one's feet firmly planted in mid-air"! However, logically, the existence of rival religious worldviews only implies that all of them cannot be valid (Craig, 1995, p. 77). Christians hold to **religious exclusivism**, because we comprehend that divine self-disclosure has come to humankind in two specific ways—the Word incarnated (in the person of Jesus Christ) and the Word propositionally (in the Scriptures). These revelations from God point us away from **religious pluralism** while relatively freeing us to celebrate other forms of diversity.

What Goes Around Comes Around

Worth reflecting on and deciphering, as we seek to critique globalization and pluralization scripturally, is how the church met the challenge of multiculturalism and religious pluralism in the first few centuries of its existence. At that time, the Roman Empire provided religious and social dynamics not dissimilar to our own in the Western world today (Green, 1971). The same dynamic is found in other parts of the world too, such as India, which is the nation to which I have been most exposed cross-culturally. The church in India has developed a theology of mission for over 200 years in a milieu of religious diversity that we in North America are only now discovering. India is dominated by Hinduism but is also crowded by Islam, Sikhism, Buddhism, Jainism, etc. In the West, the cultural landscape is encroached upon by these same world religions and people groups, as well as by a secular

Jazz Band or Classical Orchestra?

Are we going to play in a jazz band or a classical orchestra as we worship God in heaven? I suspect it might be a jazz band! You see, the conductor of an orchestra is in complete control. His or her baton and gestures control every nuance of how the music is played by the individual musicians. The interpretation of a classical masterpiece is recognized by all as the conductor's. However, in a jazz band, the conductor encourages improvisation. Diversity and unity are enhanced in the jazz interpretation of music. I do not think everything will be homogenized in heaven.

humanism that is the by-product of the Enlightenment and modernity, all of which have "conspired" to marginalize the church and create an incipient hostility toward the church. The new post-Constantinian reality for the church, in my view, is not a bad thing; here, I am simply raising the issue to make a comparison.

Perhaps it is not by accident that Lesslie Newbigin, longtime missionary to India, upon his return to the West, prophetically analyzed the need to re-evangelize the West and develop a new apologetic for doing so, in which the uniqueness of Christ would be defended.[2] He it is who gave us the tool of understanding that Christians could be *cultural pluralists* without being *religious pluralists*. Not coincidentally, another voice from South Asia, Ajith Fernando (1987), has passionately called for tolerance in terms of our attitude of respect to those of other faiths, while remaining unswerving in our defense of there being but one way. Similarly, fellow Sri Lankan, Vinoth

Ramachandra (1996, 1997), out of his context of religious and cultural pluralism, has been able to show how the West can be recaptured from its bedazzlement by such idols as inclusivism and relativism. The South Asian church's response to its longstanding existence in a context of multiculturalism (e.g., India has 18 major languages, each spoken by at least 50 million people) and religious pluralism (we have not even mentioned the 350 million Muslims of the subcontinent) may enlighten the global church as she wrestles with a similar cultural and religious environment as a result of globalization—a trivializing and yet a tribalizing of culture and truth claims.[3]

About the early church's response to the pluralization challenge, she sought to emerge and be resilient in the face of enormous pressures. In a sense, the Roman Empire created conditions of globalization, as common features of the nations in its far-flung empire were observable everywhere, whether it be the presence of Greek as

---

[2] These musings may be found in Newbigin (1989, 1995).

[3] The dual development of universals and particulars in the phenomenon we now call globalization was noticed early on by John Naisbitt (1994).

the *lingua franca*, the economic and communication advantages produced by its extensive road system, or its tolerance of local religions as long as its polytheistic state religion was given lip service. In the Roman Empire, *religio* meant the state religion, a formal connection between humans and their gods. In this agreement, the gods, especially Jupiter, would look after Rome's security and welfare, while the state would look after the gods' needs by appropriate sacrifice and worship. While citizens of the Roman Empire did not really have to believe in the divinity of the gods or their human representative, the Emperor, they must participate in the public offerings and ceremonies. Belief was a private matter, but everyone was expected to participate in the state cult. Failure to do so could result in imprisonment or death. Of course, this posed an ethical dilemma for Christians, who could offer allegiance only to the true and living God. To appease conquered peoples, the Romans absorbed the local deities into their pantheon of gods. Mutual respect for each other's gods was a way around the clash of cultures. However, that did not work for the Christians, who could not agree with the Roman distinction between *religio* (public faith) and *superstitio* (private faith).

While seeking to be good citizens, early Christians refused to participate in cultic emperor worship, often with fatal consequences. They had no problem with the gospel taking root and finding expression in cultures other than

The Tower of Babel: Proof for the Christian That Globalization Is Wrong?

Homogenized uniformity seems to have existed millennia ago, for Genesis 11:1 announces that "the whole world had one language and a common speech." How do we know that the pluralization that diverse cultures create is not a judgment, for in indignation, God subsequently confuses their languages and scatters them across the planet (vv. 5-7)?

The reason for the nations' indictment is not the homogenization of humankind, but their misuse of the benefits of that homogenization, so as to make themselves godlike in their grasping for a larger-than-life role in relation to their Creator as they built the Tower of Babel (vv. 3-4). Pride has from the beginning been at the root of all evil.

Even more telling is realizing that the nations had been allowed to develop in advance of the Tower of Babel incident. Genesis 10 describes what God in His grace had encouraged—the evolution of diverse cultures (a table of 70 nations is outlined in this chapter). One is left with the distinct impression that the mandate of Genesis 1:28 in part is to be fulfilled by the diversity of the 12,000 people groups now inhabiting the earth.

Jewish (even documented as early as the New Testament through the disputes referred to in Acts 15 and the book of Galatians). They were respectful of pluralization but resisted any leveling effects (akin to the pressures of globalization) that required them to compromise faith. Faithfulness to the uniqueness of Christ and his salvation required consistent behavior in both the public and private spheres. The early Christians understood that they could be cultural pluralists (not insisting that others believe as they did, in the sense of physically forcing them to believe, which would have been a form of pre-Islamic jihad) while being religious exclusivists (holding firmly to their convictions for themselves).

Returning to our own day, we pick up with Newbigin again in his development of a theology of culture. He sees cultural plurality emanating from the diversity found within the unity of the Triune Godhead, and so he is able to distinguish between the "diversity [which] is part of God's gracious purpose for the human family" and the "separation and mutual rejection [that] is not," so that diversity is not necessarily at odds with unity (Hunsberger, 1998, p. 253).

Some Applications

Although it is not possible to develop a full-blown Christian response to multiculturalism and pluralization vis-à-vis globalization in a single chapter, a number of missiological principles and applications are proffered briefly.

1. Multiculturalism is consistent with the peaceful acceptance of racial and cultural diversity and equality inherent in the human race "made in the image of God" and made realizable through Christ (Gen. 10; Eph. 2:11-21; Acts 10:1–11:18; Gal. 3:28). It is therefore to be embraced by Christians, who must be the true "cultural pluralists."[4] Another way of putting this is that the Christian mindset is of inclusivism, in the sense of recognizing that all cultures and individuals have divine aspects ("made in the image of God") and are loved by God, even though they also have fallen aspects to them, which come under judgment. Furthermore, there is no Christian culture or race, per se, and so we love and appreciate without discrimination all that God has made, while critiquing the sinful dimensions of everyone and everything. Moreover, this critiquing is especially done in the household of faith, where the presence of the Holy Spirit empowers us to effect the change and repent of sins, whereas we cannot expect or require that transformation from the unconverted, who are dead in their trespasses and sins. Charles Van Engen (1999, p. 167) sums up this fine balance as follows: "This world-encountering church is as broad as all humanity (pluralist), as accepting as Christ's cosmic lordship (inclusivist), and as incorporating and gathering as Christ's disciples (exclusivist)."

2. Pluralization as a philosophy that has arisen out of globalization and multiculturalism, in part, **is to be resisted where it compromises the**

---

[4] A full elaboration of this love of God for human kinds, not just humankind, is found in Lundy (1999, chapter 3).

absolute truths of the Bible. Our behavior should therefore in society be expressed much the same way as it was by Christians in the ancient Roman Empire who did not bow to the pressure to separate their public and private lives. They remained religious exclusivists in the public place, while showing respect to the peoples around them, also part of their morality, thus being cultural pluralists. Nonetheless, their cultural inclusivism was a subset of their religious exclusivism, not the other way around! Revelation takes precedence over relevance, even though the revelation of "God made flesh" signals to humankind that for divine revelation to be fully understood, it needs a human/cultural context in which to be expressed (1 Cor. 15:3-4; Jude 3).

3. The genuine respecting of opposite points of view about fundamental issues, while holding to the uniqueness of Christ, can be demonstrated through friendship building; through gentle, thoughtful, engaged disagreement (2 Tim. 2:22); and through living out the truth practically (James 1:22-25). This mindset and matching behavior have been described aptly as "the ability to temporarily set aside one's own point of view and enter sympathetically, but critically, into those of other persons and groups" (Osmer, 2000, p. 68). Related to this is the role that hospitality should have in the Christian's lifestyle (Rom. 12:13; Heb. 13:2). There is an Arab proverb that resonates here that suggests, "If you have room in your heart, you have room in your home." Our homes should not be fortresses to protect us from the world. Rather, they should be gateways (Grand Central Stations or Staten Islands) for diverse strangers to find a welcome that mirrors for them the inclusive and self-giving love of Christ (cf. Lev. 19:33-34).

4. Pluralization in the sense of a public attitude of tolerance should be promoted by Christians, for, as Walsh (2001) has noted, "Evangelicals know that a pluralism that does not favour one faith over another actually provides an ideal context for mission and ministry." Post-Constantinian models of the church in society are truer to the biblical picture of a church—a faith community that is in the minority—which is the reality when pluralization rules.[5] In this sense, Christians should be "pro-choice," while still living counter-culturally, and therefore prophetically, in order to be faithful to God's Word and morality and to be a kind of "conscience" to those of their barrio, high-rise, and souk. As Rodney Clapp (1996, pp. 170-171) eloquently phrases it:

> Non-Constantinian evangelism means recognizing the differences of others, ... of requir[ing] that Christians understand and practice evangelism as proposing rather than imposing Christ.... The God of Israel and Jesus Christ makes himself known by entering into vulnerable relationship with his creatures. This God—preeminently in the life of Christ—does not force people to faith but attempts to persuade them to faith.

---

[5] The defense of Christianity as a "narrow way" is well expressed by Poston (1995).

5. Pluralization, properly held, **means that we are given over**, as messengers of the gospel, **not only to persuade the masses or individuals to accept Christ** (the emphasis of the Mark 16:15 version of the Great Commission), **but also to intentionalize the planting of churches in every people group** (the Matthew 28:19-20 emphasis of the Great Commission). God's glory then is furthered by a pluralization mentality which sees his intention that a people for himself is to be rooted in every tribe, tongue, and culture (Rev. 5:9-10; cf. Gen. 12:3) (Piper, 1999, pp. 113-117). After all, God himself is trinitarian, communal.

6. Globalization as a phenomenon **is not inconsistent with biblical values**, insofar as it is inclusive of diversity, in the sense of freedom to make informed choices, and of pluralization, in the sense of ethnicity. Therefore, uniformity (the blurring of cultural distinctions) in the fashioning of multicultural churches is not a necessary expression of unity in the sense that we shall expect to see it displayed in heaven. (Do the peoples of the tribes, tongues, and nations lose their racial and cultural distinctives in glory just because they are unified by being in the immediate presence of the Lord and the Lamb? Not according to my reading of Rev. 7:9!) This understanding of God's ultimate intentions, therefore, is that he is glorified "not [by] a diversity on the way to unity but a diversity on the way to unified diversity" (Hunsberger, 1998, p. 253). On the other hand, where a set-ting engenders multiculturalism, such as in a world class city, a multicultural church is contextually sound and a foretaste of one aspect of our worship in heaven. We need both multicultural churches and homogenous unit principle style churches.

7. Where technology and relational networking enable the worldwide church to harness the disparate strengths of her presence found in virtually every nation on earth, in order to complete the task of world evangelization, without domination by any one side of her, **an invaluable synergy and witness are formed**. For example, Brazilians may be more effective on tentmaking/church planting teams in North Africa than the membership of the largely Anglo-American agency with which they choose to partner but which has the training resources and experience to enhance the Latin effort. Or British money wedded to Indian human resources in a joint-venture NGO to uplift the downtrodden may be embraced by the Dalit community in India more readily than traditional ways of parachuting assistance in from abroad.

8. The complexities of a globalized and pluralized world cry out for discernment. Furthermore, the vulnerability and uncertainty created by living in such a world as a faithful follower of Christ should drive us to our knees: "Prayer and the seeking of God's will amid the complex circumstances of human life lie at the heart of discernment" (Osmer, 2000, p. 71).

The Uniqueness of Christ

"All things are yours." What does it mean? All true Christian teachers of every name—Paul and Apollos and Cephas and Wesley and Phillip Brooks and Cardinal Newman and Barth and Pascal and Papini and Spurgeon and William Booth—we do not belong to them; no, they belong to us. Every faithful minister profits the whole church; and every member of the church may, and ought to, derive benefit from the teachings of all. It is thus our minds are expanded beyond mere party limits and party cries into a true catholicity....

The declaration, "All is yours," also promises the world to Christians, pre-eminently in this sense, that all secular art and all the sciences help furnish mortar for the temple of God. Christians are not called to leave the world, or to curse the world, or to ignore the world, but to overcome the world and to rule the world for God. Music, painting, sculpture, architecture, all the fine arts—they were given by God from the beginning to be used for the glory of God.

— Comment made by Samuel Zwemer,
a great missionary statesman to the Muslim World,
at the Keswick Convention of 1937 in England (Zwemer, 1937)

Study Questions

1. Do you agree with Zwemer's interpretation of 1 Corinthians 3:21-22?
2. Was Zwemer a globalizationalist ahead of his time?
3. Was he uncritically celebrating pluralization?
4. How did he integrate globalization and pluralization in such a way so as to be true to Scripture?

References

Carson, D. A. (1996). *The gagging of God: Christianity confronts pluralism.* Grand Rapids, MI: Zondervan Publishing House.

Clapp, R. (1996). *A peculiar people: The church as culture in a post-Christian society.* Downers Grove, IL: InterVarsity Press.

Clark, D. (1991). Is special revelation necessary for salvation? In W. Crockett & J. Sigountos (Eds.), *Through no fault of their own? The fate of those who have never heard.* Grand Rapids, MI: Baker Book House.

Colson, C. W. (2000, August 7). Salad-bar Christianity: Too many believers pick and choose their own truths. *Christianity Today, 44*(9), p. 80.

Couto, J. (2001, May 1). Multicultural diversity growing in Canadian churches. *Christian Week*, p. 3.

Craig, W. (1995). Politically incorrect salvation. In T. R. Phillips & D. L. Okholm (Eds.), *Christian apologetics in the postmodern world.* Downers Grove, IL: InterVarsity Press.

Csillag, R. (2001, May 12). Census reveals how we worship. *Toronto Star*, p. M16.

Fernando, A. (1987). *The Christian's attitude toward world religions.* Wheaton, IL: Tyndale House.

Friedman, T. L. (2000). *The Lexus and the olive tree.* New York, NY: Anchor Books.

Green, M. (1971). *Evangelism in the early church.* Grand Rapids, MI: Wm. B. Eerdmans.

Greenway, R. S., & Monsma, T. M. (1989). *Cities: Missions' new frontier.* Grand Rapids, MI: Baker Book House.

Grenz, S. J. (1996). *A primer on postmodernism.* Grand Rapids, MI: Wm. B. Eerdmans.

Hunsberger, G. R. (1998). *Bearing the witness of the spirit: Lesslie Newbigin's theology of cultural plurality.* Grand Rapids, MI: Wm. B. Eerdmans.

Kim, G. Sangok. (1996). Asian North American youth: A ministry of self-identity. In D. Ng (Ed.), *People of the way: Asian North Americans discovering Christ, culture, and community.* Valley Forge, PA: Judson Press.

Lundy, D. (1999). *We are the world: Globalisation and the changing face of missions.* Carlisle, UK: OM Publishing.

Muck, T. C. (1990). *Alien gods on American turf.* Wheaton, IL: Victor Books.

Naisbitt, J. (1994). *Global paradox: The bigger the world economy, the more powerful its smallest players.* New York, NY: W. Morrow.

Newbigin, L. (1989). *The gospel in a pluralist society.* Grand Rapids, MI: Wm. B. Eerdmans.

———. (1995). *The open secret: An introduction to the theology of mission.* Grand Rapids, MI: Wm. B. Eerdmans.

Osmer, R. (2000). The teaching ministry in a multicultural world. In M. L. Stackhouse, T. Dearborn, & S. Paeth (Eds.), *The local church in a global era: Reflections for a new century.* Grand Rapids, MI: Wm. B. Eerdmans.

Piper, J. (1999). Discipling all the peoples. In R. D. Winter & S. C. Hawthorne (Eds.), *Perspectives on the world Christian movement* (3rd ed., pp. 113-117). Pasadena, CA: William Carey Library.

Poston, L. (1995). Christianity as a minority religion. In E. Rommen & H. A. Netland (Eds.), *Christianity and the religions: A biblical theology of world religions.* Pasadena, CA: William Carey Library.

Ramachandra, V. (1996). *Gods that fail: Modern idolatry and Christian mission.* Carlisle, UK: Paternoster Press.

———. (1997). *The recovery of mission: Beyond the pluralist paradigm.* Grand Rapids, MI: Wm. B. Eerdmans.

Ripley, D. (1994, April). Reaching the world at our doorstep. *Evangelical Missions Quarterly, 30*(2), p. 142.

Seim, B. (Ed.). (1999). *Canada's new harvest: Helping churches touch newcomers* (2nd ed.). Toronto, Ontario: SIM Canada.

Thomas, T. V. (1998, March 9-12). *Mobilizing a church on the move.* Paper presented at the International Leadership Conference hosted by Lausanne Canada, Toronto, Ontario.

Van Engen, C. (1999). The uniqueness of Christ. In R. D. Winter & S. C. Hawthorne (Eds.), *Perspectives on the world Christian movement* (3rd ed., pp. 162-168). Pasadena, CA: William Carey Library.

Walsh, G. (2001, January/February). Pluralism and faith communities. *Faith Today,* p. 7.

Zoba, W. M. (2000, April 3). Islam, USA: Are Christians prepared for Muslims in the mainstream? *Christianity Today, 44*(4), pp. 40-46, 48, 50.

Zwemer, S. (1937). *The solitary throne.* London, UK: Pickering & Inglis.

David Lundy is the International Director of Arab World Ministries and is currently serving with his wife Linda at AWM's international headquarters in the UK. Previously, David spent seven years pastoring a church in Toronto. He also served as the Canadian Director of AWM for seven years and as the Canadian Director of Operation Mobilization for nine years. He is the author of **We Are the World: Globalization and the Changing Face of Missions** and **Servant Leadership for Slow Learners**, as well as numerous articles. Email: davidl@wornet.org.

Part 2
Specific Issues

5

Is God colorblind or colorful? The gospel, globalization, and ethnicity

Miriam Adeney

Isabell Ides was 101 years old when she died last June. A Makah Indian, a member of a whale-hunting people, she lived in the last house on the last road on the farthest northwest tip of the United States. Isabell was known far and wide because she loved and taught Makah culture and language. Hundreds of people learned to weave baskets under her hands. Several generations learned words in their language from her lips. Young mothers brought her their alder-smoked salmon. After chewing a bit, she could tell whether their wood was too dry. Archaeologists brought her newly excavated 3,000-year-old baskets, and she could identify what the baskets were, how they were made, and how they had been used. "It's like losing a library," an anthropologist said at her funeral.

Isabell also taught Sunday school at the Assembly of God church on the reservation. She attributed her long life to her Christian faith.

Did Isabell's basketry matter to God, as well as her Sunday school teaching? How important was her ethnic heritage in the Kingdom's big picture? This question reverberates as we explore globalization.[1]

Creative Destruction

In the spring of 2001, representatives of 34 nations gathered in Quebec to discuss a free trade agreement that would cover the whole of the Americas. There were many worries. How can there be a level playing field between the US or Canada and Honduras or Bolivia, between some of the richest and some of the poorest countries on the planet? Won't the small ones be gobbled up? Even Brazil, Latin America's largest economy, was skittish.

Into this discussion, US federal economics chairman Alan Greenspan dropped the phrase "creative destruction." Yes, he said, more open global trade means some "creative destruction." Businesses will close. Jobs will be lost. "There is no doubt," Greenspan (as cited in Workers, 2001) stated, "that this transition to the new high-tech economy, of which rising trade is a part, is proving difficult for a large segment of our work force…. The adjustment process is wrenching to an existing work force made redundant largely through no fault of their own." But, he said, that's just part of the price of progress. You can't make an omelet without breaking eggs. You can't gar-

den without pruning. You can't use the computer without pressing the delete button now and then. You can't train as an athlete without sloughing off bad habits. Honing, sharpening, weeding out, paring down—these are positive terms. So Greenspan spoke of the "creative destruction" inherent in globalization. But, he added, "History tells us that not only is it unwise to try to hold back innovation, it is also not possible."

Ethnicity is one arena of destruction. In today's global system, local ethnic values are being trampled (see box on page 89).

Cultural values are more than commodities. There are valuable things in our heritages on which we cannot put a price. Just as the ecology movement speaks of endangered species, cultural values too may be seen as endangered. During the 1999 world trade talks, for example, when the Canadian government wanted to limit the amount of US entertainment media pouring into their country, they argued, "Canadian culture represents the values that make us unique from other nations. The Canadian government … recognizes that cultural diversity, like biodiversity, must be preserved and nurtured" (report issued in February 1999 by the Cultural Industries' Sectoral Advisory Group on International Trade, as cited in Virgin, 1999).

---

[1] What is ethnicity? Ethnicity's most fundamental criterion is self-ascription as a member of a shared culture. Other-ascription limits this but is secondary. Components of ethnic identity may or may not include the following: an ancestral land (whether or not inhabited by members of the group today), an ancestral language (whether or not spoken by members of the group today), shared history (especially if this includes suffering and heroes), food, humor, and behavior appropriate between close relatives. The actual distinctives shared may be trivial; it is the self-classification that is significant. What a given ethnicity means is reshaped continually. For a fuller discussion of ethnicity, see Williams (2001).

The Trampling of Ethnic Values

Take myself, father of a family, and others like me: We are no longer typical, living examples for our children. It's the cinema, the TV, the video which are the channels for the new cultures, the new values. We, the older generation, are absent in our own families.

I was born in the colonial era. I witnessed all the humiliation and self-abasement my father had to put up with in order to survive. But in the evenings when we came home to our huts, we rediscovered our culture. It was a refuge. We were ourselves again, we were free. Nowadays the TV is right there inside the hut where in the old days the father, the mother, the aunt held sway and the grandma told her stories and legends. Even that time is now taken away from us. So we are left with a society which is growing more and more impoverished, emptying itself of its creative substance, turning more and more to values it does not create.

— Sembene Ousmane,
West African novelist
(Chreachain, 1992, p. 244)

While globalization threatens ethnic heritages, ethnicity does remain resilient. Consider languages. In the US, where English is the official language, the number of Spanish speakers grew by 50% from 1980 to 1990. Spanish speakers now make up 30% of the population of New York City. In the same decade, the number of Chinese speakers in the US increased by 98%, and four-fifths of these continue to prefer to speak Chinese at home. In the former Soviet bloc, Russian is spoken less and less, while local languages are spoken more. By 2050, it is estimated that the world will hold 1,384 million native speakers of Chinese, 556 million native speakers of Hindi and Urdu, and 508 million native speakers of English. As native languages, Spanish and Arabic will be almost as common as English (Wallraff, 2000).

Sometimes global technology strengthens ethnic ties. Members of an ethnic group spread around the world can find each other on the Internet and communicate intensely. Software makers recognize this felt need. Just a few years ago, the Microsoft Windows computer-operating system was designed for English speakers only. The latest version is available in 28 languages.

More often, however, globalization threatens ethnicity. How should we respond to this destructive potential? We turn first to God. Jorge and Gail Atiencia of Colombia have offered a prayer in which we may join (see box on page 90):

A Prayer of Repentance

Padre nuestro, Dios de la ira venidera, Tu palabra nos convoca hoy a arrepentirnos. No vivimos bajo el imperio romano pero bajo otros imperios:

- *el imperio del capital*
- *el imperio tecnologico*
- *el monstro militar*
- *el tentaculo de los medios*

Our Father, God of the wrath to come, your Word calls us today to repentance. We no longer live under the Roman Empire, but we do live under other empires:

- the empire of capital
- the empire of technological power
- the empire of the military monster
- and the empire whose tentacles are the media.

Son estos poderes los que estan articulando nuestra cosmovision:

- *lo que hemos de ser*
- *como hemos de vivir*
- *cuantos debemos tener*
- *como hemos de solucionar los problemas*
- *y aun nos dicen como hemos de buscarte.*

These are the powers that articulate the worldview under which we live, molding:

- who we should be
- how we should live
- how much we should have
- how our problems should be solved
- and they even tell us how we should seek you.

Revelanos, Padre, lo que precisa ser: <<llenado>>, <<desmoronado>>, <<enderezado>>, <<allanado>>. Que por el arrepentimiento podemos ordenar todo lo desordenado causado por los imperios de turno. Entonces, <<la gente vera tu salvacion>>.

Reveal to us, Father, what in our lives needs to be "filled in," "brought low," "made straight," and "smoothed out." By our repentance, may we begin to order all that has been disordered by the powers of our time, so "all flesh will see the salvation of the Lord."

Padre, libranos de reducir <<arrepentimiento>> a emocion o aun a oracion. Lo que tu pides es: Frutos de arrepentimiento. Esto no cabe en la cosmovision que nos dan los poderes, esto es mas de lo que nuestra piedad alcanza.

Father, do not allow us to reduce "repentance" to mere emotion or just another prayer. What you are asking for is "fruit in keeping with repentance." There is no place for such things in the worldview of the powers; this is more than our spirituality can muster.

Dador del Espiritu Santo, venga sobre nosotros tu Espiritu, solo el hace fructificar en medio de la esterilidad.

Oh Giver of the Holy Spirit, may your Spirit come upon us, because only He can make us fruitful in the midst of sterility.

Que por la exposicion de tu Palabra hoy, tu Espiritu nos conduzca a preguntarnos, <<Y nosotros, que haremos?>>

Contronted by your Word today, may your Spirit lead us to the point where we too ask, "What then should we do?"

Que con frutos dignos de arrepentimiento preparemos el camino para la venida del Senor. Amen.

With fruits worthy of repentance, may we prepare the way for the Lord. Amen.

— Jorge and Gail Atiencia (2002)

God Left the Challenge in the Earth

When God made the earth, he could have finished it. But he didn't. He left it as a raw material—to tease us, to tantalize us, to set us thinking, and experimenting, and risking, and God adventuring. And therein we find our supreme interest in living.

He gave us the challenge of raw materials, not the satisfaction of perfect, finished things. He left the music unsung, and the dramas unplayed. He left the poetry undreamed, in order that men and women might not become bored, but engaged in stimulating, exciting, creative activities that keep them thinking, working, experimenting, and experiencing all the joys and satisfactions of achievement.

— A. A. Stockdale (1964)

A Place in the Story

What is God's view of ethnicity? God created us in his image, endowed us with creativity, and set us in a world of possibilities and challenges. Applying our God-given creativity, we have developed the cultures of the world.

In the beginning, God affirmed that it was not good for humans to be alone. Humans were made to live in communities of meaning. So God gave his blessing to cultural areas such as the family, the state, work, worship, arts, education, and even festivals. He gave attention to laws which preserved a balanced ecology, ordered social relations, provided for sanitation, and protected the rights of the weak, the blind, the deaf, widows, orphans, foreigners, the poor, and debtors.

He affirmed the physical world, out of which material culture is developed. He delighted in the very soil and rivers that He gave his people. It was "a land which the Lord your God cares for. The eyes of the Lord your God are always upon it from the beginning of the year even unto the end of the year" (Deut.

11:12). Knowing the material delights of his people, God put them in:

A good land, a land of brooks of water, of fountains and depths that spring out of valleys and hills.

A land of wheat, and barley, and vines, and fig trees, and pomegranates.

A land of olive oil, and honey.

A land where you will eat bread without scarceness, you will not lack anything in it.

A land whose stones are iron, and out of whose hills you may dig brass (Deut. 8:7-9).

In the picture language of the Old Testament, God gave people oil to make their faces shine, wine to make their hearts glad, friends like iron to sharpen them, wives like fruitful vines, and children like arrows shot out of their bows.

Economic, social, and artistic patterns combine to make up a culture. This is the context within which we live. It is where we were designed to live. Global systems may immerse us in **virtual** realities—media, packaged music, the stock market, sports scores, and news flashes in which great tragedies are juxtaposed with beer ads. Yet if we are absorbed in the global or virtual level, we miss out on the real rhythms of nature and society. Seed time and harvest, and the health of our soil, trees, and water. Friendship, courtship, marriage, parenting, aging, and dying. Creation, use, maintenance, and repair. There are rhythms to living in God's world. These are expressed locally, through specific cultural patterns. Knowing these helps us know ourselves, our potentialities and our limits, and the resources and sequences that weave the fabric for happy choices. They cannot be known at the abstract, global level. Disciplining a child, for example, is not virtual. Being fired from a job is not a media experience. Having a baby is not a game. Coping with cancer is not abstract.

During the 2001 Davos world economic forum, columnist Thomas Friedman (2001) observed:

> There was a panel about the 21st century corporation, during which the participants described this age of digital Darwinism in chilling terms. The key to winning in business today is adapt or die, get wired or get killed, work 24 hours a day from everywhere or be left behind.

Finally Howard Stringer, chairman of SONY America, stood up and said, "Doesn't anyone here think this sounds like a vision of hell? While we are all competing or dying, when will there be time for sex or music or books? Stop the world, I want to get off."

Sex, music, books, and business are gifts from God who calls us to live vigorously and abundantly (John 10:10), pressing toward a goal (Phil. 3:13-14), doing everything heartily, as to the Lord (Col. 3:23). Whatever our hand finds to do, we are to do with all our might (Eccl. 9:10).[2]

When I lived in the Philippines, I saw strong families. Warm hospitality. Lots of time lavished on children. Enduring friendships. A heritage of economic freedom for women. The ability to live graciously on little money. Sauces that extended a small amount of meat to many people. A delight in sharing. Skill in the art of relaxation. Lithe, limber bodies. The ability to enjoy being with a large number of people continuously. Since every good gift is from above (James 1:17) and since all wisdom and knowledge come from Jesus Christ (Col. 2:3), such beautiful qualities in Filipino culture must be seen as gifts of God. Our Creator delights in

---

[2] Erich Sauer (1962, p. 81) commented, "[God's words to Adam] call man to progressive growth in culture. Far from being something in conflict with God, cultural achievements are an essential attribute of the nobility of man as he possessed it in Paradise. Inventions and discoveries, the sciences and the arts, refinement and ennobling, in short, the advance of the human mind, are throughout the will of God. They are the taking possession of the earth by the royal human race, the performance of a commission.

"Man has a position of authority, under God and over the rest of creation.... He is expected to find out the potentialities of earth, air, and sea, to use nature and its resources.... In this we can see the scientific quest foreshadowed, whose aim is to understand and classify the natural world. Here is the divine charter for the immense variety of human activity: agriculture, technology, industry, craft, and art. These, according to Christianity, are God's gifts for the enrichment of man's life."

colors. He generates smells, from onion to rose. He shapes every fresh snowflake. He births billions of unique personalities. Is it any surprise if he programs us with the capacity to create an amazing kaleidoscope of cultures to enrich his world?

Cultures contain sin and must be judged, as we will discuss in the following section. But ethnic pride is not automatically sin. It is like the joy parents feel at their child's graduation. Your child marches across the platform. Your chest hammers with pride. This is not pride at the expense of your neighbor, whose face also glows as *his* child graduates. No, your heart swells because you know your child's stories. The sorrows he has suffered. And the gifts that have blossomed in him like flowers opening to the sun. You yourself have cried and laughed and given away years of your life in the shaping of some of those stories.

At its best, ethnicity is an expansion of this good family pride. Ethnicity is a sense of identification with people who share a culture and a history, with its suffering and successes, heroes and martyrs. Like membership in the family, ethnicity is not earned. It is a birthright, received whether you want it or not.

Human beings were created to live in community. In today's world, we still feel that need. "Even when our material needs are met, still our motivation … emotional resilience … and moral strength … must come from somewhere, from some vision of public purpose anchored in a compelling image of social reality," according to anthropologist Clifford Geertz (1964, p. 70). Being a world citizen is too vague to provide this motivation and strength, says Geertz. World citizenship makes the common person feel insignificant. Even national citizenship may breed apathy. But when you are a member of an ethnic group, you have celebrations which give zest, values which give a cognitive framework, action patterns which give direction to your days, and associational ties which root you in a human context. You have a place in time in the universe, a base for the conviction that you are part of the continuity of life flowing from the past and pulsing on into the future. You are in the story.

When Ethnicity Becomes an Idol

God ordained culture. But customs that glorify God are not the only reality that we observe around us. Instead of loveliness, harmonious creativity, and admirable authority, we often see fragmentation, generation gaps, alienation, lust, hate, corruption, selfishness, injustice, laziness, disorder, and violence cultivated by our culture. No part remains pure. Science tends to serve militarism or hedonism, ignoring morals. Art often becomes worship without God. Mass media is full of verbal prostitutes. Advertisers exploit sex. Businessmen pull shady deals whenever they can. Politicians fill their own pockets with the people's money. Teachers don't bother about scholarship after a few years in the profession. Workers do shoddy work. Husbands deceive their wives. Wives manipulate their husbands. Parents neglect their children or dominate them. Children ignore their parents as persons.

We are not only created in God's image. We are also sinners. Because we have cut ourselves off from God, the cultures we create reek with evil. We are called, then, not only to rejoice in the patterns of wisdom, beauty, and kindness in our culture, but also to confront and judge the patterns of idolatry and exploitation.

Sometimes ethnicity is turned into an idol. Like other idols of modern society—money, sex, and power, for example—ethnicity is not bad in itself. When we exalt it as though it were the highest good, however, ethnicity becomes evil. Racism, feuds, wars, and "ethnic cleansing" result.

When ethnicity becomes an idol, it must be confronted and judged. Nearly 100 years ago, some German Mennonites in Canada faced this situation. Their churches increasingly were filled with nominal Christians who wanted roots more than they wanted Jesus. Spiritual stagnation loomed. So the people made a choice. They decided to send their children to Prairie Bible Institute and other nondenominational schools. When they did this, they lost the German language. Many lost strong convictions about pacifism, a theme the group had cherished for centuries. But they recovered evangelistic zeal, and they considered the trade worth the cost. Ultimately, faith matters more than ethnicity. These German-Canadian Mennonites were willing to pay with their ethnicity in order to keep their faith alive for the next generations (Epp, 1978).

Implications for Mission

Ethnicity counters the dehumanizing bent of globalization. Even at its best, economic globalization tends to treat cultural values as commodities. Ethnicity reminds us to keep faith with our grandparents and with our human communities. It is a vital counterbalance.

What does ethnicity mean for mission? We will suggest four applications.

1. Affirm the local

First, mission should affirm local cultures. We do not do this uncritically. Working with and under local Christians, we judge patterns of idolatry and exploitation, as explained above. Yet we love the local culture. We receive it as a gift of God. And while we live in that place, we adapt gladly to those dimensions of local values that are wholesome.

We speak the local language. Everywhere Christians go, they translate the Bible. This has been noted by Lamin Sanneh, a Muslim-background Christian who is professor of history at Yale University. Muslims insist that people learn Arabic, because that is the language of God. But Christians say, "God speaks our language."

We patronize local businessmen and businesswomen. We encourage local artists, musicians, and writers, rather than routinely importing foreign books or translating them. We stay in locally owned hotels and homes. We learn from the lore of local herbalists. We safeguard local forests. We gain skills in local sports and games. We make efforts to be present at local parties and funerals. We empathize with local social reformers. If we are missionaries, we discipline our thoughts so that we are not preoccupied with our homeland's culture patterns.

A quarter of a century ago, I studied the Tagalog language in a premier university in the Philippines. What a shock it was to see the word "beautiful" illustrated in our curriculum by a European face, and the word "ugly" by a Filipino face. It made a sad kind of sense after I learned about "reverse ethnocentrism," in which people value what is foreign over what is local. Filipinos live at the crossroads of big powers. Regularly they have been overrun. They have absorbed cultural veneers from Muslims, Chinese, Spanish, Japanese, Americans, and now the global media. For some Filipinos, what is true, good, and beautiful is what looks Greek, Semitic, or general Caucasian. But Pastor William Girao gives us a very different view of what it means to be a Filipino. His Christian faith has unleashed a passionate love for his heritage (see box).

Is Nationalism a Friend or Foe of the Gospel?

Nationalism is imbedded in the Scriptures. As the chosen people of God, Israel was fiercely nationalistic. The Psalms are replete with nationalistic sentiments. The Prophets were messengers primarily concerned for Israel and Judah (Isa. 1:2; Jer. 4:5; Ezek. 2:3). They identified passionately with their people (Neh. 1:5-6).

Nationalism is in the New Testament. The Lord Jesus himself identified with the Jews. They were "his own" (John 1:11). He was sent to Israel first and primarily (Matt. 15:23-28). He dedicated his public ministry to the Jews and rarely reached beyond them.

Although Paul held Roman citizenship, he was proud to be a "Hebrew of the Hebrews." Of course, he considered this less than nothing when compared with identification with Christ (Phil. 3:5, 8). But in fact Paul loved his own people so much that he was willing to go to hell if that would bring them to Christ (Rom. 9:3-5)....

The brain drain is not a rhetorical device. Every year our [Philippine] churches' most crucial lay leaders go abroad. Many choose never to return.

When Filipinos leave the Philippines rather than stay and help bail it out of its problems, something is drastically wrong with our society and also with those who are leaving. Nationalism draws us back where we belong—to our home, where our leadership is most needed....

Nationalism is the foundation of internationalism. The self-respect and the sense of dignity and worth fostered by nationalism challenge us to try the more complicated task of witnessing to people of a different culture. This merging of national strains, when based on distinct national identities, results in an authentic fellowship in diversity rather than a hypocritical fellowship of conformity.

Is nationalism a friend or foe of the gospel? Nationalism is a friend, an ally in our evangelizing and discipling. But like any other abstraction, nationalism may be misunderstood. Like any other popular movement, it will draw false followers. Like any love, it can be perverted.

Should we repudiate nationalism because we are afraid of the risks? We would have to reject many other necessary movements and abstract realities—even the idea of love itself, since love has so often been abused, misunderstood, and made an excuse for countless crimes.

I maintain that as a nationalist I can serve God better.

— William Girao (1971)

Specific heritages matter. Even the 20th century epic *The Lord of the Rings* (Tolkien, 1954) affirms the local. Columnist Mike Hickerson (2002) observes:

> *The Lord of the Rings* suggests that God's victory on Earth (or Middle-Earth) is incomplete unless and until the victory fills the "small places."… The final battle between good and evil is not some gigantic historic battle—like the destruction of the Death Star—but rather a small fight, followed by a small reconstruction of a very small place. The Good News fills every valley….

In their return to the Shire, the Hobbits continued their mission to its proper conclusion. Without their humble work among their own humble folk, evil would have retained a stronghold in Middle-Earth. The global is important, and so too is the local.

In missionary training programs, this emphasis must be made. There is a tendency for missionaries from dominant cultures to assert their ethnic heritage as though it were God's pattern for everybody. Western missionaries do this.

Chinese and Korean missionaries do it in Central and Southeast Asia. Latinos do it in indigenous communities.

Even within a single nation, missionaries who are from the majority population may lack appreciation for minority cultures and treat them shabbily. Consider an email invitation that arrived this morning. The message reads:

> When you come, would you conduct a workshop on theology of culture? In our country, we have so many different ethnic groups, and the prejudices are amazing. So we may have people from one ethnic group working in a village with multiple ethnic groups. But they tend to work only with their own, and come up with all sorts of reasons not to work with the others.

Throughout history, some missionaries have equated their heritage with God's preferred way.[3] It is easy to criticize them in hindsight. However, we dare not dismiss them too glibly. While early missionaries' theology of culture may have been skimpy, their practice often was robust. They learned local

---

[3] Even evangelical Anglicans associated with the Clapham Sect, that small group of influential Christians in early 19th century England who accomplished so much in eliminating the slave trade, nepotism in civil service, child labor, unsafe factory conditions, prison squalor, harsh punishments, etc.—even some of these dedicated evangelicals, blinded by triumphalism, viewed Indians and Africans ambivalently, almost, in Kipling's famous phrase, "half-devil and half-child." According to Samuel Wilberforce, it was "the vocation of the British people to leave as the impress of their intercourse with inferior nations marks of moral teaching and religious training, to have made a nation of children see what it was to be men." Charles Grant, "taking as his starting point the utter depravity and corruption of the Hindu race," argued that Britain must assume "the task of instructing the Indian population in Christian civilization which providence had so clearly ordained for it, by putting the country under British control," and further that "there was no foreseeable future 'in which we may not govern our Asiatic subjects more happily for them than they can for themselves.'" After all, as John Lawrence explained, "in doing the best we can for the people, we are bound by our conscience and not theirs" (Bradley, 1975, pp. 89, 81, 87, 93).

languages. They were major sources of cultural information for the first anthropologists. Without airplanes, they stayed put through wars, epidemics, droughts, and floods. Their children and wives were buried in local dirt.

By contrast, today's missionaries love to talk about contextualization. But do we have time to live it?

Jesus spent 33 years immersed in one local culture.

2. Be pilgrims

Local cultures are gifts of God, but they are never enough. They are stained with sin. So on one hand, like Jeremiah, we want to "seek the welfare of the city" (Jer. 29:7) where God has placed us. On the other hand, like Abraham, we know that this culture is not our final resting place. We are always pilgrims, "seeking the city whose builder and maker is God" (Heb. 11:8-10).

In his novel *The Blue Mountains of China*, Rudy Wiebe (1975) tells of German Mennonites who were invited by Catherine the Great to settle in Russia. Later, under Stalin, they found themselves removed to a commune in central Asia. It was hard to live as God's people should. As they looked across the border to the blue mountains of

The House of Christmas

There fared a mother driven forth out of the inn to roam.
In the place where she was homeless, all men are at home.
The crazy stable, close at hand, with shaking timber and shivering sand,
Grew a stronger thing to abide and stand than the square stones of Rome.

For men are homesick in their homes, and strangers under the sun,
And they lay their heads in a foreign land whenever the day is done.
Here we have battle, and blazing eyes, and chance, and honor, and high surprise,
But our homes are under miraculous skies where the yule tale was begun.

A Child in a foul stable where the beasts feed and foam,
Only where He was homeless are you and I at home.
We have hands that fashion, and heads that know, but our hearts we lost—
    how long ago!—
In a place no chart nor ship can show under the sky's dome.

This world is as wild as an old wives' tale, and strange the plain things are.
The earth is enough, and the air is enough, for our wonder, and our war.
But our rest is as far as the fire-drake swings, and our peace is put in impossible
    things,
Where clashed and thundered unthinkable wings round an incredible star.

To an open house in the evening home shall men come.
To an older place than Eden, to a taller town than Rome,
To the end of the way of the wandering star, to the things that cannot be,
    and that are,
To the place where God was homeless, and all men are at home.

— G. K. Chesterton (1948)

China, they dreamed, "If only we lived there, *then* we could truly be the people of God." Almost miraculously, they escaped. But being the people of God in China turned out to be harder than it had appeared. So in time they migrated to Paraguay and eventually to Canada. Here they became wealthy wheat farmers with many distractions They discovered that there is no place on earth where it is easy to be the people of God. We remain pilgrims, trekking toward Jerusalem, trusting that in God's time he will prepare a place for us.

How this comforts uprooted people! The immigrant. The biracial child. The Navaho who wonders whether home is the reservation or the city. The cosmopolitans and the youth who buy and wear goods from everywhere and who read, listen to, and watch media from everywhere. What is their identity? Who are their people? Are they destined to be global nomads?

The gospel offers them a home. God doesn't stereotype us. He meets us each as the exceptions that we are, with our multiple and overlapping identities, our unique pilgrimages, our individual quirks. God doesn't slot us into pigeonholes. Whether we have permanently lost our community, or are temporarily adrift, or have patched together bits of several heritages, God welcomes us into his people. The gospel offers us a home beyond the structures of this world.

3. Build bridges

In 1964, when he was 14, Zia entered a school for the blind in Afghanistan. He became a joyful Christian. Over the next years, he learned to speak the Dari, Pushtu, Arabic, English, German, Russian, and Urdu languages, and to read these languages where Braille script was available. During the Russian occupation of Afghanistan, Zia was put in charge of the school for the blind. Later, because he would not join the Communist Party, he was thrown into prison. He escaped to Pakistan in the disguise of a blind beggar, which was his actual state.

In Pakistan, because Zia was translating the Old Testament, he was offered a scholarship to go to the United States to study Hebrew. He declined the opportunity. Why? He was too busy ministering locally. Although he didn't think he had time to extract himself to learn Hebrew, he did learn Urdu as his seventh language in order to reach Pakistanis. Eventually he was martyred.

Moses: Psalm 90

Remember
the slave shack?
the rush bed
on the river?
the pagan palace
which was your splendid prison?
the dust
of Midian's deserts?
the skin tents?
the wanderings in
a wilderness
walled in with thirst
and unthankfulness—
pot-holed
with graves?

Remember? How
could I forget, Lord?
Yet always You
have been
my dwelling place.

— Luci Shaw (1971)

Zia represents the millions of Christian witnesses over the centuries who have discovered that the gospel links us with the globe. We begin locally, but we do not stop there.

Today the world desperately needs people like Zia. Economic and technological globalization connect us at superficial levels. Societies must have people who can make deeper connections. Thomas Friedman (1999) explores this idea in his powerful book *The Lexus and the Olive Tree*, where the Lexus represents the global economy and the olive tree represents local traditions. Clifford Geertz (1973) writes about the tension between epochalism and essentialism, between the need to be part of the contemporary epoch versus the need to maintain our essential identities, to know who we are. Manuel Castells (1996, p. 459) in *The Rise of the Networked Society* argues that although a networked globe means an integration of power, this happens on a level increasingly divorced from our personal lives. He calls it "structural schizophrenia" and warns, "Unless cultural, political, and physical bridges are deliberately built … we may be heading toward life in parallel universes whose times cannot meet."

Who can build bridges? What movement spans nations, races, genders, ethne, rich and poor, illiterates and Ph.D.'s? It is an awesome thing to realize that there are scarcely any people more suitably poised to connect interculturally than the church universal. Praise rises from every time zone, as a classic hymn describes (Ellerton, n.d.)[4]:

"As o'er each continent and island
The sun moves toward another day
The voice of praise is never silent
Nor dies the sound of prayer away."

As a result, when civil ties break down, it is often believers who can lead societies across bridges of reconciliation, reaching out to clasp hands with brothers and sisters on the other side.

Our loyalties do not stop at the edges of our culture. We are pilgrims. We can step out into the margins. Indeed, that has always been the Christian mandate. Abraham was called to be a blessing to all the families of the earth (Gen. 12:1-3). Moses charged God's people to "love the aliens as you love yourselves" (Lev. 19:34). David sang, "May *all* the peoples praise you, O God" (Psalm 67:3, 5). Isaiah envisioned God's followers being light to the nations (Isa. 42:6). Habakkuk, in the pit of Israel's despair, pictured the day when "the earth will be filled with the knowledge of the glory of the Lord, as the waters cover the sea" (Hab. 2:14). Paul was propelled by a passion for the unreached peoples (Rom. 15:20-21). John vibrated with a vision of peoples and tribes and kindreds and nations gathered together around the throne of God at the end of time (Rev. 4–5).

Making cross-cultural connections has been our mandate from the beginning. Our involvement in globalization is rooted not in economics but in God's love for his world. We cannot be isolationists, content in our cocoons. The love of God compels us to step outside our boundaries. Where there is conflict, we step out as peacemakers. Where the

---

[4] For a description of the current rise of global Christianity, see Jenkins (2002).

gospel is not known, we step out as witnesses. Global connections also make it possible for us to step out to serve the church of Jesus Christ worldwide more swiftly and comprehensively than ever before.

To whom much has been given, from them much is required. Are we building bridges?

4. Nurture ethnic churches

Finally, we must consider ethnic churches. Are they racist? Some theologians think so. Although they recognize that ethnic churches facilitate evangelism and fellowship, they argue that what works is not always what is right.[5]

In this chapter, we have argued that ethnic churches are justified not only for pragmatic reasons—because they work—but also because they are rooted in the doctrine of creation. In God's image, expressing God-given creativity, people have developed different cultures. These cultures offer complementary glimpses of beauty and truth and complementary critiques of evil. Like a mosaic, like the design of a kaleidoscope, the whole spectrum of cultures—and ethnic churches—enriches God's world. In an extensive recent essay, "The First Globalization: The Internationalization of the Protestant Missionary Movement Between the Wars," historian Dana Robert (2002) argues that, just as strong bridges require strong supporting columns on each side, so strong international Christian connections require strong indigenous churches. And just as strong, healthy families are the building blocks for strong, healthy communities, so strong ethnic churches can be the building blocks for strong multicultural and international fellowships. It is when we learn commitment and cooperation at home that we are prepared to practice those skills at large.

People gather together in ethnic churches to pray in their heart language, with meaningful gestures, ululations, and prostrations. Their culture will affect the way they do evangelism, discipling, teaching, administration, counseling, finances, youth work, leader training, discipline, curriculum development, relief, development, and advocacy. Their theologians will bring culturally specific questions to the Scripture, generating insights that will complement other cultures' understanding of the texts. The missionaries who serve them must avoid "dumping" theologies or teaching aids or ministry procedures from outside, just as foreign corporations in the secular arena should be kept from "dumping" products that may kill locally owned businesses.

Separate congregations are not bad. What is bad is the lack of love, especially from the dominant culture's churches. There are numerous ways to combat the problem, if we will just commit ourselves to the task (see box on page 101).

---

[5] For an argument against ethnic churches, see Padilla (1983).

Combating a Lack of Love
in Ethnic Churches

- We must **teach**, over and over, the contrasting **biblical** truths of **unity** and **creativity**.

- We must **pray with each other** regularly across ethnic boundaries.

- We must **invest** our time and money sacrificially, and **risk** ourselves emotionally, in strong **partnership** and **exchange** patterns.

- Each church should **commission a "culture broker"** to link it with specific churches or communities of other heritages, and to hold the church members accountable for maintaining faithful relationships of depth and substance.

- When people of other cultures want to join our church, we must **welcome them fully** into our body, yet help them find niches where they can **worship in familiar ways**.

- If minority parents so desire, majority churches must make special effort to serve the **youth**, while encouraging them to maintain pride in their heritage.

- Majority churches must ask minority partners how we can **help them evangelize** their people.

- Majority churches must actively support **leadership training** and **publishing** of training materials to serve minority partners.

- We must repent of **hegemonic dominance** or **neglect** on one side and of **resentment** or **dependency** on the other.

- We must be ready to **learn from each other**, believing that the word of the Lord may come to us through people very different from ourselves.

Ethnic churches are a good place to begin our global mission work too. We can partner with the foreign Christians who live in our own cities—international students, businessmen, temporary visitors, asylum seekers, refugees, immigrants. Many represent relatively "unreached" peoples. Many regularly return to their homeland to help dig wells, set up clinics, teach in Bible schools, publish hymn books and training textbooks, etc. We can pray with them, help them grow to maturity as Christ's disciples, and reach out together to their peoples.

When ethnicity is treasured as a gift but not worshiped as an idol, God's world is blessed, and we enjoy a foretaste of heaven. Let us keep that vision before us.

Japanese and Cherokees
Sing "Holy, Holy, Holy"

There is a vision according to which all peoples and nations and tribes and languages must bow before the beast and worship it. This is the vision of Nebuchadnezzar: "You are commanded, O peoples, nations, and languages, that ... you are to fall down and worship the golden statue" (Dan. 3:4-5). There is a vision that takes for granted that there will always be a great harlot who sits upon many waters; and these waters are the many nations and tribes and languages and peoples who must bring their wealth to her.... If we live by that vision, we shall be content with a world order in which many nations and tribes and peoples and cultures have no other purpose in life but to enrich those who sit upon many waters. According to that vision, the nations and peoples and tribes can and should remain subjected, for that is their place in the scheme of things. According to that vision, our task is to make sure that we, and others like us, are the ones who sit upon many waters, while the rest of the world enriches us.

But that is not the vision of John of Patmos. According to his vision, out of these many nations and tribes and peoples and languages, God will build a kingdom in which all have royal and priestly honor. According to that vision, a great multitude, from all different nations and cultures, will jointly sing, "Holy, Holy, Holy, Lord God Almighty...." Our music and our worship must be multicultural, not simply because our society is multicultural, but because the future from which God is calling us is multicultural. We must be multicultural, not just so that those from other cultures may feel at home among us, but also so that we may feel at home in God's future ... because like John of Patmos, our eyes have seen the glory of the coming of the Lord; because we know and we believe that on that great waking-up morning when the stars begin to fall, when we gather at the river where angel feet have trod, we shall all, from all nations and tribes and peoples and languages—we shall all sing without ceasing: "Holy, holy, holy! All the saints adore thee, casting down our golden crowns before the glassy sea: cherubim and seraphim, Japanese and Swahili, American and European, Cherokee and Ukrainian, falling down before thee, who wert, and art, and evermore shall be!" Amen.

— Justo Gonzalez (1999, pp. 111-112)

References

Atiencia, J., & Atiencia, G. (2002, Winter). Prayer from chapel, March 12, 2002. *Et Cetera: Newsletter of Regent College Students*. Vancouver, British Columbia, Canada.

Bradley, I. (1975). *The call to seriousness: The evangelical impact on the Victorians*. New York, NY: Macmillan.

Castells, M. (1996). *The rise of the networked society*. London, UK: Blackwell Publishers.

Chesterton, G. K. (1948). The house of Christmas. In J. D. Morrison (Ed.), *Masterpieces of religious verse* (p. 162). Grand Rapids, MI: Baker Book House.

Chreachain, Firinne Ni. (1992). If I were a woman, I'd never marry an African. *African Affairs, 91*, pp. 241-247.

Ellerton, J. (n.d.). The day thou gavest, Lord, is ended. *Presbyterian hymnal* (USA), p. 60.

Epp, F. (1978). The Mennonite experience in Canada. In H. Coward & L. Kawamura (Eds.), *Religion and ethnicity*. Calgary, Alberta, Canada: Wilfred Laurier University Press and The Calgary Institute for the Humanities.

Friedman, T. L. (1999). *The Lexus and the olive tree*. New York, NY: Farrar, Straus, Giroux.

———. (2001, January 30). Buzz from Davos: Backlash brewing against technology. *Seattle Post-Intelligencer*.

Geertz, C. (1964). Ideology as a cultural system. In D. Apter (Ed.), *Ideology and discontent* (pp. 47-56). New York, NY: Macmillan Publishing Company.

———. (1973). After the revolution: The fate of nationalism in the new states. In *The interpretation of culture* (pp. 243-254). New York, NY: Basic Books.

Girao, W. (1971). Is nationalism a friend or foe of the gospel? In *The message, men, and mission* (pp. 80-86). Manila, Philippines: InterVarsity Christian Fellowship.

Gonzalez, J. (1999). *For the healing of the nations*. Maryknoll, NY: Orbis Books.

Hickerson, M. (2002, Winter). Editor's note. *Et Cetera: Newsletter of Regent College Students*. Vancouver, British Columbia, Canada.

Jenkins, P. (2002, October). The next Christianity. *Atlantic Monthly*, pp. 53-68.

Padilla, R. (1983). The unity of the church and the homogenous unit principle. In W. Shenk (Ed.), *Exploring church growth*. Grand Rapids, MI: Wm. B. Eerdmans Publishing Company.

Robert, D. (2002, April). The first globalization: The internationalization of the Protestant missionary movement between the wars. *International Bulletin of Missionary Research, 26*(2), pp. 50-66.

Sauer, E. (1962). *The king of the earth*. Grand Rapids, MI: Wm. B. Eerdmans Publishing Company.

Shaw, L. (1971). Moses: Psalm 90. *Listen to the green*. Wheaton, IL: Harold Shaw Publishers.

Stockdale, A. A. (1964, December). God left the challenge in the earth. *His, 25*, p. 20.

Tolkien, J. R. R. (1954). *The lord of the rings*. London, UK: Allen & Unwin.

Virgin, B. (1999, November). Trading away their identity? *Seattle Post-Intelligencer*, pp. C1-2.

Wallraff, B. (2000, November). What global language? *Atlantic Monthly*, pp. 52-66.

Wiebe, R. (1975). *The blue mountains of China*. Grand Rapids, MI: Wm. B. Eerdmans Publishing Company.

Williams, D. (2001). *Castrating culture: A Christian perspective on ethnic identity from the margins*. Cumbria, UK: Paternoster Press.

Workers can face wrenching adjustments. (2001, April 5). *Seattle Post-Intelligencer*, p. C8.

Miriam Adeney *is Associate Professor of Global and Urban Ministries at Seattle Pacific University, and Teaching Fellow at Regent College. She is the author of five books and over 100 articles, including* **God's Foreign Policy: Practical Ways to Help the World's Poor** *and* **A Time for Risking: Priorities for Women** *. An anthropologist, Miriam has worked in Nepal, Brazil, Ecuador, Mali, Russia, a Canadian Indian reserve, and many countries in Southeast Asia. Through the program in Bookwriting for Asia, Africa, and Latin America based at Regent College, Miriam nurtures people as they write biblically rich, culturally contextualized books in their own languages. She is Editor-at-Large for* **Christianity Today** *and serves on the Advisory Boards of both the Institute for the Study of Asian Church and Culture and the Magazine Training Institutes for Eastern Europe. She is married and the mother of three sons, Daniel, Joel, and Michael. Email: miriamsea@aol.com.*

6

Chainsaws, planes, and Komodo dragons: globalisation and the environment

RUTH VALERIO

A few years ago, I went to Indonesia to visit my brother who was living there. We went travelling across the Indonesian islands—a wonderful adventure seeing Komodo dragons, riding on horse-drawn carts, snorkelling off islands untouched by tourists, watching dolphins jump…. One of my most vivid memories was crossing from one island to another on a local boat. There were quite a few bins which people frequently used to relieve themselves. As we drew near to the shore, I leant over the side of the boat to take in the view—stunning white beach, clear blue coralled sea, coconut palms lining the beach—and watched as, to my horror, the crew took all the bins and one by one tipped their contents into the sea!

Similar stories could be told by every reader of this book, no matter what country we come from—stories of both careless and deliberate abuse of the world in which we live. However, stories also abound of people and communities with a deep respect for God's world—stories of beauty, joy, wonder, and hard work. Listen to one man's understanding:

Upon our land, our island, we are caretakers and stewards between a thousand generations. Our footprints are slow to disappear. The view of our wake, the vision back down the trail of our history, gives us a sense of where we have been and are going. Changing conditions demand our attention or teach us hard lessons. We respond individually or as teams, all on this life raft we call Earth, our Mother. A ferry captain steers a half-mile off course so as not to frighten a flock of seabirds. A gardener takes better care of her compost pile than her jewelry. A commuter rides a bicycle, rather than foul forest-filtered breezes. We adopt streams, roads, beaches, animals, children, the less fortunate, a new attitude.[1]

Occasional tractor sound apart, the countryside was silent, if in this silence you include, as I do, the irregular calling of farm animals, the singing of the birds, and the hum of insects. It was unimaginable then that I was to witness the end of quiet and the dimming of the starry firmament. Half a century later, millions of cars, lawn-mowers, strimmers, chain saws, and aeroplanes have seen off the silence, just as street lights have become the enemy of the stars.

— Gerard Morgan-Grenville (2001)

As I write this, the Johannesburg World Summit on Sustainable Development is drawing to a close, and it is clear that "a new attitude" is what is desperately needed. In this chapter, we want to look at some of the negative as well as the positive stories that are happening today. Through these accounts, we will consider the effects that globalisation is having on God's creation and what new attitude is required of us. We will also explore how globalisation impinges on our lives and our mission as we seek to worship God.

Environmental Problems

Climate change, deforestation, loss of biodiversity, and clean water shortages are the main environmental problems facing the planet today. We will look at each area briefly.

Climate change

Climate change is now recognised as being the biggest threat to our world today. It is caused by the releasing of harmful gases into the atmosphere (predominantly carbon dioxide) when fossil fuels are burned. These greenhouse gases trap the sun's heat in the atmosphere, leading to global warming, which in turn results in a change in climate. Global warming is having a devastating effect on our world, with floods, droughts, storms, and heatwaves trebling over the last 30 years and wreaking havoc the world over. In 1998, for example, 26 million people were made homeless through flooding in Bangladesh. As temperatures rise and glaciers melt, sea levels are rising around the world, threatening low-lying coastal

---

[1] From an interview with Gerald Elfendahl in Sacket (n.d.).

> Hunched over, his wiry muscles bunched on his shoulders, Nur Mohammed points out to sea, to where his house used to be—a half mile from the shore. He sits outside the tiny shack that is now his home, on the beach at the north end of Hatiya Island, in the Bay of Bengal. "We had to move fast," he says. "It was the rainy season and the sea was rough—worse than before. There was a flood and it came quickly. We managed to save some of our things and come here."
> — Teartimes (2002, pp. 4-5)

areas. The Maldives, for example, are likely to disappear altogether.

Global warming is directly related to the high consumption of fossil fuels on the part of the richer industrial nations. Nearly everything I have done today has been reliant on fossil fuels, from having a shower to boiling a kettle, cooking my lunch, and working here on my computer—and this says nothing about the fossil fuels used by businesses around the world. One particular problem, directly linked to globalisation, is that of global trade and the energy used in transporting goods all around the world. For example, each kilogramme of apples from New Zealand that is imported into the UK produces its own weight in carbon dioxide emissions (Ecologist, 2001, p. 60). Nearly three-quarters of the energy that is used globally comes from fossil fuels (oil, coal, and gas), and the rest is from nuclear, hydro, and biomass. In the UK, nearly 90% of the energy comes from fossil fuels.

Central to the issue of climate change is oil, because oil is essential to agriculture, to petro-chemicals, and to the production of the petrol and electricity that we use. The extraction of oil causes environmental degradation, which will only worsen as new reserves become harder to find and are opened in such fragile and beautiful places as Alaska, officially a National Wildlife Refuge.

The story of the Ogoni people in Nigeria, where Shell and others have been involved in oil extraction, is telling. Protests from the Ogoni people that their land has been ruined and their livelihoods destroyed have been met by violence from the Nigerian government. Since 1993, the Nigerian Internal Security forces have killed over 1,000 Ogonis (McLaren, Bullock, & Yousuf, 1998, p. 86). Oil now accounts for 80% of the country's GDP and 90% of government revenues, yet the industry employs only 2% of all Nigerians, and deep corruption means that the nation as a whole does not feel the benefit of the oil money.

Because of the central place of oil in the global economy and because we cannot survive without this "black gold," oil is a major factor in world politics. The Gulf War was waged mainly because of the need for the West to access Kuwait's oil (*New Internationalist*, 2001, p. 12). Another example is the Global Climate Coalition, which was formed by the fossil fuel companies to protect their profits and lobby against any action taken to prevent further climate change.[2]

---

[2] One of the positive outcomes of the World Summit on Sustainable Development is that the Kyoto Protocol (the only international agreement on climate change) could be made law. By the time you read this book, you will know whether this has happened!

Deforestation

Deforestation is the second highest contributor to climate change, behind burning fossil fuels. It is responsible for 20-30% of all carbon dioxide in the atmosphere.[3] Deforestation contributes to climate change through the carbon that the trees absorb through photosynthesis. In fact, scientists describe rainforests as "carbon sinks." They are one of the main ways in which carbon is absorbed out of the atmosphere. However, because they absorb so much carbon, when forests are felled and burned, the carbon is then released back into the atmosphere (as also are nitrous oxide and ozone). Recent calculations suggest that "frontier forests" (i.e., original forests remaining in large, relatively natural ecosystems) store more carbon than is likely to be released by burning fossil fuels and manufacturing cement over the next 70 years or so (World, n.d.).

Rainforests are incredibly precious.[4] They are the earth's oldest living ecosystems: forests in Southeast Asia have existed for 70 to 100 million years. Whilst they cover a relatively small amount of land area, they house half of all the plant and animal species in the world. Still, scientists estimate that there could be as many as 30,000 plant species yet to be discovered. Rainforests are amazingly rich in both medical and food stuffs. A quarter of the medicine we use today comes from rainforest

> Ruwi lives in the forests of Sumatra. Here, thousands of trees are being clear-cut by multinational forestry corporations. This ruthless exploitation is destroying the forests and the livelihoods of the forest dwellers. Ruwi is only 10, but he can still remember the awful polluting fog caused by the corporations setting fire to the forests a few years back.
>
> — Friends of the Earth (2002)

plants, and much of our food had its origin in the rainforests. The genetic material from the wild strains of food is needed to keep the modern stock strong and healthy, but less than 1% of rainforest plants have been examined thoroughly for their chemical compounds.

Despite their importance, rainforests are facing intense pressure, and the figures on how they are disappearing are staggering. All of the primary (i.e., original) rainforests in India, Bangladesh, Sri Lanka, and Haiti have been destroyed, and the destruction is nearly complete in Ivory Coast. The Philippines lost 55% of its forests between 1960 and 1985. Thailand had lost 45% by 1985. The destruction continues today. Around the world, 2.4 acres of rainforests are destroyed every second. This translates to

---

[3] Unless otherwise indicated, all the information on the rainforests comes from Rainforest Action Network factsheets.

[4] In addition to tropical rainforests, there are a number of other types of forests in the world: temperate forests (in northern Russia, North America, Chile, and Australia), boreal forests (in the cold north of Europe and North America), and temperate rainforests (on the west coast of North America). All of these contain huge varieties of wildlife, and all are increasingly under threat from the demand for timber and the resources these forests hold. However, it is the tropical rainforests that are particularly significant.

149 acres every minute, or 214,000 acres each day (an area larger than that of New York City), or 78 million acres each year (larger than Poland).

There are five primary causes of deforestation:

- the demand for goods made from wood (including paper products)[5]
- farming for beef for richer countries[6]
- mineral and oil extraction[7]
- hydroelectric dams (built to provide the energy for mineral and oil extraction)[8]
- subsistence farming

All of these factors have strong links to globalisation.

Two things are of particular note. Firstly is the fact that all of the activities of corporations in the rainforests depend on having enormous amounts of money. The World Bank and many of our national banks are involved in providing the necessary capital. Secondly, deforestation is clearly linked with issues of poverty, as the uneven distribution of land and money are both caused by and a cause of the forests' destruction. There is a direct link between deforestation and the global structures that we saw in chapter 1 on globalisation and economics. David Gosling (as cited in Reed, 2001, p. 54) cites the example of Brazil, where repayment of international debt takes place primarily through the exporting of cash crops, which then leads to the inevitable clear-cutting of the forests.

Loss of biodiversity

Alongside climate change, one of the most pressing concerns over deforestation is the loss of biodiversity, which is resulting in an alarming rate of species extinction. There are incredibly complex systems of relationships existing in the rainforest. If just one part of that network is disrupted, the whole ecosystem is harmed. One extinction leads to another, which leads to another, and so on. It is thought that 10% of the world's species could disappear within 25 years because of the breakdown of rainforest ecosystems.

The destruction of the rainforests is the primary cause of species extinction, but it is not the only one. Intensive agriculture, commercial fishing, the car and its roads, and the effects of industrial activity in general all combine to contribute to a devastating loss of the planet's ecosystems. The authoritative 2002 Red List of Threatened Species (IUCN, 2002) says that 11,167 creatures

---

[5] Britain is the fifth largest paper user in the world, despite being so small.

[6] In 1993 and 1994, America imported over 200 million pounds of fresh and frozen beef from Central American countries. Whether the forest is cleared for cattle grazing or for crop farming, the thin rainforest soil can grow pasture for only a few years. When the soil is worn out, the cattle ranchers and farmers are forced to move on, which results in yet more forest being cut down.

[7] Large areas are threatened through mining for minerals such as aluminum and tin and through oil extraction. BP, Chevron, Shell, Exxon, Conoco Inc, and Occidental are all involved in "exploring" different rainforest areas. Mineral and oil extraction leads to massive degradation and pollution. It also affects human rights as tribal territories are invaded.

[8] These dams flood extensive areas of forest and displace the people who lived in those areas.

> "Extinction is a loss of our knowledge of God—erasing his fingerprints."
>
> — Metropolitan Archbishop Daniel of Moldova

face extinction; this is already 121 more species than were listed in the 2000 edition. Incredibly, a third of the world's primate species face a serious risk of extinction (Conservation, n.d.).

We will consider a fuller theological response to these issues later, but it is worth pausing now to consider the spiritual nature of species extinction. Romans 1:20 makes it clear that creation reveals the character of God.[9] The story of Noah is about God's saving and loving care for all living things. The purpose of including two of every living creature in the ark was "to keep their various kinds alive throughout the earth" (Gen. 7:3). Looked at from this perspective, then, "extinction is blasphemy," as John Stott has noted.

Clean water shortages

One of the most devastating effects of climate change is drought. Lack of clean water is becoming one of the biggest problems facing our world and its people. Global water consumption rose sixfold between 1900 and 1995 (more than double the rate of population growth) and is continuing to grow rapidly as agricultural, industrial, and domestic demand increase. Currently, 41% of the world's population (2.3 billion people) live in areas of water scarcity. Of these 2.3 billion, 1.7 billion people do not have the resources to tackle the shortage. The effects become severe,

leading to problems with local food production and economic development. It is thought that by 2050 nearly half of the world's population (48%, or 3.5 billion people) will face severe water shortages (Revenga, 2000). The health implications are catastrophic, while armed conflict over dwindling water resources, particularly in the Middle East, will become an increasing threat (Townsend, 2002).

As with so many environmental issues, it is the poor who suffer most but who are least responsible for the problems (Tearfund, n.d.). As competition for water increases, the rich and powerful are the ones who have the most influence. One major cause of water shortages is the migration of people to the cities, leading to a demand that far outstrips supply, as people desperately try to survive in slums and shanty towns. The economic demands placed on poorer countries by the rich nations include the privatisation of public amenities. As a result, water prices are

> Arby Nia Souwailou lives in the village of Ngorfuhondu, six hours from Timbuktu, the capital of Mali. Mother to three children, she has a plot of land, but she says that water is a chronic problem. "The soil is just sand," she laments. "We have to buy water to cultivate it. Often the whole harvest goes toward paying back the debts we've taken on to grow it. It's a vicious circle: cultivation, harvest, famine. Hunger is our daily lot."
>
> — Teartimes (2000, pp. 5-6)

---

[9] See also Psalm 104 and Job 38–42.

> "Our most precious resources are clean air, clean water, and clean soil. These are our birthright, and yet they are all under threat. Those who contaminate them are our certain enemies, and it is the duty of every citizen to fight them."
> — Gerard Morgan-Grenville (2001)

hiked up in the cities, and the needs of those in urban areas are ignored. Water problems are growing, too, because of the increasing consumption of water due to economic development and higher standards of living. The tourism industry, for example, can worsen shortages as hotels and golf courses take the majority of water away from the local community.[10] Industry and agriculture consume huge amounts of water (agriculture uses 70% of the world's water). They lead to deforestation, soil erosion, and water pollution, all of which exacerbate water problems.

As consumer demands increase and the volume of world trade rises, untold pressure is being put on the planet and its resources. What may not be quite so obvious is that it is the economic global structures maintained by the wealthy countries that keep this situation as it is. Northcott (1996, pp. 31, 30) makes it clear that "the system of resource extraction in the South and capital accumulation in the North is still the basic economic context for relations between North and South." Consequently, "The environment of indebted countries is being raided to meet payments to Western bankers under structural adjustment programmes imposed by the World Bank and the IMF."

Deep Magic[11]

Any theological reflection on the subject matter of this chapter must, inevitably, start with the story of creation because, whatever may have happened subsequently, Christians believe in a trinitarian God who made the universe and the world we live in and who declared everything to be "very good" (Gen. 1:31).

In chapter 1, dealing with economics and globalisation, we saw that our mission is defined by our being created "in the image of God" (Gen. 1:27), emphasising the relationality involved in that: our relationships with God and with his creation. As I looked previously at our relationship with God's human creation, so now I want to focus on our relationship with the rest of creation. This relationship is a vital element of our identity, but a false understanding of the word "dominion" in Genesis 1:26,[12] Enlightenment values that viewed the environment as a resource for mankind, and eschatological beliefs that see the destruction of this world as part of God's end-time

---

[10] On a similar note, the Sheraton Hotel in Addis Ababa, Ethiopia, consumes a quarter of the entire city's electricity.

[11] "Deep magic" is what Lewis (1950) calls the mystery of the gospel in *The Lion, the Witch, and the Wardrobe*.

[12] Elsewhere in the Old Testament, the idea of dominion is used of the Hebrew kings and embodies the idea of "servant kingship" rather than of domination (Osborn, 1993, p. 29).

The Singer

"In the darkness something was happening at last. A voice had begun to sing. Its lower notes were deep enough to be the voice of the earth herself. There were no words. There was hardly even a tune. But it was, beyond comparison, the most beautiful noise he had ever heard. It was so beautiful that he could hardly bear it. The blackness overhead, all at once, was blazing with stars. They didn't come out gently one by one, as they do on a summer evening. One moment there had been nothing but darkness; next moment a thousand, thousand points of bright leaped out. Far away, the sky began to turn grey. A light wind, very fresh, began to stir. All the time the Voice went on singing. The eastern sky changed from white to pink and from pink to gold. The Voice rose and rose, till all the air was shaking with it. And just as it swelled to the mightiest and most glorious sound it had yet produced, the sun arose. And as its beams shot across the land, the travellers could see for the first time what sort of place they were in. The earth was of many colours: they were fresh, hot, and vivid. They made you feel excited—until you saw the Singer himself, and then you forgot everything else."

— C. S. Lewis (1955)

plans have all contributed to our missing this truth. The reality is that we are a part of creation. Yes, we have been given a special role within that creation, which is a part of our calling as the only creatures made in the image of God. It is an inescapable fact, however, that we are part of the same ecosystems and structures that are formed with the rest of creation. This is readily apparent in the creation narrative of Genesis 1:1–2:3. Contrary to popular thought, humanity is not the pinnacle of creation, although it is clearly a special part of creation. The pinnacle comes on the seventh day with the establishment of the Sabbath rest.

Nature, represented by the garden of Eden, was the first place where humanity met with God (Osborn, 1993, p. 92), and this is something that surely resonates loudly with us today. The people of Israel certainly recognised the natural world as they filled their temple with reminders of that world (e.g., Ex. 25:31-33; Osborn, 1993, p. 92). In addition, the Psalms are full of the praises of creation, with Psalm 104 being the most obvious example. These things are not simply reminders, however. Gunton (1992, p. 98) makes the point, "The enabling of creation's praise of the Creator becomes a central part of the human offering of thanks to God for his creating and redeeming love."

However, our ability to image God perfectly was marred by the Fall, in which humanity turned away from God and chose to go their own way. The Fall broke humanity's relationship with God, with each other, and with the rest of creation. Creation would now carry within itself the curse of God, as well as his blessing. The rest of the Bible tells the story of the unfolding plan of God for salvation. Israel is called to be his people and model his purposes for the land.

True Worship

Space does not permit a full consideration of the attitudes towards nature contained in the Old Testament.[13] However, one aspect that is relevant to the discussion of this chapter is that the two dimensions of social justice and ecological harmony are inextricably linked, and they are linked together by the concept of the true worship of Yahweh, Israel's God. We have seen already in chapter 1 how significant it is that the primary command of Exodus 20 is against idolatry; this has relevance here too. Deuteronomy 30 picks up on this theme and explicitly relates faithfulness to God with social and ecological prosperity (vs. 15-16). The Prophets (e.g., Jer. 5:23-25; Isa. 5:8-10; 24:1-6) emphasise this particularly: where disobedience to God leads to social injustice, there the land will fail and become desolate and fruitless. The importance of this truth for today can hardly be denied, as the greed and idolatry of globalisation trample over human beings and destroy the rest of creation. It is now almost universally acknowledged that environmental and social issues, far from being in competition, have to be tackled together.[14]

If any consideration of our relationship with the rest of creation inevitably

Diamonds That Leap

When the leaf fell and brushed my hand
I began to reverse the world. I asked:
What if this warped willow leaf, yellow,

scaled with age, could smooth
to a green blade and flicker into
the knot of a spring twig, like

a grass snake's tail disappearing, slick
and chill, into his home? That one question—
it was a whirlpool, pulling in

others: What about a river?
Might its waters rush up these indigo
hills of Shenandoah and split into a scatter

of diamonds that leap to their rain
clouds, homing? Can a love
shrink back and back to like,

and the crack of a small, investigative
smile? Could God ever suck away creation
into his mouth, like a word regretted,

and start us over?
— Luci Shaw (1994)

starts with the story of creation itself, it must also find its centre in the coming of Jesus to live on earth as a human being, to die, and to be raised to life again. If we see human beings as part of creation, rather than separate from it, then the incarnation affirms the goodness and intrinsic worth of the whole of creation. When Jesus died on the cross, he brought about not only the means of reconciliation between God and humanity and between humans one to another, but that reconciliation is

---

[13] For more on this, see Northcott (1996, chapter 5) and Osborn (1993, chapters 5-6).

[14] The difficulty of doing this, however, was amply demonstrated at Johannesburg.

extended to include the whole of the cosmos. Romans 8:18-25 and Colossians 1:15-20 demonstrate that Jesus is Lord over *all* things, and *all* things will be involved in the final act of consummation. However, that consummation is only guaranteed because of the resurrection. That is the pivotal point for Christianity and, indeed, for the history of the world. As Northcott (1996, pp. 199-200) says:

> The relational alienation ... which issues from the Fall is transformed and redeemed by the restoration of created order which is presaged in the resurrection of Jesus Christ who, Christians came to see, was indeed God incarnate, God in a human body, transforming from within the disorder of a fallen creation.

Revelation 4 gives us a glimpse of the future to which all of God's creation is oriented: the future that is begun with the "firstfruits" of the resurrection. This is the end for which we have been made: to worship God completely and to enable the rest of creation to be made perfect in order to praise its Creator. In this way, we understand "the new creation itself not as a replacement for the present world but as the eschatological future of this world" (Bauckham & Hart, 1999, p. 137). This is a wonderful privilege, but it is also an awesome responsibility. As Gunton (1992, p. 64) says, "We human creatures are the centre of the world's problems, and only by our redirection will the whole creation be set free."

Implications for Mission

Clearly, our mission work bears immense significance. Ultimately, it is only as people come to recognise the Lordship of Jesus, trust in his saving power, and be filled with his Holy Spirit that the rest of creation will also be liberated. However, as both history and the present demonstrate, eschatology is too often used as an excuse for inaction regarding the environment, causing many to focus solely on saving human beings whilst ignoring the land around them.

Realising God's promised future

Biblically, the opposite is true. We live as children of the future, living our lives now in the light of what we know the future holds, guaranteed by the working of the Holy Spirit (Eph. 1:13-14).[15] Bauckham and Hart (1999, p. 82) argue forcibly for this understanding of the Christian life as motivated by the vision of the future, saying, "Christianity is a faith which is essentially forward looking and forward moving, orientated towards and living now ever in the light cast backwards by God's promised future." If the promised future involves all of creation, then our mission today must do likewise. Let me quote again from Bauckham and Hart (1999, p. 71), who express the idea far better than I can:

---

[15] Paul provides us with a clear example of such an eschatological orientation (e.g., Eph. 5:8; Phil. 3:20), so much so that Fee (1994, p. 13) says, "It seems impossible to understand Paul without beginning with eschatology as the essential framework of all his theological reflection."

It is a vital part of a Christian perspective on this world to identify within it scattered acts of re-creative anticipation of God's promised future.... Such anticipations are to be found *in* this world, but they are not *of* this world in the sense of having identifiable and sufficient natural antecedents in it. They belong to God's future, of which they are heralds and towards which they direct our hopeful gaze. In such happenings, the power of the future-made-present is manifest, the lustre of the new creation shines provocatively from behind the heavy clouds of history. In the meanwhile, Christians are called to identify and to become involved with God's Spirit in all that he is doing to fashion a genuine presence of the new within the midst of the old, drawing it into self-transcendent albeit partial anticipations of what it will ultimately be.

What might some of these anticipations look like? Two possibilities are given in the boxes below.

A Rocha

A Rocha was established in Portugal in 1983 by Peter and Miranda Harris. The organisation now has centres in Lebanon, Kenya, France, the UK, the Czech Republic, Canada, the USA, and Finland. Five "Cs" characterise A Rocha's approach:

- **Christian** – We are motivated by our biblical faith, particularly in God the Creator.
- **Conservation** – We focus on scientific studies of important habitats and species.
- **Community** – We bring people together for environmental education and action, with special emphasis on students and school children.
- **Cross-cultural** – We involve staff and volunteers internationally and give priority to parts of the world where resources for conservation and Christian witness are limited.
- **Campaigning** – We work with local and international agencies for the protection of key areas and environments.

A Rocha is an example of a Christian organisation that is not mere words but has attempted to express its theology in practical projects. A Rocha, however imperfectly, gives a view of Christian mission in the world, where common humanity forms the basis for community, where care for creation forms part of one great commission along with care for people. It is not theories and ideas which change people in their attitudes to the environment, but relationships in community, shared experiences in story form, and working together in practical tasks at a local level. For more information, visit **www.arocha.org**.

A Christian Environmental Workshop

In 1997, a two-week Christian environmental workshop took place at the Ortho-dox Cultural-Pastoral Centre at Durau, in Romania's Carpathian mountains. The event was organised by Youth With a Mission and the Metropolitan's Department of Pro-tocol and Pilgrimage in Iasi. It brought together Romanian and Western European students to study environmental problems and their management from a Christian perspective. The purpose of the workshop was to introduce the theology of creation and Christian responsibility towards the environment, to compare different world-views, and to present a model for conflict resolution in environmental management. The workshop provided the experience of working on a simple, practical project and gave an opportunity for cultural and spiritual exchange between Western European and Romanian participants.

Choosing simplicity

The examples given above are just two of the ways people are attempting to realise "God's promised future" to-day. One key response that many people are making is choosing a life-style of simplicity. Indeed, once we recognise that it is primarily the greed and idolatry of the wealthier nations that are causing ecological destruction in the first place, it could be argued that for those of us who have the choice, there is no excuse *not* to simplify our lives. Lane (2001, p. 19) recognises this when he writes that one reason people are choosing to live more frugally "arises out of their heart-felt concern at the devastating consequences of what capi-talist exploitation and technology are doing to the natural world, and the con-sequences for their children and grand-children. Gandhi expresses this as a basic law: if you want to change soci-ety, you must change yourself at the same time."

For many people, the idea of sim-plicity makes their toes curl, carrying connotations of woolly jumpers and mungbean stew, living in poverty in a draughty hut! However, simplicity is actually about something far more ex-citing. Henry Thoreau, one of the pio-neers of the simplicity movement, said, "A person is rich in proportion to the things he can leave alone." Simplicity is not about scarcity and misery, but about discovering what it really means to be rich. It is about having true life in abundance: "life to the full," as Jesus said (John 10:10). As we have seen in this chapter and in chapter 1, true life is found not in the accumulation of money and possessions, but in our re-lationships with God, with one another, and with the rest of creation. Simplic-ity, therefore, is about getting rid of the clutter that stands in the way of devel-oping those relationships.[16]

---

[16] Focussing on our time is often therefore central to developing a life of simplicity (see Valerio, 2002, pp. 4-6).

Food considerations

One underlying theme that comes through many approaches to simplicity is our attitude towards food. Seemingly innocuous, actually food connects us to all three of the relationships we have looked at. Food has a profoundly spiritual dimension to it. It is one of the main ways by which we nourish ourselves and our relationships with each other.[17] It is no coincidence that the Bible so often links food/eating with central biblical concepts (communion, water of life, fasting, "taste and see that the Lord is good" (Ps. 34:8), the eschatological banquet, etc.). Indeed, Mike Schut (2001, p. 11) sees food as a sacrament and talks of "the spirituality embodied in our personal and cultural relationship to food."

Food also stands at the heart of many of our environmental problems. Consider, for example, the fact that people in the richer countries now eat more beef, pork, poultry, eggs, and dairy products, which in turn means a greater demand for grain to feed animals. More grain means more water is needed for irrigation. A US diet annually requires 800 kg of grain per person, compared to just 200 kg for an Indian diet (Tearfund, n.d.). Or consider the fact that on organic farms in the UK, there are five times as many wild plants in arable fields and 57% more species as on those that are intensively farmed. Some endangered species are found only on organic farms.[18]

The factors involved in the food we eat are many, and there is no doubt that it is a political issue involving, amongst other things, the vital question of freedom.[19] Sticking to the brief of this chapter, though, if we are to realise our calling in relation to the rest of God's creation, then it is vital that we consider the food that passes our lips, rediscovering the connection between it and the land it came from.

Relating rightly to creation

From all that we have seen above, it is clear that the salvation of humanity is closely intertwined with the redemption of the rest of creation (Rom. 8:19ff). Based on this understanding, an important mark of those who are saved is that they are in a right relationship with all of God's creation. To be a disciple and neglect creation is a contradiction in terms. For so much mission work, this is a lost dimension that needs to be recovered. In a similar way to that of social concerns over previous decades, environmental concerns now must be integrated into all that we do.

---

[17] Issues relating to trade and working/producing conditions mean that the food we eat affects our relationships with other people, even if those people live thousands of miles away.

[18] There were also 44% more birds in fields outside the breeding season. Endangered birds, such as the song thrush, were significantly more numerous on organic farms. In particular, there were more than twice as many breeding skylarks (Soil, 2001).

[19] As Wendell Berry (1999, p. 106) says, "We still (sometimes) remember that we cannot be free if our minds and voices are controlled by someone else. But we have neglected to understand that we cannot be free if our food and our sources are controlled by someone else. The condition of the passive consumer of food is not a democratic condition. One reason to eat responsibly is to eat free."

We need to do this, in part, because a neglect of creation can stand against the integrity of the gospel we preach. Peter Harris (personal communication) cites the example of an Australian who sees missionaries' complete lack of concern for the land as being a large part of the long-term failure of Christian missions in reaching aboriginal people, for whom the land is a fundamental aspect of their culture. We have seen how globalisation can lead to the exporting of American/Western values in all areas of life. Those missionaries/ agencies coming from the predominantly wealthy countries must ensure that they do not bring with them the attitudes towards God's creation that are embedded in the culture of consumerism. In contrast, as we recover an understanding that includes the whole of creation, our mission work will be enhanced, demonstrating through our words and our actions what life is like when it experiences relational redemption on all levels.

Whether we are planting churches, drilling teeth, discipling new converts, or building schools, then, one of the questions at the front of our minds will be, How can we anticipate the new creation in our present work? In order for missionaries both to ask the question in the first place and then be equipped to find an answer, teaching on God's creation and its significance for mission must be included in missionary training. For example, Redcliffe College in the UK has a lecture on "Development and the Environment" in their Development Studies course, and the topic is included as an important ongoing theme in their Globalisation and Mission course. They also have an annual lecture from A Rocha as part of their missionary speaker programme. Redcliffe, of course, is not alone in doing these things.

Understanding local ecology

One important area is gaining a knowledge of local environmental issues. Any missionaries worth their salt should ensure that they know the language and culture of any area in which they work. The same should be true of the area's ecology (P. Harris, personal communication). For many missonaries, it is second nature to attempt to live in the same way the local people do. This can now be extended to consider living sustainably. For example, a friend moving to Tanzania wanted to have a nice garden and so water it. Her first thought, though, was to consider the water situation in the area and find out if that would be taking valuable water away from land and people who needed it more. Whatever work we do, we will be touching creation somehow. Peter Harris (2000) writes:

We all turn on taps or fetch water, we all switch on or off lights or light fires, we all breathe and eat. All of these things involve us in choices, and responses to God's good gift of creation. They may well also involve us in the suffering that has been brought into the world through the Fall. The water may be polluted, the light comes at a high cost to creation... So, whether we live in a mega-city or a tiny hut in the rainforest, we live in creation, and its care is our concern.

Conclusion

We do, indeed, live in creation. More than that, we *are* creation. As such, we owe our very beings to our Creator God. That Creator God has made us to be like him and to reflect the relationality that is at the very heart of the Trinity. Our calling is to be his ambassadors—working to see the restoration of the broken relationships that came as a result of the Fall. As we do that—through our gospel proclamation, our social concern, and our caring for the rest of creation—so we will begin to experience the new creation, inaugurated by Jesus' life, death, and resurrection. Perhaps no one expresses this better than G. K. Chesterton (as cited in Gunton, 1992, p. 63):

On the third day, the friends of Christ coming at daybreak to the place found the grave empty and the stone rolled away. In varying ways, they realised the new wonder, but even they hardly realised that the world had died in the night. What they were lookng at was the first day of a new creation, with a new heaven and a new earth; and in the semblance of the gardener, God walked again in the garden, in the cool not of the evening, but the dawn.

The Song of the Inexhaustible Sun

Can I ever repay my gratitude to the sea
whose quiet waves come out to seek me
as I am led astray, day after day? —
and to the sun
for not spurning me, its journey done,
and for keeping evening and dawn
not far apart?

What can I give you for the nearness which
you kindle in this immensity
like fire,
like hearts poised on their equanimity?

What can I give you for that familiarity
which you start in a child's eye
and complete in the glory, untouched
by shadows of sorrow?

And for defencelessness what reward?
It gives me day in abundance.
Am I so strong that I can last?
A creature such as I, my Lord,
you should not trust.

Can I ever repay my gratitude to the sea
whose quiet waves come out to seek me
as I am led astray, day after day?
and to the sun
for not spurning me, its journey done,
and for keeping evening and dawn
not far apart?

Forgive my thought, Lord, for not loving enough.
My love is so mind-manacled, forgive that, Lord;
it subtracts You from thought, leaving it cool as
    a stream,
where you want an embrace of fire.

But accept, Lord the wonder that leaps from my
    heart—
as a brook leaps up from its source—
a sign that heat may yet burn.
So, Lord, do not spurn
even that cool wonderment.
One day You will nourish it with a burning stone:
a flame in my mouth.

— Pope John Paul II (Dent, 1997)

References

Bauckham, R., & Hart, T. (1999). *Hope against hope: Christian eschatology in contemporary context*. London, UK: Dartman, Longman, & Todd.

Berry, R. J. (Ed.). (2000). *The care of creation: Focusing concern and action*. Leicester, UK: InterVarsity Press.

Berry, W. (1999). The pleasures of eating. In M. Schut (Ed.), *Simpler living, compassionate life: A Christian perspective*. Denver, CO: Living the Good News.

Bruges, J. (2000). *The little earth book*. Bristol, UK: Alistair Sawday Publishing.

Conservation International and the Primate Specialist Group of the IUCN. (n.d.). Retrieved from http://www.conservation.org.

Cootsona, G. (2002). *Creation and last things: At the intersection of theology and science*. Louisville, KY: Geneva Press.

Dent, Sr. A. (Ed.). (1997). *Ecology and faith: The writings of Pope John Paul II*. Berkhamsted, UK: Arthur James.

Department for International Development (DFID). (n.d.). Literature on environment, poverty, and development. London, UK: Author.

The Ecologist. (2001). *Go M.A.D.! 365 daily ways to save the planet*. London, UK: Think Publishing.

Fee, G. D. (1994). *God's empowering presence: The Holy Spirit in the letters of Paul*. Peabody, MA: Hendrickson Publishers.

Friends of the Earth. (2002, July). *Earth summit briefing*.

Gunton, C. (1992). *Christ and creation*. Carlisle, UK: Paternoster Press.

Harris, P. (2000). Creation care and everyday cross-cultural mission. In W. D. Roberts (Ed.), *Down-to-earth Christianity: Creation-care ministry: A manual for relief and development workers, missionaries, pastors, and all Christians interested in caring for God's creation*. Wynnewood, PA: Pub. for the Association of Evangelical Relief and Development Organizations by the Evangelicals for Social Action/Evangelical Environmental Network.

Hughes, D. (1998). *God of the poor: A biblical vision of God's present rule*. Carlisle, UK: OM Publishing.

IUCN Red List of threatened species. (2002). Retrieved from http://www.redlist.org.

Lane, J. (2001). *Timeless simplicity: Creative living in a consumer society*. Totnes, UK: Green Books.

Lawrence, D. (1995). *Heaven: It's not the end of the world!* Reading, UK: Cox & Wyman Ltd.

Lewis, C. S. (1950). *The lion, the witch, and the wardrobe*. New York, NY: Harper Collins.

———. (1955). *The magician's nephew*. New York, NY: Macmillan.

McLaren, D., Bullock, S., & Yousuf, N. (1998). *Tomorrow's world: Britain's share in a sustainable future*. London, UK: Earthscan Publications.

Morgan-Grenville, G. (2001). *Breaking free*. Bridport, UK: Milton Mill Publishing.

New Internationalist (2001, June).

Northcott, M. (1996). *The environment and Christian ethics*. Cambridge, UK: CUP.

———. (1999). *Life after debt: Christianity and global justice*. London, UK: SPCK.

Osborn, L. (1993). *Guardians of creation: Nature in theology and the Christian life*. Leicester, UK: Apollos.

Prance, G. (1996). *The earth under threat: A Christian perspective*. Glasgow, UK: Wild Goose.

Rainforest Action Network. (n.d.). Fact sheets.

Reed, C. (Ed.). (2001). *Development matters: Christian perspectives on globalisation*. London, UK: Church House Publishing.

Revenga, C. (2000, October). *Will there be enough water?* Retrieved from http://www.earthtrends.wri.org/conditions_trends/feature_select_action.cfm?theme=2.

Sackett, J., & Association of Bainbridge Communities. *In praise of island stewards: Portraits and views in passing.*

Schut, M. (Ed.). (1999). *Simpler living, compassionate life.* Denver, CO: Living the Good News.

———. (2001, November). Food as sacrament. *Earth Letter.*

Shaw, L. (1994). *Writing the river.* Colorado Springs, CO: Pinon Press.

The Soil Association. (2001). *The truth about food* [Brochure].

Tearfund. (n.d.). *Water matters.* Campaign material.

Teartimes. (2000, Autumn).

———. (2002, Spring).

Townsend, M. (2002, August 18). Who will save the world? *The Observer.*

Valerio, R. (2002). *Simplicity: Living life to the full.* Cred Papers.

World Resources Program. (1998). *Fragmenting forests: The loss of large frontier forests.* Retrieved from http://www.earthtrends.wri.org/conditions_trends/feature_select_action.cfm?theme=9.

Wright, T. (1999). *New heavens, new earth: The biblical picture of Christian hope.* Cambridge, UK: Grove Books Ltd.

Ruth Valerio *works with the organisation Cred, teaching and resourcing the church on globalisation, justice and poverty, environment, and lifestyle issues. She is on the Council of the World Development Movement and on the Tearfund Theological Resources Team. Ruth is based in Chichester, UK, with two preschool children, and is chair of her local Community Association. Email: ruth.valerio@virgin.net.*

7

Globalisation and healthcare mission

STEVEN FOUCH

He was 30 years old—only two years my senior at the time. With a master's degree in civil engineering, he was already a gifted leader at what his own culture regarded as a very young age. He had an intelligent, loving wife and a growing, happy young family. Seemingly, he had everything to live for. When I first met him, he could do little more than smile and tell me his name; his mental condition had deteriorated to that of a two-year-old in the space of a fortnight. On two occasions, we had to conduct a massive manhunt to find him after he had wandered off around the streets of South London, too confused to be able to remember where he lived. Once we found him wearing no more than his pyjamas on a frosty November morning three miles from his home.

During the year I spent caring for Tim and his family, I watched this young man become increasingly childlike, until he could no longer be trusted to care for himself in even the most basic of bodily needs. HIV-related dementia had robbed his wife and children of a husband and father, and it had robbed his country of a future leader of industry and education, long before death claimed him. And claim him it did, after a long, traumatic year, with his wife following him 18 months later. To the best of my knowledge, his eldest child is still healthy and virus free, but her younger brother died not long after his father.

This was neither my first nor my most traumatic exposure to the devastation of AIDS, but it highlighted for me the global nature of this epidemic. Tim was from sub-Saharan Africa and was only in the UK to complete a doctoral thesis. His infection had been acquired in his home country, but for more than half of the Africans I have met, HIV was acquired here in the UK. HIV/AIDS may be the first disease of modern globalisation; it is certainly the most widespread and devastating. It has become apparent to me that the complex global community of which we are a part is both a causative agent in the health problems that I meet daily and also is being shaped by these self-same illnesses.

I must lay my cards on the table as I write this chapter. I am not a hands-on expert in what used to be called "medical mission." I have relatively limited overseas experience, and I possess no qualifications in international health. I write not from firsthand experience but from the experiences of those with whom I have come into contact in my various areas of work down through the years. As a nurse, I have worked in the field of HIV and AIDS in the UK for many years, and as a medical anthropologist, I have experience in analysing critically the complex interplay of society, culture, and health. With my limitations in mind, I have included a suggested reading list at the end of the chapter for those who are interested in exploring this whole complex field in more depth.

Healthcare and Mission: From Jesus to Today

"Then he sent them out to preach the kingdom of God and to heal the sick" (Luke 9:2).

It was the gospel that compelled me into nursing and that further compelled me into working with people with AIDS, at a time when such a focus was both deeply unfashionable and rather "beyond the pale" in most of the Christian community in the UK. The same compulsion has moved countless others down through the ages, both in their homelands and across the globe.

Jesus sent out the first disciples with the commission to preach and heal. When confronted by John's disciples asking if he was the Messiah, Jesus replied, "The blind can see, the lame can walk, lepers are made clean, the deaf can hear, the dead are raised, and the gospel is preached to the poor" (Luke 7:22). You can almost hear him adding, "So what on earth do *you* think is going on then?" In Luke 4:16-21, when Jesus stood up in the synagogue in Nazareth and read from Isaiah 61:1-2, he proclaimed (among other things) recovery of sight to the blind and care and freedom for the poor and oppressed. In short, healing, care for the sick and the weak, and the proclamation of the good news have always gone hand in hand. Saving people from spiritual death was one half of a mission that was also about bringing physical wholeness and restored human social relationships.

This "wholistic" approach to mission was very much a part of the life of the early church. Examples abound of the early church caring for the sick, as

Christians travelled across the known world—both in miraculous healing and in the more mundane areas of care for the chronically ill and dying. For example, during the bubonic plague epidemic of AD 256 in Alexandria, Egypt, while the rest of the city fled, the Christians stayed behind to care for the sick and dying. Many of them paid for their compassion with their own lives (Davey, 1985).

Our modern words "hospice" and "hospital" share the same root as "hospitality," recognising that the early church took people into their own homes to care for them (many of whom were suffering from plague, leprosy, and other diseases that would usually have left them outside the bounds of normal society).

As Hans Küng (1976) wrote, "The message of Jesus culminates in love of neighbour.... In this light, the young community of faith from the very beginning recognised active care of the suffering as a special task. Hence systematic care of the sick became a specifically Christian affair."

This emphasis was largely lost after the "Christianisation" of the Roman Empire under Constantine in the fourth century, but even as late as the Middle Ages, monastic orders were still being established that saw care for the sick as a central ministry (Davey, 1985).

The modern missionary movement has involved medical care through much of its existence, although it may be argued that, with honourable exceptions, many early missions did not see that saving lives and mending bodies were as important as saving souls. Indeed, it may arguably have been the phenomenally high morbidity and mortality among the early missionaries that persuaded some societies to begin to set up hospitals. In time, those hospitals pioneered medical care for many communities in what we would now call the developing world (Davey, 1985). Today there are thousands of hospitals, clinics, and healthcare projects around the globe set up and run by various Christian groups. India alone can boast over a thousand Christian hospitals, now run almost exclusively by the national church.

Globalisation, Poverty, and Health

"The poor you will always have among you" (John 12:8).

Jesus' comment to Judas was not just a statement of fact, but also an indictment. Poverty is as real and horrifying in our day as it was in the first century, but the scale has grown beyond all imagining.

Consider these few stark facts:

■ Around 1.3 billion people live in grinding poverty (income less than $1 per day).

■ Growth of the world economy doubled in the 25 years before 1998.

■ The population of the developing world numbers 4.4 billion.

■ Significant proportions of this population lack:

- sanitation (3/5)
- clean water (1/3)
- healthcare (1/5)
- enough dietary energy and protein (1/5) (WHO/6, 2000)

Economic disparities both within and between countries have grown over the past decade, and incomes are lower in real terms in about 100 countries.

Life Expectancy and Mortality Rates, by Country Development Category (1995–2000)

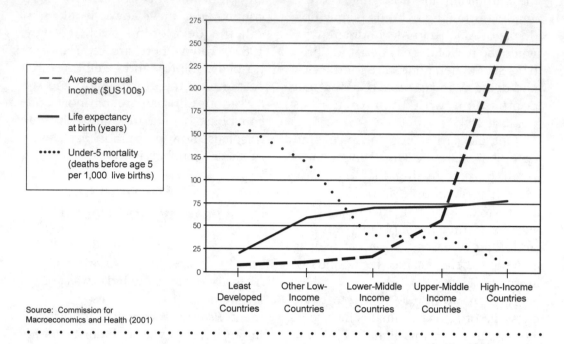

Source: Commission for
Macroeconomics and Health (2001)

It is often assumed that poor health and poverty are automatically linked. Indeed, as the chart above indicates, the increasing wealth of a nation does show marked changes in many basic indicators of health, such as the under-5 mortality rate and average life expectancy. If a nation is wealthy as a whole, it can (theoretically) afford better health infrastructures, so that more people can access healthcare. If people are wealthier, then they can afford to pay for healthcare (either directly or indirectly through taxation) so they become more healthy. More fundamentally, they can afford to eat better, can afford better housing and sanitation, etc.

However, this is not the whole picture. According to the International Poverty and Health Network (IPHN), the link between economic growth and

health is not automatic. Poverty is multi-dimensional. Improving the average health of a nation may widen inequalities, with the rich getting healthier and the poor getting less healthy (Haines, Heath, & Smith, 2000).

In practice, increases in national wealth often tend to benefit the health only of those who are already wealthy. New wealth tends to congregate around those already "better off," while healthcare services become more costly as they improve. Both of these factors tend to disadvantage the poor (Haines, Heath, & Smith, 2000). Furthermore, this new wealth is often built around the owners of factories in free-trade zones. These zones are effectively tax havens for sweatshop factories, where workers are required to work long hours in poor working conditions for minimal wages. Unable to afford to eat well and working in sometimes hazardous and often arduous conditions, the workers often suffer from poor health. Access to healthcare is minimal, if not non-existent (Klein, 2000, pp. 195-229). In these cases, increasing wealth in one sector of the population is bought at the price of dramatically reducing the health of another sector.

However, health also affects wealth. As people's overall health improves, so their ability to earn a living improves (where a reasonable job at a reasonable wage is available), and the drain on their incomes by medical bills is reduced. The wealth of the nation as a whole is also affected, because the drain caused by an overburdened health system and a large unproductive population is reduced. A report by the Commission for Macroeconomics and Health (CMH) (2001) suggests that if the basic health inequalities in the poorest nations of the world were met, over US$186 billion per annum could be added to the global economy, and the resultant economic uplift could take many nations out of poverty. More significantly, 8 million lives would be saved each year.

To achieve this level, CMH calculates that all of the developed nations would need to give a total of $27 billion per annum, and the developing nations would need to increase their spending on health by $38 billion. If we consider that in 2001 the US mobilised $40 billion in a few weeks to fight a war in Afghanistan, or that the costs of the proposed health development programme are equivalent to only $25 per person per year in the developed world, it becomes apparent that the missing ingredient is not money but political willpower in developed nations.

However, a lack of political will (or, indeed, infrastructure to sustain the development of health services) on the part of the governments of many developing nations is equally a part of the problem (Terrorism, 2001). Perhaps tackling this political apathy may be a role for healthcare mission work. We tend to focus on the local and the specific needs of communities, but these needs are affected by bigger issues with which we are often less engaged.

The focus of the secular pro-globalisation development agenda is primarily economic and at this macro level. For example, a recent initiative (the Global Health Initiative or GHI) which came out of the World Economic Forum (WEF) seeks to get businesses to tackle the health needs of both their employees and the communities in which they operate, on the basis that investing in health will yield economic benefits in the long term. This initiative is being seen as a major driver in the international fight against HIV, malaria, and TB (World, 2002).

Opponents of economic globalisation argue that this approach is naïve, as the major causes of poverty in the developing world are often these self-same businesses, and self-interest is unlikely ultimately to benefit the poor. As the WEF was meeting in New York in February of 2002, an even larger gathering in Porto Alegre, Brazil, was looking at how to tackle corporate power on behalf of the poor (Campaigners, 2002). One example of such power held by businesses is in the area of Intellectual Property Rights (IPR) for pharmaceuticals.

The Agreement on Trade-Related Aspects of Intellectual Property Rights (TRIPS) ensures that all pharmaceuticals are protected globally for a minimum period after they are patented, to ensure that the transnational companies that develop them are able to recoup the cost of research and development. Since most of these new drugs are priced at a level above the health budgets of most developing nations or individual incomes, there is no access to many new, life-saving medicines for a large part of the world's poorest people. Some firms (in particular, in Brazil and India) have manufactured some of these drugs without licensing agreements, making them available to developing nations at a fraction of the costs of the licensed versions. However, TRIPS has significantly limited this practice until relatively recently.

A recent campaign and international court ruling have encouraged the World Trade Organization (WTO) to ease some aspects of the TRIPS regulations with respect to HIV anti-retroviral drugs, and some developing companies have reached agreements on licensing, allowing them to manufacture these drugs at low cost. In addition, many pharmaceutical companies have been encouraged to supply these drugs at cost to developing nations (African, 2001; Africa's, 2002).

However, these successes have not tackled the chronic under-investment in developing drugs that primarily benefit people in the developing world (e.g., treatments for common tropical diseases such as sleeping sickness, Leishmaniasis, or Chaga's disease). The capitalist economic model encourages pharmaceutical companies to invest primarily in drugs that will be profitable, which in practice means those that treat primarily Western conditions (Griffins, 2002). It is more profitable to invest in drugs that correct male sexual dysfunction, for example, than those that will effectively control the current epidemic of drug resistant malaria. A recent report shows that many leading pharmaceutical companies spend less than 1% of their research and development budgets on the major illnesses of the developing world (Médecins, 2001).

Globalisation and Global Health

"Be fruitful and multiply, and fill the earth and subdue it" (Gen. 1:28).

Economic globalisation is a hot topic as either the cause or cure for world poverty and thus of health inequalities. However, it is not the only factor. Globalisation in its wider sense also has a major impact on health and always has. The ancient world was globalised, in a manner of speaking—especially under Rome, where travel was relatively safe, free trade was encouraged, and movements of knowledge, communities, cultures, philosophies, and religions happened largely unchecked. Throughout the ages, these movements of people through trade, exploration, world mission, and (latterly) tourism have enabled many infectious diseases to be moved from one corner of the globe to another. The lack of local resistance to these newly imported illnesses often has transformed a relatively minor illness in one region into a major, life-threatening epidemic in another. Hence, the devastation wrought on the native Amerindians by 16th century

Spanish explorers carrying smallpox, or the impact of the common cold and influenza upon the Alaskan Inuit (Diamond, 1998).

Movements of people are usually tied in with the forces of wealth and poverty, war and ecology. For example, the poor increasingly move into urban areas looking for work as rural economies collapse (e.g., as a result of the fall in coffee and cocoa prices in recent years, or as a result of drought and famine driving subsistence farmers out of their traditional homelands). This large-scale urban migration, usually into crowded shanty towns and slums, makes these incomers vulnerable to infectious diseases, waterborne illnesses, and diseases usually thought of as diseases of affluence, such as cardiovascular disease and cancer (WHO/51, 2000).[1] Meanwhile, sex tourists from the West have introduced HIV and other sexually transmitted diseases (most notably into Haiti and Thailand), and they are now acting as vectors to bring those diseases back to the West (Panos, 1988, pp. 88-91).

It is not just migration into cities that presents a health problem. People moving into new rural areas to escape war, famine, or overpopulation also make themselves vulnerable to illnesses such as Leishmaniasis, Ebola, Kayasanur Forest Disease, etc. These illnesses are exacerbated by environmental damage (Hellman, 1994, pp. 380-381).[2]

In short, the complex dynamics of human global relationships have a major impact on the social and environmental causes of disease and on access to healthcare. We are naïve if we think that life in the West is not impacted too. Global health issues are on our own doorstep. For example, AIDS, malaria, and TB are now endemic problems worldwide. In the UK, where I live, on the borders of Kent and Greater London, we are seeing outbreaks of TB in schools (Sharp, 2000). In addition, health workers in Kent have voiced concerns to me about the imminent arrival of malaria in coastal regions, where mosquitoes coming off cargo ships from the South are once again beginning to breed in the marshlands. Meanwhile, AIDS is now one of the leading causes of death of young men and women in the Greater London Area. More and more of those who are affected are from the sub-Saharan African communities. Similar patterns can be discerned throughout the Western world.

In addition to these movements of people and disease, there is movement of cultural ideas. Western biomedicine is as culturally bound as any healthcare

---

[1] For example, smoking—a habit imported from the West and supported by international tobacco firms who pump a large part of the advertising budget into the developing world—is a growing health problem among the world's poor, especially in cities.

[2] For instance, Kayasanur Forest Disease (KFD) in southern India is transmitted (like Lyme disease) by ticks, whose normal hosts (small mammals and birds) were driven from their habitats due to extensive deforestation. The clearance of the forests created scrubland that was colonised by poor agricultural communities. These communities kept cattle that were ideal hosts to ticks. Significantly, the Indian government for many years played down the links between deforestation and KFD.

system.[3] This realisation has undermined the standing of biomedicine in Western culture, so that in the postmodern West, Eastern medical paradigms such as the Ayurveda and Traditional Chinese Medicine (TCM) are increasingly popular. They offer an alternative for those who perceive the limitations of Western medicine, particularly in dealing with chronic illnesses. The concern that these Eastern forms of medicine raise for Christian mission is that the worldview of many of these healing systems is based in non-Christian religions. However, we often do not look critically at the Greco-Roman pagan origins of our own scientific Western medicine, nor at the secular and atomistic view of the human body and health, from which Western medicine works—a view which is hardly any more biblical than that of Eastern medicine.

In developing nations, these and numerous other local healing traditions compete with Western Christian medical services—often to the detriment of patients. In some cultures, Western medicine is only used to treat certain conditions. Some cultures believe that the soul is lost or damaged if one dies in a hospital, so they will not seek treatment for serious conditions. Others see Western medicine as useful for treating certain acute illnesses or as a quick "pick me up." In some West African cultures, it is believed that a man will lose his soul if his body is pierced by metal, leading to a dangerously low uptake in vaccinations for male children.

The failure in the past of some Western health practitioners to realise the interaction of local and Western health beliefs has added to the problem, and we have often assumed the primacy of our views over local beliefs. Poverty is

---

[3] Being "culture bound" does not imply arbitrary or unproven. Rather, in acknowledging that in all spheres of human activity culture is a fundamental factor and that beliefs are not just based on "hard evidence" but also on deeper cultural values and assumptions, we can understand how any activity we undertake, however scientifically objective we believe it to be, is affected by the social and cultural environment in which it is undertaken.

To give two examples of how cultural and socio-political factors affect medical knowledge in the West, consider the cases of homosexuality and AIDS. Homosexuality was listed for many years as a mental illness in psychiatric textbooks. For a long time, it was considered a treatable condition, until the closing decades of the 20th century, when gay rights campaigning and (ironically) the onset of the AIDS pandemic resulted in a sea change in cultural attitudes in much of the Western world towards sexuality. Homosexuality is no longer regarded as an illness by the medical establishment. Now the condition is not only tolerated, but is also being seen increasingly as an acceptable and positive lifestyle.

Meanwhile, medical opinion in the US during the early 1990s redefined the point at which a diagnosis of AIDS could be made, relying on certain clinical markers rather than presentation of disease. This gave people an AIDS diagnosis often before they showed any signs of illness. Being diagnosed with AIDS gave access to the benefits system in the US that a simple HIV positive diagnosis did not. In the UK, where this was not an issue, the criteria for diagnosing AIDS did not change and remained based on disease presentation. Cultural, social, and political values can shape the way in which disease is diagnosed, defined, and treated, as much as scientific research (which is itself a culturally shaped activity).

not the sole reason people do not come to the doctor for help (Hellman, 1994).

Global Crisis in Healthcare

Another big issue facing the global health environment is the emerging crisis affecting healthcare provision across the globe. We are aware in the West from almost daily headlines that our health systems are in crisis. In the UK, there is a huge debate on how state funding of the National Health Service should continue, as the costs of raising the funds through direct taxation escalate. Meanwhile, in the US, around 40 million people with middle incomes have no medical insurance. They do not qualify for the government Medicare or Medicaid programmes, thus creating a new underclass of the medically untouched and untouchable (Kenay & Christensen, 2002). The costs of modern health provision are a major economic stress in the West.

There are two major reasons for this stress, both of which are, in part, ironic consequences of the advances in modern medicine. First, social policies and medical care have increased our life expectancies, although our overall health in old age has not increased as rapidly. The result is an increasingly aged population, a large proportion of whom will require long-term medical and/or nursing care, while the proportion of taxpayers able to fund this care is decreasing (Meek, 2002).

The second problem is cost—mainly in the medical technologies that increase life expectancy. New treatments are highly expensive, but an informed, consumerist population wants access to these treatments as soon as they become available. Consumer culture has pervaded healthcare, as it has all other aspects of Western life, and consumer demands for the best treatment available, as a right, are now attitudes firmly entrenched both in Western cultural beliefs and law. More people requiring (and demanding) more expensive treatments, with fewer taxpayers to support services, is an equation that is slowly driving the Western healthcare systems to the brink of collapse (Meek, 2002).

How does this crisis in the West affect other parts of the globe? Obviously, this is a problem facing all developed nations (not just in the West), but the developing nations have a somewhat different issue. Lacking the financial resources to provide new technologies, and with life expectancies actually being driven downwards by HIV, the issue here is how to provide even a basic level of service to the poor.

The problem is exacerbated by the fact that locally trained health professionals want to find more lucrative work, either in their own cities, in private hospitals, or by emigrating to the West. One set of figures that I heard recently suggested that out of every seven doctors qualifying in one sub-Saharan nation, only one was still practising in the country a year later. This is one reason that mission hospitals still tend to be staffed by expatriates (especially in Africa, where these pressures are most acute). Nurses, for example, are being actively recruited from developing nations such as Malawi and the Philippines by private recruiting agencies in the UK[4] to fill the growing

---

[4] The British Government maintains that this is not its policy, however.

gap in nurse recruitment and training from the indigenous population. The result is devastating to a country like Malawi, where already under-resourced hospitals cannot find any staff to man their wards, threatening the well-being of patients (Laurance, 2002).

AIDS is one of the other major new factors in this equation. It is most prevalent in the 20-45 age group, removing the most productive adults from the working population, thus reducing tax revenues, increasing the need for care for vast numbers of infirm adults, and killing large numbers of health professionals. In Zimbabwe, for instance, as many as one in two nursing students is HIV positive.

Another factor is war. In Angola, Democratic Republic of Congo, and Sudan, hospitals and clinics have been bombed out of existence in some areas. Transport infrastructures have been equally decimated, and access to food, clean water supplies, work, etc., have all been virtually eliminated by many years of civil war. In many parts of both these countries and many others, there is no health system at all. The move-

ment of large populations of men at times of war also creates a sex industry, in which the spread of HIV, hepatitis, TB, and sexually transmitted diseases can accelerate dangerously.

Faced with health systems that are in many cases in a state of collapse or even non-existent, with the growing health inequalities between rich and poor, and with the impact on health of environmental and social exploitation and war, it is hard for Christian mission to engage with local communities without engaging with their health needs as well. The challenge for mission hospitals is to become sustainable and locally led. Yet when local health professionals do not want to stay, and when the local community is too poor to support a hospital or clinic by itself, how can sustainable healthcare be achieved without continued input from expatriate missionaries? The only solution is for all these other factors to be addressed as well, making communities wealthy enough and healthy enough to maintain their own healthcare infrastructures.

Sustainable Healthcare in Zambia

Chikankata Hospital in Zambia was founded on the edge of the Gwembe Valley in 1946 by The Salvation Army, to provide a health service for some of the poorest people in the country.

The Present

As one of the epicentres of the AIDS pandemic in sub-Saharan Africa, in a situation of economic restructuring and declining net national and international aid to Zambia, the hospital in its original form had become unsustainable. At the same time, the local community's existence was threatened by poverty and by the growing AIDS problem.

continued on page 133

continued from page 132

Recognising that hospital based care was too expensive to keep pace with the demands in the long term, the hospital turned its focus outwards to the local community itself. A programme of home based care that is clinical, pastoral, and educational has been linked to family and neighbourhood based counselling. This has enabled the neighbourhood groups in the areas covered by the programme to recognise and respond to the problem of HIV infection themselves, rather than relying on hospital personnel. The response is seen in the expression of care for each other and in sustained commitment to change, where this is needed, in attitudes and behaviours. This process has happened in both low and high prevalence areas. A team approach is used in hospital care, as well as in home visits to those infected, affected, in danger of being infected, or connected in other ways. Such an approach widens the circle of prevention.

The Future

Led by its traditional headmen, the community around the hospital has begun to recognise that it has the capacity to care for its own health, and it has begun to accept the responsibility to do so. It can discuss its own problems, recognise their causes, decide how to solve them, and determine the priorities in light of the resources available. This process can extend to all aspects of healthcare and not just to HIV/AIDS. The hospital and home care staff, most of whom are Zambian and many of whom are locally employed, have increasingly become identified with the community in this process. They are facilitating change by:

1. drawing attention to problems.
2. exploring concerns and hopes when people discuss what they see.
3. encouraging the living and giving hope to the dying by working for better relationships and a more secure future.
4. planning with the community a sustainable use of hospital resources.
5. seeking within the church a holistic spiritual response to sickness and poverty.
6. helping home care programmes in other areas and countries.

This process of facilitating participation and change causes the solutions to become community-owned rather than being imposed from outside. The hospital and clinics become resource centres for the community. A community confidentiality develops, and a degree of "community informed consent" is found, which may allow HIV testing without time-consuming pre-test counselling. The process of care resulting in change "is as simple and yet as profound as the recognition that the love of Christ transforms" (Campbell & Clegg, 1999).

Mission hospitals have long been seen as the mainstay of Christian healthcare mission, and indeed in many parts of the world, they were the first hospitals of any kind. Inevitably, in most countries, state and private hospitals now provide the majority of services, but Christian hospitals still have a role. These hospitals are often based in the poorest communities, which the private sector does not want to service (because there is no profit) and which the state cannot afford to serve. However, most Western missions are shedding their hospitals, as they become huge drains on cash and other resources.

The aim for many mission agencies is now to get local churches to take over the running of these hospitals. In some cases, this is successful; in others, it is an ongoing struggle, as a poor church and community seek to find the resources to run a health facility that may simply not be part of their vision for their ministry to the local area. In still other cases, running a hospital is

Emmanuel Hospital Association in India

The Emmanuel Hospital Association (EHA) in India is an indigenous mission that brought together a number of previously Western-run mission hospitals under an umbrella network over 20 years ago. It now includes 19 hospitals and 27 local community health projects. Its main thrust has been to develop appropriate local responses to the health needs of the vast communities it serves in North India.

Staffed almost exclusively by Indian personnel (mainly from South India), EHA has benefited from the two major Christian medical colleges in Ludhiana (in the Punjab) and Vellore (in Southeastern India). EHA has thus created a strongly Indian Christian response to health and community outreach. It has also seen, as a direct result of its work, many new churches established and growing in the regions near its hospitals.

Using its expertise gained in locally running and developing not just hospitals, but also community health programmes, literacy, and income-generation projects, EHA is now increasingly developing a vision for sharing that expertise elsewhere, especially into the Christian hospitals of sub-Saharan Africa, Nepal, and many other parts of the globe. It has become a lead partner in the Indian Christian AIDS National Alliance, sharing its experience gained in HIV prevention and AIDS treatment programmes in North India with the rest of the country.

EHA is an example of how a previously Western-run healthcare mission service has been successfully translated into a locally run and mainly locally resourced Christian healthcare outreach.

impossible, and outside Western input remains the only way to keep going. Sometimes this leads to a failure to develop local skills and leadership, thus perpetuating the problem. At other times, the facility remains so wedded to expensive Western medical technologies that sustainable healthcare appropriate to the local setting is never fully achieved.

Overall, Christian hospitals as vehicles of Christian mission are in a state of crisis at a time when effective, affordable, and local healthcare is becoming a greater need than ever. It is becoming increasingly apparent that Christian hospitals can become effective and sustainable only through the development of local skills, through the ownership and participation of the local community and church, and through the use of health technologies and strategies appropriate to the local economic and cultural context (Crespo, 2000).

AIDS: A Pandemic of Globalisation

If we are to consider globalisation, health, and mission in the 21st century, we have to consider the phenomenon of HIV and AIDS. The virus has been spread by people movements, like many other illnesses in history. However, the rate of spread and its devastating consequences on a global scale mark out a new kind of epidemic—one intimately tied into the forces of modern globalisation. AIDS is perhaps a good model for the way that modern globalisation is shaping not only disease patterns and socio-medical responses, but also cultural and religious ideas.

We have already seen how global trade, tourism, and migration (both economic migration and migration enforced by war and famine) have helped spread the virus with remarkable speed, and how activism at a global level has begun to see treatments being made available (at least on a limited scale) to most affected developing nations (AIDS, 2002).[5] Yet, undeniably, the situation is getting worse. Some 40 million people have been infected in the last 20 years. Half of these have died, and new infections occur at a rate of 15,000 per day worldwide. In some countries, as many as 40% of the population may be infected in the next few years, almost all of whom will suffer periods of debilitating illness before they die, effectively wiping out the 20-45 age group in some nations.

HIV also remains inextricably linked to poverty. As an HIV positive African women recently told me, "People do not have more sex in Africa than in Europe, we are not less moral, yet we have a worse AIDS problem. The difference between AIDS/HIV in the West and the developing world is one of poverty. Why do Christians always emphasise sex as the primary prevention issue and not poverty?"

---

[5] The effects of this activism are such that talk globally is now about treatment and prevention, rather than just prevention. This change of emphasis has taken a mere two years to come about, between the World AIDS Conference held in Durban, South Africa, in 2000 and the conference held in Barcelona, Spain, in 2002.

The two most populous nations on the planet, India and China, are at the early stages of the epidemic. This still means there are around 1 million infected people in each nation, which is a similar proportion to that found in South Africa 12 years ago. If the trend in South Africa is replicated, so that by the middle of the next decade 20-30% of the adult population of India and China are infected, we are looking at an epidemic the likes of which history will never have seen before—nearly a billion people worldwide living with a terminal viral infection. The consequences socially, politically, economically, and spiritually are too horrific to take in.

The response has, as a matter of mounting urgency, become truly global. AIDS is the only illness to have both a specific UN organisation to deal with it (UNAIDS) and, with malaria and TB (with which it co-occurs on a large scale), a Global Fund for treatment and prevention. AIDS has been an example of how governments, international agencies, and other bodies can work together globally and strategically to tackle a major health issue (with limited success so far, admittedly).

The cultural ramifications of HIV/AIDS are significant. A recent Channel 4 documentary on the history of the portrayal of sex on British television noted that the 1980s marked a watershed—mainly because of AIDS. Suddenly, people had to talk about sexual practices and had to be open about the lifestyles that increase the risk of infection. Sex was discussed in a public way that could never have been envisioned before, even in the liberal West. Similar shifts in the approach to AIDS are true in many other nations.

Uganda is often cited as an example of a country that has seen a marked reduction in HIV transmission rates, mainly due to frank government education programmes in the media and schools. Significantly, a lot of this education has been in partnership with churches and mission agencies, such that the role of faith based (especially Christian) agencies in HIV prevention as well as care is being recognised more and more by such bodies as UNAIDS and the Global Fund for HIV, TB and Malaria (Allen, 2002; Christian, 2002). AIDS is creating a doorway for Christian mission in many parts of the world.

An open attitude to talking about sex is now more prevalent in Ugandan society and in the churches—something unimaginable a decade ago. In fact, there is evidence to suggest that African and Asian attitudes to sexuality and the body have been widely influenced (not necessarily for the better) by Western attitudes as a result of the AIDS prevention campaigns that continue across the globe. Indeed, the global response to AIDS has so entrenched Western attitudes to illness, disease, and treatment as a whole in developing nations that it has become more effectively the dominant discourse in all matters of health and illness than at any other time in history (Altman, 2002). AIDS is not just caused by the forces of globalisation; it has become a vehicle for those forces, especially in the Westernisation of discourse and action around AIDS.

The Good News

One might conclude from this discussion that globalisation can only mean bad news for the health of the poor, but this is far from the truth. The reality is more complex. The Western-isation of health practice and discourse is widely beneficial, but it is also problematic, as we have seen. Nonetheless, Western medicine is extremely effective in eliminating morbidity and mortality from many infectious diseases and in dealing with the consequences of trauma.

One example of how Western medicine and globalised technology and communications can come together beneficially is in the whole area of **telemedicine**. New technologies, from digital cameras to the Internet, allow the sharing of complex medical knowledge between centres of excellence in major cities in the developing world or the West, with smaller district hospitals and clinics.

For example, a patient presenting with an extremely unusual or rare injury can have the lesion photographed and clinical measurements taken. The photo and measurements can then be emailed to a doctor thousands of miles away, who can review the information and send back a suggested diagnosis and treatment course, or the doctor can suggest other lines of enquiry in making a full diagnosis and a plan of treatment and care. The review and feedback can all happen within a few hours after a patient presents at a hospital in a remote region, far from any specialist centre. In the past, such consultation was either impossible or at best would require a lengthy referral process, which would probably fall through because the patient would be unable to afford the travel, let alone the medical costs of going to a major hospital in a big city.

The impact that this kind of telemedicine is having is immense. Although more remote bush hospitals that have access to email only by long-wave radio may not be able to make use of this technology yet, other centres are increasingly availing themselves of this kind of networking.

International travel now means that experts can travel from different corners of the globe to provide training and input, share models of practice, and provide expert consultancy to new health projects, helping the sharing of expertise and models of best practice between quite remote areas. Medics from the North are not the only ones going to the South to impart their wisdom as the "great white doctor." Increasingly, health professionals from other Southern nations are sharing their knowledge with one another. For instance, India, a nation which boasts at least three Christian teaching hospitals, turns out hundreds of Christian doctors, nurses, physiotherapists, dentists, pharmacists, and hospital managers each year. Many go on to work in other Indian Christian hospitals. The skills and experience that they have developed and the pioneering health work happening in so many Indian Christian health institutions are increasingly being disseminated to other parts of Asia (particularly Nepal), to Africa, and even further afield. Healthcare mission, like all mission work, is increasingly from everywhere to everywhere.

Thus, although widespread travel, technology, and economic globalisation have been major sources of health problems, they also allow creative local and global responses to the self-same issues.

AIDS Care in Uganda

Uganda, a nation that has seen a significant turnaround in rates of new HIV infection, has achieved this largely by close co-operation between churches, missions, and government. ACET (AIDS Care Education and Training) is a Christian NGO that has developed some pioneering work in peer education, community based care programmes, and the production of HIV educational literature. Their experience has enabled them to share the lessons learnt with related organisations in Thailand, India, and even Eastern Europe. They have significant input into CANA (Christian AIDS National Alliance in India) and have been instrumental in setting up the first Pan-African Christian AIDS Network (which first met in Gabarone, Botswana, in June 2002). Through a network of related Christian AIDS NGOs under the umbrella of ACET International, ACET Uganda continues to have major input into the development of co-ordinated Christian responses to HIV and AIDS across the globe, in a way that a North-led organisation could not.

Conclusions

How does Christian mission respond to the globalisation of health, illness, and healthcare?

We face a lot of questions as we seek to tackle the vast, complex web of problems that impact the health of the many communities we seek to reach with the gospel. What structural issues can we and should we address to help the health situation of the poor? Where does the line come between mission, political activism, and healthcare provision—or should there be a line? How can we best meet the health needs of the poor—through mission hospitals or other mechanisms—and what is suitable or even affordable? How do we fund healthcare—from local churches, from charges to patients, from national governments, from Christian or secular donor agencies, or from individual supporters in the West? And how can we address all the questions that are raised

and still actually get on with the day-to-day business of stitching up the injured, caring for the dying, helping mothers give birth safely, and giving their children a chance to grow up healthy in body, mind, and spirit?

I would suggest that there are three domains that need to be addressed further—economics, activism, and contextualisation.

What is apparent to me is that we cannot view health as an issue that is separate from justice and evangelism. If, to take an example, we are to see the lives of workers in Philippine sweatshops improve, we must ensure that their health needs are being addressed, that their sense of community empowerment and their awareness of their rights are heightened, and, above all, that they learn that there is a God who has come to save them. All these areas are limited if the Western corporate giants and national Third World governments are not prepared to change the way that they do business. This issue can only be addressed by consumers and governments in the West, in particular, putting pressure on these companies. Health, education, evangelism, and local and global activism necessarily go hand in hand.

It seems an impossible task for us to address all these issues at the same time, especially when we ourselves come from environments where they are not addressed. We in the West do not see the links between our own consumer culture and our health needs or our attitude to churches. (For instance, how many people talk of "shopping around" for the right church?) Can we reconcile Western medicine (which tends to objectify the body and separate out the spiritual and socio-political and cultural causes of illness) with Christian faith? Have Westerners become consumers of faith and health, and are we guilty of exporting these Western ideas of spirituality, health, and illness to our mission environments—ideas that are not of themselves necessarily based on biblical values? I would argue that the church worldwide, not just in the West, needs to regain a truly biblical understanding of health, not as an absence of disease, but as a state of right relationship between God, one another, and our environment. Disruptions in any of these relationships have health consequences. Ironically, many non-Western, non-Christian health systems understand the nature of health in this way far more fully (Ngong Teh, 1998).

This also raises the question of how much we engage with local health beliefs. If locals do not approach Western medicine in the way the practitioners would like (i.e., as the first recourse for all illnesses), can we find ways of bridging that gap? In fact, a better question may be, How do we meet people's health needs in a manner that is appropriate to their local situations and understanding of health? Most non-Western cultures see health in the context of a spiritual and social network. For them, healing must encompass social and spiritual dimensions, as well as the physical realm, to be truly effective.

Many illnesses seen in developing nations are known as "culture bound syndromes." These conditions do not correspond to biomedical models of illness and may involve witchcraft, spirit possession, loss of face or loss of some other notion of self, and physical/spiritual energy. Local witch doctors, shamans, and traditional healers will often be the main recourse for treatment. By leaving these illnesses outside the boundaries of Christian medical work, we are missing the opportunity to show a God who can tackle all levels of illness. Effective Christian healthcare has always seen prayer, exorcism, and other spiritual ministries as a central part of its role—tackling the real needs and issues of people whose cultural context for illness and healing does not fit into Western notions. It is not just in the preaching of the gospel and the practice of the faith where contextualisation is an issue; it is also in the provision of healthcare.

Non-Western health practitioners (particularly, as already discussed, from India and Africa) are also a key resource. How can we facilitate more African, Asian, and Latin American health professionals staying and working as missionaries to their own communities, and sharing their learning and perspectives with one another? How can we resource Christian hospitals, clinics, and church-run health initiatives to meet the needs of their own communities, using local skills and knowledge as well as local resources, while drawing on Western skills and resources where appropriate?

These are some of the questions and challenges facing healthcare mission in the 21st century. Globalisation is forcing us to re-evaluate the links between economic justice, health, culture, and disease, and to look again at the way that addressing these needs creates a wide-open doorway for sharing the gospel.

Further Reading

Browne, S. G. (Ed.). (1985). *Heralds of health: The saga of Christian medical initiatives.* London, UK: Published for the Medical Committee of the Conference for World Mission by Christian Medical Fellowship. ISBN 0-906747-17-1. A good potted history of 19th and 20th century Christian contributions to global health.

Diamond, J. (1998). *Guns, germs and steel: A short history of everybody for the last 13,000 years.* London, UK: Vintage. ISBN 0099302780. A fascinating study of how geography, the domestication of livestock, the growth of population, and the emergence of new diseases have interacted to give one region of the world dominance over others at different times in history.

Dixon, P. (1990). *The truth about AIDS.* Eastbourne, UK: Kingsway. ISBN 0-86065-880-5. (A new edition is due to be published very shortly.) Gives a clear Christian response to the global AIDS pandemic, as well as being a great source of health information.

Hellman, C. (1994). *Culture health and illness: An introduction for health professionals.* Oxford, UK: Butterworth-Heinemann. ISBN 0-7506-1919-8. A good primer in medical anthropology and global health.

References

AIDS: Hope for the best, prepare for the worst. (2002, July 13). *The Economist.*

African firm wins AIDS drug permit. (2001, October 8). *BBC news on-line.* Retrieved from http://news.bbc.co.uk/hi/english/business/newsid_1586000/1586355.stm.

Africa's AIDS drugs debate heats up. (2002, January 30). *BBC news on-line.* Retrieved from http://news.bbc.co.uk/hi/english/business/newsid_1789000/1789524.stm.

Allen, A. (2002, May 27). Sex change: Uganda and condoms. *New Republic.*

Altman, D. (2002). *AIDS, sex, and globalization.* Chicago, IL: University of Chicago Press.

Campaigners set to focus on world's biggest corporations. (2002, February 4). *Financial Times.*

Campbell, I., & Clegg. D. (1999, Winter). Tradition in transition. *Among All Nations, 10.* London, UK: MMA Health Serve and the Christian Medical Fellowship.

Christian Connections for International Health. (2002, May 11). *Global Fund responsiveness to faith based organizations.* Retrieved from http://www.ccih.org/globalfundsurvey-results.html.

Commission for Macroeconomics and Health. (2001, December). *Investing in health for economic development.*

Crespo, R. (2000, August). The future of Christian hospitals in developing countries: The call for a new paradigm of ministry. *The CCIH Forum,* Special Issue #8. Retrieved from http://www.ccih.org/forum/0008-00.htm.

Davey, T. F. (1985). Introduction. In S. G. Browne (Ed.), *Heralds of health: The saga of Christian medical initiatives* (pp. 1-11). London, UK: Published for the Medical Committee of the Conference for World Mission by Christian Medical Fellowship.

Diamond, J. (1998). *Guns, germs and steel: A short history of everybody for the last 13,000 years.* London, UK: Vintage.

Griffins, J. (2002, Spring). Developing world drugs. *Triple Helix.*

Haines, A., Heath, I., & Smith, R. (2000). Joining together to combat poverty. *British Medical Journal, 320,* pp. 1-2.

Hellman, C. (1994). *Culture health and illness: An introduction for health professionals.* Oxford, UK: Butterworth-Heinemann.

Kenay, J. W., & Christensen, C. M. (2002). *Disruptive innovation: New diagnosis and treatment for the systemic maladies of healthcare.* Business briefing: Global Healthcare, World Markets Research Centre.

Klein, N. (2000). *No logo.* London, UK: Flamingo.

Küng, H. (1976). *On being a Christian.* Garden City, NY: Doubleday & Co.

Laurance, J. (2002, June 19). Hands off their nurses. *The Independent Review,* p. 12.

Médecins Sans Frontières Access to Essential Medicines Campaign and the Drugs for Neglected Diseases Working Group. (2001, September). *Fatal imbalance: The crisis in research and development for drugs for neglected diseases.* Geneva, Switzerland: Author. Retrieved from http://www.doctorswithoutborders.org/publications/reports/2001/fatal_imbalance_short.pdf.

Meek, J. (2002, May 10). Health crisis looms as life expectancy soars: Average ageing forecasts far too low, say scientists. *Guardian.*

Ngong Teh, R. (1998, December). *The role of traditional medical practitioners in the context of the African traditional concept of health and healing.* International Mental Health Workshop. Retrieved from http://www.globalconnections.co.uk/pdfs/HealersMentalHealth.pdf.

Panos Dossier. (1988). *AIDS and the Third World.* London, UK: Panos Institute.

Sharp increase in tuberculosis. (2000, October 23). *BBC news on-line.* Retrieved from http://news.bbc.co.uk/hi/english/health/newsid_986000/986406.stm.

Terrorism is not the only scourge. (2001, December 22). *The Economist.*

WHO. (2000, January 26). *WHO bulletin spotlights serious inequalities in health.* WHO press release WHO/6.

WHO. (2000, August 14). *One in five school children smoke in developing countries.* WHO press release WHO/51.

World Economic Forum. (2002, February 2). *World Economic Forum CEOs call for greater corporate engagement against AIDS/HIV, TB and malaria.* Press release. New York, NY: Author.

*After working in London for many years with the Christian AIDS organisation ACET, since 2000 **Steve Fouch** has been Director of Health Serve, developing resources for global healthcare mission. He has worked short-term in North Africa and spent 13 years church planting in South London. He now lives in North Kent with his wife Debbi and their daughter, Hannah. Email: steve@healthserve.org.*

8

Globalisation, women, and mission

Rose Dowsett

Glimpses From Around the World

Altaa

Altaa busied herself inside the family ger preparing the meal. In almost every respect, she could have been her mother, or her grandmother, or a distant forebear. The movements of her hands, the rituals she performed, and the dish she prepared were an echo of the centuries. Yet as she worked, the thoughts passing through her mind found little resonance with the past.

Altaa had never heard the word "globalisation" and wouldn't have known what to make of it if she had. All she knew was that the traditional way of life, unassailed by many centuries or by natural disaster, all of a sudden was melting like snow in early summer. She doubted whether her children would adopt this way of life. By the time they grew up, the call of the city would be overwhelming, and they would desert their nomadic heritage. They would not observe the customs of marriage by which she had been bound, nor would they bear their children in remote places, as she had. And if she herself lived to be old, would she be forced to leave the land and go to the strangeness of the city? Perhaps one day she and her husband would simply die of weakness and starvation and cold, alone in their ger, unable any longer to care for themselves.

Altaa thought enviously of her mother, who had never known that there were other ways of life, that other people in other countries lived differently, or that there was a world of possessions and sounds and ideas that was no longer invisible and that called into question the old, familiar ways. For Altaa, inescapably, confusingly, this new world battered at the very door of her ger.

She came to the opening in the heavy felt and gazed at her husband's proud purchase from when he trekked to town to trade last year. It was a satellite dish. Truly, the world was on Altaa's doorstep.

Femi

Femi scratched helplessly at the sun-baked earth. Where there should be fat cobs of maize, ready to feed her hungry grandchildren, there was only a handful of dried leaves, not even enough to feed her last remaining scrawny chicken. The rains had failed again. After four years of drought, the land that once had been fertile had become dust, and the streams had turned into dried beds. Femi no longer had the strength to carry water from the pump, an hour's exhausting walk away, for any but the most essential use. It was a long time since she had been able to carry water for her field.

Femi wasn't alone in her predicament. The little community was a community of the old, the very young, and the very sick, and the shambas were all reduced to unyielding barrenness. Those who should have been the strong ones to work the fields and carry the water had already died or were too weak to move. Femi remembered the excitement years before, when the young men had started going to the city or to the mines to earn money with which to improve their way of life. They talked of "markets" for the goods they would make or the minerals they would dig—markets in countries far beyond the seas, which would make it possible for Africans like themselves to grow prosperous too.

At first, it had seemed that things might be as they said. But all too soon, when the men returned home with their city clothes and shoes, clutching their purchases and speaking of a great world to be explored, they brought another hidden and terrifying gift—the disease they called "the wasting disease." And now only the elderly and some of the children were free of it. Once when the pastor had visited, cycling from his village several miles away, he had told Femi that this disease had caused havoc in many countries. It had spread so rapidly, he said, because so many men moved away from home to find work and money, and then they had sexual relations with other women. When they returned home, they brought the disease with them, and their wives became sick as well. Now, he said, all over the world, but especially in poor countries, there were people who were ill with the same sickness.

Femi wondered whether the pastor would visit again. He, too, had become sick of the wasting disease.

She didn't think she would be strong enough again ever to walk to the little church where he taught. She didn't know when last she had seen an able-bodied man. Nobody cared very much about the tragedy of a dying village in an impoverished country. She tried to teach the little ones about God and about Jesus, as best she could. But some days, like today, she wondered whether God either knew or cared about the sickness, the hunger, the hopelessness. Perhaps the world was too big for him to manage properly, or perhaps he preferred to help white people. Perhaps he was punishing her family because they were not good enough. Perhaps the old ways of her people were right after all. Why should some distant land's hunger for copper or cheap cloth have led to this tragic conclusion? It was all very confusing.

When you're starving, it's hard to believe.

Rani

Rani and her husband walked together into the lake. They were going to be baptised as Christians, along with 10 others from their country. Even on this warm summer's day, the Scottish water was cold. But Rani scarcely noticed. Boldly she declared her faith in Jesus Christ and entrusted herself to the gentle arms of the pastor to be plunged into the water. They held her safely, and she stood again, praying quietly as she dedicated her life to the One she had come to know and follow. The crowd watching from the shore responded with a song of praise to God.

Looking back over the past two years since she and her husband had first fled their country, Rani could scarcely believe the events that had led to today. In their home country, they had been deeply committed to another religion, a religion moreover that was deeply hostile to Christianity. In fact, neither Rani nor her husband had ever met a Christian, and they had only heard bad things about them. It was not on religious grounds that they had left, but because her husband had offended the authorities by some mild protest against an injustice. Such criticism wasn't tolerated, and, distraught, they'd fled for their lives. They had taken nearly a year to reach Britain, where they had claimed asylum.

They had been sent to a Scottish city, along with many other asylum seekers, including a number from their own country. It had been very hard to adjust to the strange culture, to the cold wet climate, and to the extraordinary racial mix among which they found themselves. For the first time, they rubbed shoulders with Africans, Asians, and Eastern Europeans, all seeking the right to make their home there permanently. As was the custom back home, Rani did not go out much, but her husband explored freely. Almost at once, he met up with fellow-countrymen who told him of the kindness of a local church, where food, clothing, and English lessons were offered to the asylum seekers. Curious, he went to investigate. He asked many questions and discovered that Christians were different from the way they had been portrayed back home. He began to attend a Bible study along with some compatriots. They watched the *Jesus* film in their own language. Soon, several believed, and within a year nearly 90 from that country had become Christians.

At first, Rani was furious. She decided to go along to stick up for their own religion and to prevent such awful apostasy. But before long, she too was gripped by the gospel and by the person of Jesus Christ. Eagerly she talked to other women who had never heard the gospel before, and soon she was leading others to faith.

And so, on this day beside the lake, she thanked God for his love in bringing them thousands of miles, through heartbreak and danger and suffering, in order that they should meet with him. She did not understand all the forces at work in the world that were leading to such mass migrations of peoples back and forth across the globe. But she knew with deep assurance that the God and Father of the Lord Jesus Christ was using the refugee movement to enable many like herself to hear the gospel. She and her husband had craved freedom and safety. They had found it in a profound dimension.

Globalisation in Biblical Perspective

A true understanding of the nature of "real" globalisation begins in the character of God. Without any apology, the Bible declares him to be not some tribal god, concerned with the welfare of a small people group at the eastern end of the Mediterranean, but the Lord and King and Creator of the whole earth, the one to whom every knee in the whole universe shall bow, the one who is Judge of all humankind, whether or not they know and recognise him. The Old Testament as well as the New rings with the world-wide claims of the God of the globe. The Lord Jesus Christ is the only Saviour throughout the universe. The church is to be a global community of disciples and worshippers. The gospel transcends barriers of race and colour and language. It is central to the eternal well-being of people in Peru as well as in Portugal, in China as well as in Chile, in Alaska as well as in Australia. North to south, east to west, the gospel is global, because the God whom it celebrates is global.

Our problem with globalisation is that we have created a human construct which is as outrageous as the Tower of Babel. It challenges the divine reality of globalisation—that which takes its starting point in God—and functions instead on the basis of human control, power, and ambition.

Insofar as globalisation reflects human fallenness, it will magnify on a huge canvas sin, corruption, and domination of the weak by the powerful. It thus portrays on a world-wide scale the tragic impact of sin. And yet, because as human beings we are inescapably made in the image of our Creator, alongside the subversion of globalisation that comes from our fallenness, there are still redemptive possibilities. There is great potential to do good and to serve the cause of mission. There is also great potential to make visible the world-wideness of the church as the true global humanity—the global worshipping community that is committed to the one true God of the whole earth.

It is critical that we discern both aspects of globalisation. We must reinforce that which displays the character and purposes of God, while vigorously seeking to challenge and counteract that which entrenches sin. In this endeavour, women as well as men have a strategic responsibility. We are called in this global setting to ensure that on both the micro level and the macro level we demonstrate what the universal kingship of God looks like, as we put off sin and put on righteousness.

Men, Women, and God

Much of what happens as part of globalisation today is driven by men and benefits men more than women. Of course, some women, especially Western women, fully share in the positive benefits of globalisation, such as ease of travel, horizons that have been expanded through communications, and incredible consumer choice (if that really is a benefit!). Nonetheless, globally, women are more likely to experience the negatives of globalisation and less likely to experience the positives.

The biblical truth is that God cares passionately about women as well as men. Women are equally created by him. They are equally redeemed by him. They are equally the recipients and dwelling place of the Holy Spirit. They are equally the church on earth. They are equally destined for eternity in his presence. All of God's grace-designs for humankind are equally for women as well as for men.

It is a great outrage and offence to God when women are exploited or abused, when justice is denied them, or when structures exclude them from encountering the gospel message. Of course, God equally hates these same things done to men. Genesis 3 clearly predicts, however, that one outcome of the Fall is that women will be exploited and dominated by men (just as women will be manipulative towards men). Just as in general terms men are likely to have greater physical power than women, so in most cultures men have greater economic and social power than women. At the domestic and community level, this means that in many cultures women suffer more than men and have fewer resources with which to change their circumstances. They will be likely to have less access to financial and economic resources, less education, less access to work beyond the home, less access to medical care, and less access to justice. Of course, these are generalisations, and we could all cite many exceptions. But where there is superior power in the hands of men and too little to balance that power, women suffer.

We see the same principle at work on a much larger scale when we note how rich nations exercise power through their resources of money and technology. Western nations do not expand their markets out of philanthropy. Many poorer nations angrily but helplessly find themselves unable to operate on the world stage as equal players. They are frequently forced into arrangements that benefit the richer countries at the expense of the poorer ones.

In thinking about globalisation, then, we need to think about the impact upon those who have historically and almost universally had less voice, who have less say in determining their lives, and who may find themselves caught up in powerful forces they neither understand nor can control. A traditional Chinese saying describes women as "holding up half the sky." This proverb is wiser than the original author could have dreamed. It is because of the way God created us that women are indeed destined to "hold up half the sky."

With the foregoing discussion as background, let us now consider the specific challenges that globalisation presents for women. We will also look at some of the specific opportunities for mission to and by women, in the context of globalisation.

Pluses and Minuses

Migration

As the thumb-nail sketches at the beginning of this chapter illustrate, the impact of globalisation on women is both universal and confused.

Take Rani's story. On the one hand, the massive migration movements of the past 20 years or so have undoubtedly been fuelled by global factors. Equally certain, the vast uprootings of people from their familiar environments, whether through war, famine, or economic opportunism, have brought both alienation from the gospel and openness to it. In parts of Africa, for example, migration has resulted in either forced conversion from Christianity or voluntary abandoning of Christianity to embrace materialism. At the same time, there are many stories like Rani's, involving people from many different countries.

It is not only in the West that people are coming to faith. You may find the same glorious evidence of God's sovereign care in China, Turkey, Thailand, and many more countries. For the first time, perhaps, or in the context of all the familiar structures of life being taken away, there has been an opportunity to question the old assumptions. Perhaps there has also been a first encounter with vibrant Christianity. Where compassion and practical help have been offered to refugees, there has often followed an opportunity to point to God as our great motivator—the one who teaches us to love the stranger in our midst and to welcome her in the name of the Lord.

While migration is as ancient as the human race, globalisation has intensified, diversified, and fed the movement of people. Travel, information, awareness of alternative ways of life, and inequity of wealth distribution on an international scale have all made migration not a last resort but, for many, the means to a future.

In migration movements from some countries, the men travel first, leaving the women back in the home country. This practice is especially true of eco-nomic migration or where men have fought on the losing side in a war. This may be an especially vulnerable time for the womenfolk left behind. Not only will they probably be struggling to make a living and to feed themselves and their children, but they will also not know whether they will see their menfolk again or whether their men have taken up with other women. To compound their concerns, they may have little protection from attack or rape. In other migration movements, women travel with their men, and en route to their destination they may be caught up in begging or prostitution to pay the demands of their couriers. When (and if) women arrive at their destinations, they will face bewildering changes, probably hostility, and the unnerving problem of bearing children in a strange country whose language they do not yet speak.

As Christians, we must not exploit the weak or take advantage of their vulnerability. Instead, we must find ways of reaching out with compassion and with gospel vision to these needy women. One of the great untold stories of our time—untold because it is so sensitive—is the way in which women and men from countries where Christian activity is forbidden are coming to faith in alien countries to which they have fled. Without a doubt, globalisation has speeded up the migration phenomenon, as people become aware of the possibility of a different kind of life, if they can only reach this country or that. Just as God had compassionate purposes in the repeated migrations of his people, as recorded for us in Scripture, so today we need to look for the hand of God in this particular global dislocation and relocation. Globalisation has produced doorways for the gospel.

Collision of worlds

Altaa's experience could be repeated millions of times, with minor variations. How do you put the old world and the new world together? How do you make sense of what you see and hear through media whose origin is another world from your own? You can sidle up to the favelas of Brazil or pick your way through the shanties of some Asian or African city, and you will find yourself bombarded with the current Top Ten pop songs from London, or you can join a crowd clustered round a television screen showing some Bollywood or Hollywood blockbuster. It is almost surreal. Certainly it produces some kind of fragmentation of the personality—a cracking apart of coherence, however ill-founded.

Immediate life is lived within the boundaries of grinding poverty, with no running water or sanitation—a life that is precarious, hard, and full of suffering. And then, on the screen, there is a world of obscene wealth and unreal escapes, of fast cars and beautiful clothes, and things and things and more things. Always, the hero wins, and the virtuous heroine is carried off to a life of luxury and ease. What does a woman in a Calcutta slum make of what she sees? Does she aspire to wealth for herself or her daughters? Does she hope there might be justice for her as a woman if she's virtuous? How does she put the images together with her Hindu faith? Can she make any connection at all between what she sees and what she knows?

When a Christian woman is stirred into this context, what a marvellous opportunity there is to explain the limitations of the old world, as well as of the seductive, plastic, new world, and to deal with the realities of living differently within the world as it is. Here, too, is a doorway for the gospel, for the gospel is not escapism but deliverance.

The tyranny of world markets

Femi's life, too, is bound up with global forces. Her world may be limited to a tiny, specific geographical location, from which she will never move, and to the most basic activities of human survival. But the factors which have shaped her life's circumstances have their roots far away, quite as much as close at hand. Have industrialisation and global warming, driven by Western consumption, exacerbated the drought in her area? If there had not been a global market, perhaps her sons would not have left for the city. And then perhaps they would not have encountered HIV/AIDS and would not have left Femi struggling to care for her orphaned grandchildren, like so many other African grandmothers. Ironically, the lure of cash and access to goods drastically impoverished this community, rather than enriching it.

One of the tragedies of Western domination (through wealth) of the mass media and technology is that there is often greater export of Western values and materialism to the poorer parts of the world than there is genuine, reciprocal export to the West of understanding of life in those poor countries. So, despite some documentaries and heartbreaking images of AIDS or famine-wracked little children, we can quickly put those images aside, their place taken by other things and local concerns.

It is arguable that Femi's life is far more manipulated by the forces of globalisation than is mine, despite the fact that I am much more surrounded by the artifacts of globalisation. Certainly, Femi has far less power than I do to protest or to choose alternatives. She is much more a victim than am I. It is hard to see how any of the advantages of globalisation, as they are commonly understood, enrich her life. At the same time, if we go back to the definition of globalisation in its biblical sense of coming under the world-wide rule of God, then Femi is already a beneficiary. Sadly, the negative impact of economic globalisation has undermined her ability to live in the good of the spiritual reality.

Issues of Identity

In many cultures, women have been the guardians and primary transmitters of religion, even where they have had no public role in religious leadership and where they may be excluded from public ritual and worship. This is because they are the primary nurturers of children and are more likely to be the ones who instill in children from earliest consciousness the worldview associated with a particular faith. They may be the ones who train the next generation in home-based religious ritual and observance. Many of the rituals associated with birth, sickness, and death are performed by women, and they may shape a child quite as powerfully as any public, male-dominated ritual. If women are to be reached with the gospel, and in turn if their children are to be reached, then we need to understand and interact with these deep, often unarticulated mental maps.

One of the significant results of globalisation is that people the world over are being exposed to other ways of life, other cultures, and other belief systems, whether formal religious systems or the implicit values that betray fundamental actual beliefs. We need to be extremely sensitive to what may be going on in women's minds and worldview as a result of this exposure. There may (or may not!) be subtle (or quite major!) changes from what cultural anthropologists have noted in the past, or from what an earlier generation of missionaries has observed and passed down as "the way they think." Past observation may no longer be quite as accurate as we assume. There is an enormous amount of transition, but in women the changes may be harder to spot, because many of the traditional ritual observances continue. In this context, too, there is an exciting potential for effective ministry, in which a Christian woman can engage with women at the level of daily life and in the areas of birth, marriage, and sickness. As traditional patterns are challenged and as other possibilities are brought into focus, yet another doorway for the gospel is opened.

Despite the fact that most cultures remain male-dominated, there have been and are some high-profile women on the world stage. In the 1960s, my generation in Britain knew the name of Mrs. Bandaranaike (the Sri Lankan who became the world's first female Prime Minister), but we wouldn't have recognised her in the street, because we rarely saw a picture of her. In contrast, by the 1990s, Diana Princess of Wales and Mother Teresa were recognised by hundreds of millions all around the globe. It was not just British newspapers that were awash with pictures of them. Their images could be seen in Beijing or Bombay or Lagos. They became global icons. An icon is literally a picture that is an aid to worship, but in the hands of the unknowing, it can become an object of worship. It is worth reflecting on the response in many parts of the world to Diana's death. Here globalisation produced a counterfeit of the gospel.

Whilst there will be very few women who achieve the global familiarity of Diana or Mother Teresa, it is observable all round the world that advertising and visual images still largely present women as sex objects and as intellectually inferior. This portrayal reinforces the message that sexual exploitation of women is acceptable. The same technology that can beam wholesome information around the world can also spread pornography as fast as the most virulent physical epidemic and can become the basis of world-wide trade in child prostitution. Men travel the world to engage in the rape of little girls in Bangkok. Trade such as this, sickening and an abomination to God, has been fed by global travel, global information, and global money. It is important for Christian mission to challenge this pursuit, because it is an outrage to God as Creator and Redeemer. In some situations, though, yet one more doorway for the gospel is opened, as women discover that they are loved, valued, and respected by God.

The Challenge of Secular Feminism

The institutional church, male-dominated as it always has been, does not have a very good track record in relation to women. All around the world, the church leadership's subliminal message is designed to convince women as well as men that women are not as valuable as their husbands, their fathers, or their sons. Sadly, under the impact of globalisation, the choices being dangled before most of the non-Christian world do not include a genuinely biblical model. Rather, the choice is between the traditional ways of a people or religion (this includes fundamentalism, which seeks to ensure that the tradition remains in place), women as sex objects, or women making their claim to equality in strident and destructive ways. There are fingerprints of most kinds of Western secular feminist agendas in the most unlikely places. None of these has very much at all to do with God's loving design for men and women living in harmony and complementarity, freely and gladly serving the King of the whole earth.

There are, of course, many forms of feminism. Some come closer to God's truth than others, and feminism has highlighted many areas in which the church badly needs to change—concerns that we should share. Sadly, however, the most influential feminist movements today are driven by secular humanist values and, too often, by anger and self-assertion. This context is more dangerous than we often acknowledge, because in many parts of the world, where resistance to the gospel is strongest, the West is still (quite erroneously) equated with the Christian faith. Just as unbridled capitalism and economic imperialism (which are largely associated with the West) create enormous barriers to the gospel, so too does the powerful model of social relations exported through the feminist lobby. This model is displayed in films, books, and political policy. It can be observed in the raucous behaviour of tourists and the offensive immodesty of many Westerners. It is perceived, fairly or unfairly, as undermining family values and social stability and thus is an enemy to be resisted.

If "all the world's a stage" and if globalisation ensures that all the world can be spectators as well as players, how critical it is that we model a way of life that pulses with God's love and that points clearly to the way he has created us to live within the human family. Some feminist movements had their roots in the church, as people (rightly) protested that the church did not read the Scriptures closely when it came to treating women as God intended. Often the starting point was right, but the protest later came to be expressed in ways far removed from the biblical agenda. We need to address the challenges of feminism far more carefully and with much greater discrimination, and we need to display in practice what redeemed manhood and womanhood should look like. While there are, of course, differences in understanding from the biblical data exactly how our redemption works out, there is certainly much progress that could be made with full agreement, if only there were the will to do so. Failure to address feminist issues may greatly compromise mission and gospel ministry.

Women in Global Mission

It is one of the great ironies of church history that women have been the primary gospel pioneers in country after country and among people group after people group, yet mission strategy is normally devised by men. It remains true today that approximately two-thirds of the world's formal missionary force (i.e., members of mission agencies) are women, with a similar proportion of church members around the world. Yet mission history repeatedly shows us that as soon as a believing community emerges, it will be formalised under male leadership. Mission agencies, however heavily populated by women, are overwhelmingly led by men. Sadly, this male dominance in leadership frequently leads to the marginalisation of women in mission, as well as in church policy and practice. The result is that neither mission agencies nor churches think strategically enough about how God chooses to push back the boundaries of unbelief through the specific contributions of Christian women.

At its heart, the transmission of the gospel is highly relational. In most cultures of the world, women are instinctively (or are socialised into being) more relational than many men. Particularly in parts of the world where there is a high level of resistance to the gospel—those hard, hard places—it is only through quiet, persistent, godly living, accompanied by friendship evangelism, that people will be won to Christian faith. These are often the places, too, where traditional forms of church life, focused on buildings and institutional structures, are not possible. What a marvellous opportunity for Christian women all over the world! In almost any culture in the world, women have free access to other women and to children, with daily opportunities to disciple them, either formally or informally. In some of the countries most deeply hostile to the gospel, there is good evidence that there are countless secret believers, many of them women and children who have been quietly reached through the friendship of other women reaching into neighbours' homes and families. There is enormous potential for faith-sharing when it is properly integrated into the whole of our daily lives, wherever these may be played out—in the domestic sphere, in the community, in a workplace distanced from the home, or wherever else. It may be that some women have better captured this opportunity than those who equate mission with a more formal and separate activity.

It is not only among women and children that women are highly effective missionaries. Many of the world's tribal groups have been reached initially by women. Sometimes this is because women have appeared as less threatening than men. Women, too, have often been at the forefront of compassion ministries, nursing the sick and tending the poor and the dying. They have frequently been able to reduce deaths through childbirth, and, by teaching women primary healthcare at the level of the home and local community, they have also reduced infant and child mortality. They have sensitively taught better nutrition, have introduced small, home-based cottage industries to boost income, have listened and chatted, and so on. In wealthier settings, especially in the West, where loneliness and unhappiness are widespread, compassionate engagement in the lives of others is no less powerful a gospel tool. In a thousand small ways, Christian women, both local and expatriate, have incarnated the gospel and made it understandable, bringing word and deed together. As the contribution of women has impacted communities helpfully, the men have been more willing, in their turn, to listen too.

Another factor enhancing the effectiveness of women in missions is that many Christian women are readily content with discipling quietly in small groups or one to one. The pressure of globalisation may try to make us focus on the big scheme and the highly visible, but the spiritual reality is that the most effective mission is accomplished through deep investment in a personally known group. Yes, we need to share the Lord's vision for the whole world and not be content with a tiny fraction of it! But the paradox is that global vision will be brought into realisation through the multiplication of incarnated ministries in millions of times and places.

Men and Women Together in Global Mission

This pattern of personal discipleship, because it is biblical, is more likely to be effective in reaching today's unreached (but potentially highly reachable, thanks to globalisation) than all the complex schemes the contemporary church cares to devise. The world church has a choice facing it today. One alternative is to copy the pattern of the world and use the tools and goals so amply adopted by global business. With this approach, the church will market itself aggressively, with an emphasis on high profile, size, and success. It will devise global schemes for conquering the world, all served by efficient structures and resulting in a stress on institutional organisation. Most of the schemes will be led by men exercising power as the world knows it.

Alternatively, the church can choose to travel (not just talk about) the way of the cross. For this endeavour, the church must be prepared to be misunderstood and rejected. It must serve out of human weakness, in order that all power should be seen to be the Lord's. Structure must be emphasised less and spiritual life and godliness more. Vision rather than schemes must fire the work, with great humility. The church is called to be a global family of disciples, not a human-made empire. In this family, women and men are to stand side by side, equally loved, equally valued, and equally fruitful. In this way, the kingdom of God on earth in the here and now will more truly illustrate that fully realised Kingdom of the future, and we shall see more clearly what God truly intended globalisation to be.

Questions for Reflection

1. How have you and your neighbours been affected by globalisation? What do you think might be the gains, and what might be the losses?

2. Who are the migrants from and to your community? Why are they migrants? How could your church play its part in reaching them with the gospel?

3. Imagine yourself going to live alongside Altaa or Femi in the opening stories. How might you try to help them live with the consequences of globalisation?

4. In what ways are Christian women in your community especially effective in reaching others for Christ?

Rose Dowsett and her husband Dick are career missionaries with OMF International, parents to three adult children, grandparents—and passionate about mission! Rose is International Chairman of Interserve, leads the Global Missiology track of WEA's Missions Commission, lectures, and writes. She is the author of **Thinking Clearly About the Great Commission** *. Email: 106011.462@compuserve.com.*

9

Globalisation:
a view from Africa

WANYEKI MAHIAINI

What on earth does globalisation have to do with Africa? Might we not use our time more wisely by considering issues that are more relevant to Africa, such as AIDS and lack of clean drinking water? Should Africans spend their energies on ivory-tower concepts like globalisation?

The purpose of this chapter is to discuss this very question. I will suggest that Africans must engage with globalisation, because like the other Western experiments that have gone before, globalisation is affecting Africa in very real ways.

We first stumbled on our Western cousins conducting an experiment on our shores a long time ago. A fishing community along the River Niger was wakened one humid morning by the blast of a ship's horn. Men, women, and children stirred from their beds and made their way to the great River Niger, where a ship was berthing. It was our Western cousins come to visit!

Although our prophets and seers had warned us that these people were on their way, their appearance that morning was still a surprise. We love visitors, though, and after some awkward moments with language, they introduced themselves. (They had an interpreter with them. We quickly discovered the visitors had thought of everything!)

"We've come a long way to share a brilliant idea with you," they said, beaming.

"Wonderful!" we replied.

"Let's trade," they suggested.

It was just as our seers had prophesied. "There will come a people as colourful as butterflies seeking to trade. Things will never be the same after that."

We were hesitant at first, but after they showed us what a gun could do, we were impressed.

"So what do you want to buy from us?" we asked, thinking of the gold and ivory that Arab traders had been buying.

They responded, "Have you thought of expanding your goods and services in order to meet the emerging demands in the transatlantic trade? You could, for example, dramatically reduce the cost of running your prisoner-of-war camps by turning over the detainees to us. In one shrewd move, you will have converted your liabilities into assets, and—note this—you will have made a significant contribution to the emerging market in the Caribbean islands. As you already know, markets look with particular favour on bold investors!"

It seemed a good idea at the time to join in the experiment, but before long, we were selling one another to the highest bidder, and the land was laid bare. We suspected that we had been shortchanged, but we weren't sure how bad the situation was until the missionaries arrived with their own experiment—but more of that in a moment.

For us, the slave trade experiment spelt big trouble. We had no sooner seen the back of slavery, however, when along came the next big idea—the colonial experiment. It was sold to us in a very clever way, largely by missionaries. They did not have a good word to say about the failed experiment of the butterfly people. We were pleased and listened intently to what they had to say.

"The slave trade has brought immense suffering to you but great wealth to our country. We are ashamed of this, and we feel it is important that we put the situation right."

They continued, "First you must learn to read and write, and the best book to read is the Bible."

Amazing things happen when you read the Bible, and as a result, many of us became Christians. The missionaries were a lot more credible than the traders before them, so when they recommended that we should accept the protection of their governments, we went along with the idea. Before we could blink, we were firmly inside a scheme they called colonialism, and there was no peaceful way out.

Years after the failure of the slave trade, Sir Winston Churchill reflected on this period of history and said:

The West Indies 200 years ago bulked very largely in the minds of all the people who were making Britain and the British Empire. Our possession of the West Indies, like that of India—the colonial plantations, as they were called—gave us the strength, but especially the capital, the wealth, at a time when no European nation possessed such reserve, which enabled us, not only to acquire this world-wide appendage of possessions which we have, but also to lay the foundations of that commercial and financial leadership, which, when the world was young, when everything outside Europe was underdeveloped, enabled us to make our great position in the world (Wood, 1994, p. 26).

For us, the new colonialism project was a bitter-sweet fruit. It was bitter for three reasons. To begin with, too many people died fighting for a right that the colonialists enjoyed in their own countries of origin—the right to determine one's own political destiny. When I was in primary school in Kenya, it was usual to learn that so-and-so did not have a father because he had died in the Mau Mau freedom war. I mention this fact because whenever I meet former members of Kings African Rifles in the UK, they speak of Mau Mau as if it was no more than an administrative hiccup in what was a voluntary process of handing over Kenya to Kenyans. They tell me Mau Mau was pushing on an open door. We do not see it like that. If putting hundreds of thousands of Agikuyu women, children, and men into security "villages," or being attacked with truncheons by police, or freedom fighters being shot—if those brutalities equate to pushing on an open door, then God help us if Mau Mau had been pushing on one that was closed!

The second reason for bitterness is that colonialism compounded the sense of inferiority begun by the slave trade. Thirdly, Christianity and colonialism became linked in the minds of many. This led to many Christians losing their lives because they were seen as traitors.

But colonialism also had a sweet taste. We have the early missionaries to thank for the gospel and for reducing our languages to the written script. Ironically, it is also to the work of these early men and women of God that we turn when we trace the early beginnings of many of our nations.

The colonial stage gave rise to the last undertaking to come to us from the West—neocolonialism. Neocolonialism is an indirect means by powerful states to impose their will on weaker nations through unequal cultural, economic, and political ties. Once again, the visitors were astute at selling their ideas to us.

"We can't believe how badly things went the last time, chaps. How about we cooperate as free and independent nations for the good of our people?"

"No more slave trade, no more colonialism, and no pulling a fast one on us?" we asked.

"You haven't a thing to worry about. It will all be above board and regulated by international agreements. We are desperate to get it right this time!" the visitors said.

And so we began to tie our economies to those in the West. Soon we began to feel the pressure of the unequal relationship. For example, money was lent to our nations, with full knowledge that the dictators who were ruling our countries were promptly transferring the loans to their Swiss accounts. Pressure groups all over the continent protested vigorously, but the Western banks screamed, "Pay up or else!" We were once again in the middle of another of the visitors' bewildering experiments. We remember that phase as a period marked by loss of national pride. It is also the period during which we became weary of Western experiments.

We have now come to accept the fact that the West loves a new experiment, so when we started hearing about a new idea called globalisation, we were vitally interested to know how it would affect us. We are determined not to be caught napping again! Because of what has happened in the past, Africa

Globalisation as Interconnectedness

In my home town of Nakuru, Kenya, there is a remote neighbourhood on the rim of Menengai Crater called Maciaro. Last year I visited a friend who lives there. I arrived in the evening and found the family enjoying ugali—a kind of cornbread eaten by most East Africans. We fell talking, and I discovered that increasingly the maize used to make the ugali is imported. At 9:00 p.m. my host, as is his habit, tuned the radio to BBC World Service broadcasting in Kiswahili. I noted the radio was made in Japan. We discussed the attacks of September 11 on the World Trade Centre and compared them with Al Qaeda's attack on the American Embassy in Nairobi in 1998, in which 287 Kenyans died and hundreds more were injured. We marvelled at how quickly the BBC had buried the dead in Nairobi in comparison with the dead in America. I had a quick look around the room and concluded that at least half of us sitting there under the blinding light of a Chinese-made pressure lamp were dressed in "mitumba"—a Kiswahili word for second-hand clothes. The clothes are procured from America and the UK. It is not improbable that the clothes you are wearing now will finish up in Africa. Perhaps the word "finish" is prophetic, as second-hand clothes are likely to finish off what may be left of the local cotton industry as well. It is in this popular way that I speak of globalisation as our interconnectedness in very practical ways.

cannot afford to stand aside and wait for the outcome of this experiment. Indeed, we are already seeing the effects of globalisation in villages and towns right across the continent.

Were it not for the reality of globalisation, I would be a lot more hesitant to write on this topic. At the moment, I am living in the UK, a fair distance from the African realities I have just described. However, I read Kenyan newspapers every day. I listen to Kenyan radio broadcasts, and I watch our national TV news clips on the web. I can talk about Africa with some knowledge because of globalisation, even though the last time I was in Kenya was early last year.

I predict that this new venture, just like the last two, will fail to create a better world for mankind in general or for Africa in particular. I am prepared to believe that in the minds of their creators, these projects have been the best bet for a better world. However, I also see plenty of evidence to indicate that this new idea has all the characteristics of the other two that have gone before. They failed not only because they were morally repugnant to God, but also because they were a rejection of the created order. They failed because they were a charter of a rebel planet. They failed because they were ethnocentric. They failed because they reckoned without a God whose covenant promise is to restore to himself not only the originators of these humanist ventures, but all the children of Adam and Eve— all of mankind. Like the previous experiments, globalisation will fail to create the happy city for humankind.

I think it is critical that as Christians we understand this point. Just as the other three experiments I have described were not launched in order to serve the gospel, globalisation is not here to benefit the Christian church. You and I must not allow ourselves to be seduced in this debate from our true allegiance to the gospel by globalisation's promise of even more riches for the First World. This wooing happens most easily. If you live in those parts of the world that have bought into this and the previous projects, it is a short step from enjoying the prosperity we see in the West to thinking that God approves of the philosophy that underpins life in the West. The love of riches and of the things of this world saturates all aspects of life, to the extent that it dopes and deafens us to the cries of the poor.

Effects of Globalisation

In the rest of this chapter, I want to suggest that as evangelicals, we must not ignore the effects of globalisation in any part of the world. Certainly, we can ill afford to ignore its effects on the African church. Let us consider some of these effects in more detail.

Economic effects

Globalisation is already affecting Africa economically. It has been said that one of the starkest consequences of globalisation in Africa today, in economic terms, is the rendering redundant of the African people. This may appear to be a harsh overstatement, but I believe its validity has been demonstrated repeatedly in the past by observers such as Peter Henriot (1998), whose thoughts have influenced my own.

First of all, the policies of the International Monetary Fund in many African countries make no bones about the fact that sustained economic growth is

Redundancy and Worthlessness

Consider this true story. Carolyn is from Africa. She answered an ad in the press to come to work in Britain as a nurse. Leaving behind a husband and two children, she completed her conversion course in nursing, qualified, and took up employment in the Midlands. In the meanwhile, her husband back in Africa was made redundant and quickly began to show signs of depression. Believing she was doing her family a favour, Carolyn sent for him and for the children to join her in the UK. He showed up alone, with a head as sore as a rhino's from feelings of worthlessness. At home in the Midlands, a row erupted, and he almost took the top of Carolyn's head off with a knife. A call on the mobile saved her as she cowered in the bathroom. He did not attempt to run. When the police came, he owned up to the attempted murder, saying he did not care if he lived or died.

their main goal, not provision of employment. As a consequence, formal employment has dropped wherever Structural Adjustment Policies (SAPs) have been implemented in Africa. In recent years, employment has dipped as low as 16% in Zambia, 24% in Botswana, and 30% in South Africa, for example (ILO, n.d.).

Secondly, an acute SAP approach to kick-starting African economies only pushes the problems elsewhere. For example, cash-strapped governments are unable to prevent encroachment on nature reserves by the poor, who are desperately struggling for survival. In sub-Saharan Africa and several other places, soil erosion and deforestation through burning of charcoal are serious problems today. My own anecdotal observation is that the felling of trees for charcoal and other purposes has resulted in erratic rainfall patterns and drought in Kenya during my lifetime.

Thirdly, South Africa, which is the major beneficiary of globalisation in Africa, already accounts for over 40% of the sub-Saharan GDP. Its own GNP per capita of US$3,010 contrasts sharply with that of Zambia (US$350), Malawi (US$145), and Tanzania and Mozambique (US$80).

How has Africa responded to these problems? Our most recent reply is through the New Partnership for African Development (NEPAD). NEPAD is fronted by Thabo Mbeki of Kenya, Olusegun Obasanjo of Nigeria, Abdoulaye Wade of Senegal, and Abdelaziz Bouteflika of Algeria. Early in 2002, these men met with the G8 leaders, hoping to enlist their support for NEPAD, which is trying to attract Western capital inflow into Africa, as African governments submit to the rules of the World Trade Organisation and to democratic rule. I wish NEPAD well, and were I in a position to support it, I would. However, it is unlikely to succeed in its present state. I offer three concerns:

- The idea is modelled on trickle-down economics. At the moment, the only trickle in Kenya's economy (for example) is the leakage of foreign capital. Last year, capital inflow into the country (investment) was $23 million. In the same year, $50 million fled the country. It seems to me that growth from the grassroots is needed as well.

- The big four did not seek wide consultation across the continent before NEPAD was launched. Kenya, for example, seems to blow hot and cold on the idea, with President Moi recently saying there was nothing new to NEPAD.

- NEPAD is only as strong as its weakest link, and the presidents are the weakest link. I see little in their public behaviour to suggest that they mean business this time—either with or without the reinvented African Union.

Theological effects

We are living in an age in which, increasingly, African Christianity is becoming representative of the Christian church. This trend is related to a shift in the centre of gravity of Christianity from the North to the South. Because of this shift, we cannot afford to ignore what is happening in Africa. Globalisation is all the time increasing the integration of national economies into the global economy through trade, investment rules, and privatisation, aided by technological advancement. These trends are affecting the church in Africa in very profound ways. Not surprisingly, TV is making its own mark (see box on page 161).

Effects on the African Church

The last time I was in Nairobi, I was, as always, interested to see what was on the TV "family channel." This channel normally carries Christian programmes. The programmes I saw fell into two groups—Kenyan preachers copying American televangelists and American televangelists. Perhaps there is nothing wrong with these groups, except that as the effects of globalisation bite harder into the African church, we are beginning to see more and more African speakers holding entrenched and inflexible positions, which reflect the obstinacy and the narrow-mindedness of their Western financial and theological backers. If you ask our televangelists why they agree with T. D. Jakes, for example, or Benny Hinn, and why they disagree with John Stott or, for that matter, the Proclamation Trust stable of Bible teachers, you will find that the conclusions they have reached are not actually their own. They are merely repeating the biases and the prejudices that are common in the West. One such prejudice is the apparent divide between charismatic and non-charismatic churches in the UK. In my experience, there is less suspicion between the two church traditions in many parts of Africa. I fear that with the help of globally available TV programmes, we are already seeing the early signs of the two camps building a mental caricature of each other in Africa.

Cultural and sociological effects

Globalisation is really the way we now live. For good or for ill, it affects everyone. It puts more pressure on some cultures than on others, and the place that pressure is seen best is within the family unit. For Africa, the social pressure of globalisation is being felt most strongly by children, women, and the family. I want to say a word about each.

One of the spinoffs of globalisation is the birth of children's parliaments. From 9 May to 13 May 2001, the Labour Institute of the Trade Union Confederation hosted the spring session of the Children's Parliament. My own country, Kenya, and other several other African countries have their own children's parliaments. A part of the last session's programme was dedicated to the Global Movement in the Children's Interest, in which children and young people should play an important role. During the referendum "Say Yes for Children," the junior deputies collected signatures from their mates, teachers, parents, and public authorities. They also drafted an open letter to all those involved in children's development, education, and protection. How will the new African child conduct herself? It is yet too early to tell how this sort of empowerment will affect the development and evangelisation of the African child, but it is a trend well worth watching.

African Women as Chiefs

In May 2002, in Bulbul, Ngong, Kenya, the first woman chief in Maasailand was appointed. Susan Nampoi, a community leader, said of the appointment, "This is history being made because from the time of Laibon Olenana it has been an abomination for a woman to seek any position which would put her above men in authority" (East African Standard, 2002).

The new chief's first official act was to attack "two crimes—excessive drinking and idleness." So even the Maasai are not immune to the influences of globalisation. The chief's action demonstrated that globalisation had come to Maasailand. Firstly, time has been officially privatised. It has now become a commodity to be sold, with all the social repercussions and benefits it brings. Never again will sitting around and chatting or "chewing the fat" be regarded as an honourable thing. Such activity is now officially time wasting and is therefore, ironically, anti-social behaviour. Secondly, the centre of political and social power has made a small shift towards the women folk, as Susan Nampoi herself reminded her community.

Globalisation will speed up the emancipation of the African woman, with perceptible results on the African family. How will the two new competing centres of power—children's power and women's power—affect African cultures? I think the jury is out on that one. However, early signs suggest that we are witnessing the beginnings of new power relations within African families. For example, we are already seeing women church leaders, preachers, and evangelists. It is still too early to tell what will emerge when the situation reaches equilibrium. What sort of woman will emerge out of Africa? How will she handle her greater liberty and independence? It is anyone's guess. What we do know is that the church will do well to keep its eye on this exciting development.

There is yet a clearer example of how globalisation is affecting African families. Having signed the United Nations Convention on Human Rights, African governments are putting the rights of women and children much higher on their agenda. Take Article 2, Part 2, of the Convention on the Rights of the Child. By its nature, the Convention has a globalising agenda. It states:

> States Parties shall take all appropriate measures to ensure that the child is protected against all forms of discrimination or punishment on the basis of the status, activities, expressed opinions, or beliefs of the child's parents, legal guardians, or family members.

This statement sounds innocent enough, does it not? However, it presumes that the signatories have a Western mindset. We see this in the notion that parents are free to believe anything they want to believe. This worldview is alien to Africa. Africans still believe there is an absolute truth; moreover, we generally like to conform to communal values and beliefs. The opinion of the many is more important than my own. Hence the saying, "I am, because we are." If Africa were to implement this aspect of the Convention to the letter, we would sooner rather than later become as pluralistic and relativistic as the West. We would have to accept homosexuality too—but then I digress.

Some Suggestions

The African church has a responsibility to the Western church. Some of the things it can offer include passion for evangelism and modelling community and forgiveness. Likewise, the West has a responsibility to the African church in the age of globalisation. You might see this interdependence as one of the benefits of globalisation, but it is more than that. It is a gospel requirement. However, in order to fulfil that prophetic role, the Western church must understand that there is a common trick played on observers of Christianity in Africa. I call it the guilt trip spiel. It goes something like this:

Africa must be left alone to evolve its own home-grown solutions. After all, the African church is booming, with over 50 million people coming to the Lord in the 1990s (Brierley, 1998). It is common to hear Nigeria and Kenya given as examples of countries with the largest evangelical student movements anywhere. Such people love to cite Asian economies as an example of authentic, home-grown models. Apparently Asia was overtaking the West in

efficient manufacture, without borrowing the individualism and selfishness of the West, but that was before the bubble burst and the weakness of growth based on speculation was exposed. By implication, the suggestion was that all will end well, if only outsiders (meaning anybody who does not live in Africa) would be nice enough to leave the African church alone. The African church is in fine fettle anyway, according to this line of thinking.

Others of us from Africa play the guilt card whenever we remind outsiders of the effects of colonialism and insensitive missionary experiments in the continent. The effect of such comments is to frighten off criticism. This sort of manipulation must stop. (I readily admit that the early parts of this chapter can be said to be doing the same thing! However, I hope that the argument below demonstrates that this is not my intention at all.)

Two recent events constitute something of a watershed in the study of African Christianity, making it necessary, if not inevitable, to put a stop to such tactics. I believe the notion that Christians living outside Africa cannot comment with insight into the African church must be challenged. Recent events in Liberia and Rwanda, both of which prided themselves as Christian nations, support this conviction.[1]

Liberia

Founded by freed slaves, Liberia was modelled on American Christian values. The founders aspired for liberty and therefore called the new country Liberia. To mark their gratitude for their ex-president in America, they called the

---

[1] I am indebted to Paul Gifford's (2001) *African Christianity* for the historical material that follows.

capital Monrovia (for Monroe). The country's early presidents noted that one of the main reasons for returning to Africa was "to convert the heathen." Before Liberia degenerated into chaos, Liberian politicians were also key figures in the church. Her top three politicians were also top church leaders:

- William Tolbert, the President, was Chair of the Baptist Convention.
- Warner, his Vice President, was the President Bishop of the Methodist Church.
- Reginald Townsend, the National Chair of the True Whig Party, was the Moderator of the Presbyterian Church.

Paul Gifford (2001) reports that in Liberia one came as close as politically possible to a fusion of church and state, with the rhetoric of the latter seemingly fully church-inspired. Not surprisingly, evangelical and Pentecostal churches claimed to be apolitical, but they were not. What we saw in Liberia was the church as part of a political system that resulted in the destruction of the country in the ensuing civil war.

Rwanda

Rwanda is the birthplace of the East African Revival, which started in the 1940s. Some observers believe that the more recent spurt of growth in the East African church is still part of the original revival. Before she became a by-word for African genocide, Rwanda was the most Christianised country in Africa. It was overwhelmingly a Catholic country. However, the church turned a blind eye to the injustices in society, in return for a pole position in the management of education, health, and development.

For example, the church was linked to the regime, with the Archbishop of Kigali being a member of the ruling party's central committee for 15 years.

When the genocide finally broke out, the bishops denied it as a foreign invasion. It comes as no surprise that nuns and bishops (both Protestant and Roman Catholic) have been hauled to The Hague to answer for crimes against humanity.

These examples should demonstrate that it is no longer safe to assume that all that passes for Christianity in Africa is positive. Some of it is positively dangerous.

Opening up the church

Those of us from the African church must accept or be persuaded to accept that sometimes we are a part of the rot that has come to be associated with Africa. We must open up the church to the prophetic word of the Bible: "The time will come when people will not listen to true teaching but will find many more teachers who please them by saying the things they want to hear" (2 Tim. 4:3).

If we fail to open up to the opinion of other Christians, we may find ourselves compelled to do so after another crisis hits the church. Moreover, to turn a deaf ear to genuine concerns about the church is to play exactly the same game that was perfected by the disgraced strongmen of Africa. The latter even now dismiss all criticism as a foreign plot to discredit them.

As I have said, some people tend to dismiss suggestions by anyone who does not live within Africa as irrelevant and out of touch. Well, I believe well-meaning caution must be heard. You no longer have to live in Africa to know what is happening inside Africa. The same is true of other parts of the world, to a greater or lesser extent. Just as African governments are learning to live with scrutiny of their economic policies, the leaders of the African church should not be surprised that the church outside Africa has a few questions about the state of Evangelicalism inside the continent. The church world-wide would, in my opinion, do well to cast aside any compunction it had to ask these questions in the age of neocolonialism. In the present phase, the period of globalisation, accountability is, in fact, part of the way we now live, for we are all interconnected.

There is one more reason that we must be more open to critics from outside. There are political, economic, and social effects of a belief or a religious idea. Religious belief, especially when it makes economic and social claims, is way too big to be left to church leaders alone. What is happening within the African church has an influence that extends beyond the traditional boundaries of religion. Therefore, when the world-wide church seeks to understand more about what is happening in the African church, it is only doing its duty.

Conclusion

Others in the past have proposed a model of the church that sees the world-wide church as the family of God's people. I want to add my support to that inspiration. If we see ourselves as a world-wide community of justice and peace, and if we the church decide to share our resources as members of the same world-wide family, perhaps we shall convince the world that there is a human-friendly face to globalisation— a face based on the gospel of the first Adam and not on the economics of Adam Smith.

References

Brierley, P. W. (1998). *Future church: a global analysis of the Christian community to the year 2010*. Crowborough, East Sussex, UK: Monarch Books.

The East African Standard. (2002, May). Retrieved from http://www.eastandard.net.

Giddens, A. (2000). *Reith lectures 1-5*. Retrieved from http://news.bbc.co.uk/hi/english/static/events/reith_2000/.

Gifford, P. (2001). *African Christianity: Its public face*. London, UK: Hurst & Co.

Henriot, P. J. (1998). *Globalization: Implications for Africa*. Retrieved from http://www.sedos.org/english/global.html.

International Labour Organization (ILO). Retrieved from http://www.ilo.org.

Soros, G. (2000). *Open society: Reforming global capitalism*. London, UK: Little, Brown & Co.

Wood, W. (1994). *Keep the faith, Baby*. Oxford, UK: Bible Reading Fellowship.

Wanyeki Mahiaini *is a Kenyan and is married with two children. After graduating from the University of Nairobi and Warwick University in England, he taught at Egerton University in Kenya. He is interested in everything to do with the world and, in particular, the future of Christianity in Africa. Email: wanyeki.mahiaini@ukgateway.net.*

10

Globalisation from a grassroots, Two-Thirds World perspective: a snapshot

FIONA WILSON

In September 2001, Tearfund UK[1] held its first-ever Partner Consultation. Over a period of three days, partners were asked to comment about various aspects of Tearfund's work, and presentations were given on a wide variety of subjects. One of those subjects was globalisation. In response to that seminar, partners asked Tearfund to look at both the positive and negative effects of globalisation, so as to see both the possibilities and the disadvantages that globalisation brings with it.

Tearfund has Regional Advisors based within Africa, Asia, Central Asia and the Mediterranean, and Latin America who work with partners. The Regional Advisors helped me gather information by distributing a questionnaire from the London office to partner organisations and contacts. One helped by translating

---

[1] Tearfund UK and Ireland is an evangelical Christian relief and development agency that was founded in 1968 as the relief arm of the UK Evangelical Alliance. It became autonomous in 1970, and of the £33.2 million it received in 2001-2002, 88% was given by individuals and churches. Tearfund currently works through 364 partner organisations in approximately 80 countries around the world.

the questionnaire for partners, and some Regional Advisors gave their own opinions by filling a questionnaire in themselves.

The Questionnaire

The questionnaire was sent out by email in four languages—English, French, Spanish, and Portuguese—via Regional Advisors in Africa, Asia, and Latin America and the Caribbean. There were 77 responses from 22 different countries. The most enthusiastic responses came from Angola, with 17 questionnaires being returned, and Burkina Faso, which sent back 11. In order to keep the African enthusiasm from skewing the statistics, only the first five questionnaires returned from each country were used for the quantitative questions. All questionnaires were used for the qualitative questions.

The questionnaire was divided into five sections. The first section gave two definitions of globalisation and explained the reason for sending out the questionnaire—namely, in response to our partners' requests to look at globalisation and for this book.

The second section contained six general questions, which helped to build up a profile of the respondent. Respondents were asked to identify their nationality, their mother tongue, how many languages they speak, their gender, their age, and their general area of work.

The third section was the culture section, with questions about whether and how globalisation has affected the respondents' culture and customs. It asked more specifically about the influence or non-influence of television, where people would like to travel, and whether a change in food production and product source location had been noted. Finally, it asked about computer and Internet use.

The fourth section dealt with spiritual matters and asked respondents if they had noted changes in their church over the last 5-10 years. If change was evident, respondents were asked to assess whether and how the changes were related to globalisation. The source of any church materials was asked about, as well as which country or countries exert the most influence over the church in respondents' home countries.

The fifth section was a summary section. It asked respondents to list five benefits of globalisation and five ways in which globalisation has been harmful to the individual, the family, the church, and the culture. The final question asked what would need to happen in order for globalisation to be of benefit.

Each of the sections of the questionnaire is discussed below. Sample responses are included to illustrate the comments given.

Questionnaire Introduction

Anthony Giddens (1999) gives the following definition of globalisation in his book *The Third Way*:

Globalisation can thus be defined as the intensification of worldwide social relations which link distant localities in such a way that local happenings are shaped by events occurring miles away and vice versa.

In his book, *Globalisation and the Kingdom of God*, James Skillen (2001) expands this idea of global interconnectedness:

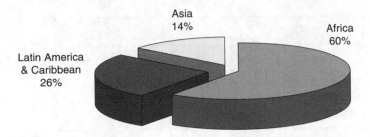

Figure 1. Questionnaire results by continent.

What is globalisation? In brief, it features the growing inter-dependence of people through-out the world. Interdependency is multiplying and intensifying by means of ever more rapid means of communication, which are helping to tie the world's billions of still-multiplying people closer and closer together economically, environmentally, technologically, and in other ways.... Globalisa-tion also means a change of per-spective on the meaning of life.

The questionnaire itself was proof of global interconnectedness in the way that it was compiled, sent out round the world, and received back within two months, as well as in the way that dis-tant localities are linked through the speed of technology.

Tearfund's Regional Advisors received the questionnaires and sent them on to partner organisations and others, who then sent them back to Tearfund. The response by continent is shown in Figure 1. Results came back from 10 African countries, eight Latin American and Caribbean countries, and four Asian countries.

Language

The majority of people answering the questionnaire spoke three lan-guages, with the second largest major-ity speaking two languages (see Figure 2). Regarding the languages spoken, it was fascinating to note that out of the

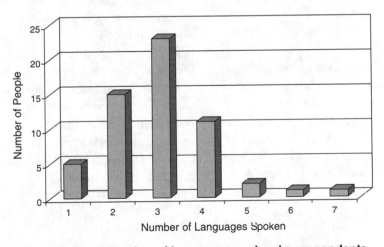

Figure 2. Number of languages spoken by respondents.

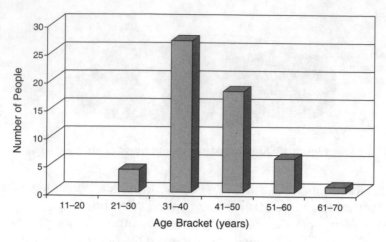

Figure 3. Age of respondents.

58 questionnaires used for statistical purposes, respondents spoke 34 different mother tongues. Only one-third of respondents answered in their first language, that is, in English, French, Spanish, or Portuguese. Two-thirds replied using their second language, or even their third, fourth, fifth, sixth, or seventh!

Gender

The gender balance was unequal, with a much higher percentage of men answering the questionnaire than women: 79% of respondents were male, and 21% were female.

Age

Half of the responses came from the 31-40 age group, and another third came from those between the ages of 41 and 50 (see Figure 3). When asking respondents to look back over the last 5-10 years, as some questions did, the majority would have been in the 21-30 age bracket.

Employment

Due to the nature of Tearfund's work, the majority of questionnaires were filled in by people involved in community development work of one type or another, including education, social work, pastoral work, local NGOs and networks, rural development, community health, HIV/AIDS work, literacy, street children's work, accountancy, and administration.

Culture

After the general details section, the second section of the questionnaire was about culture. The questions in this section centred around six main areas of life: customs, the influence of television and films, what foreign countries people want to visit and why, whether globalisation affects family life, the changes in foods and products available over the last 5-10 years, and the influence of the computer and Internet.

Customs

Local customs were highlighted by many people as having changed over the last 5-10 years, with the feeling that both local and national customs are being lost and usurped by Western values. The language used to describe the changes was strong. People talked in terms of **losing**, **abandoning**, **relinquishing**, **ignoring**, and **replacing** customs, and of customs **dying out** when old people die. Some respondents cited customs that have changed, such as village sports or traditional dances.

> "Women used to send and receive lovely cards on special occasions. Now we receive an email." *(Latin America)*
>
> "Santa Claus is replacing the Three Kings." *(Latin America)*
>
> "Changes in ancestral customs like 'Minka' (communal group working for the good of society) and 'Ayni' (mutual help)." *(Latin America)*

By far, the most commonly mentioned change was in dress or fashion. Traditional dress is being abandoned in favour of a European or American style which, to some, means a lack of modesty. Hairstyles and skin lightening were mentioned by African respondents.

> "Women don't accept their natural skin colour any more—they lighten it." *(Francophone Africa)*
>
> "Young people have extravagant hairstyles. They behave as if they are imitating famous stars." *(Francophone Africa)*

Community and family lifestyles have changed around the world, with family ties breaking down and the loss of family solidarity, as well as the feeling that the traditional extended family system is gradually being replaced by the nuclear family. There is more migration and a loss of a feeling of community living.

> "Child discipline, which belongs to everybody in the society, has changed to only parents." *(English-speaking Africa)*
>
> "Family habits are changing. On Sundays and holidays, we used to get together to eat a traditional meal together. Nowadays, every family member has their own things to do." *(Latin America)*

Language, music, and food have all changed as well. There is less use of the mother tongue and even resistance towards using it. In addition, there is the loss of traditional languages, especially in urban areas. One respondent noted that the changes in language have brought division between those who are educated and those who are not. In the areas of music and food, television has brought popular music, and Western influence has brought with it fast food and junk foods.

The main influence in the area of culture has been the technological revolution, with television having the greatest impact. The media now bring up-to-the-second information about what is happening in the world, and the Internet and telephones allow rapid communication. Through television and films, new cultures are being imported, and foreign customs are being incorporated into people's local cultures.

With these changes has come a decline in traditional moral standards. Young people especially are noted as "drifting from the social norms" through drinking, smoking, violence, and crime. They also exhibit a general increase in sexually immoral behaviour, disrespect for older people, corruption, and greed.

The profit culture has brought with it hedonism and individualism, consumerism and materialism. People want a comfortable life, and there is a real concern to earn money.

> "Social prestige used to be measured in the number of cattle and the amount of rice. Now it is measured in if one emigrates, who has a good job, and who is able to build a beautiful house." (*Francophone Africa*)
>
> "Only healthy if wealthy." (*Asia*)

Not all the changes are negative, but there were only about a half dozen respondents—definitely a minority voice—who could see the positive side of the changes that globalisation has brought. A few people mentioned the decline in idolatry; others noted better relationships and ways of behaving. The progress of women and a higher quality and standard of doing things were also brought out.

> "Improvement in relationships and ways of behaving." (*Francophone Africa*)
>
> "Start times of meetings improved." (*Portuguese-speaking Africa*)

> "Expectations in terms of quality of life increased, and there has been a 'widening' of the general population's cultural awareness." (*Latin America*)

The effect of television

Only four people did not think that television affected their culture. The vast majority talked about the effects of television in their experience, with the negative effects far outweighing the positive ones. Some people were able to see both the positive and the negative effects.

> "Some films and documentaries report about science and agriculture and the economy and are of inestimable value for our people. On the other hand, those that present foreign customs counter to morality and scenes of violence leave traces in the lives of those touched by them, especially young people." (*Francophone Africa*)

The good effects of television were seen in programmes and documentaries about things such as health, environmental protection, and new goods and services available. Such programmes improve some aspects of life for people and can give them "a glimpse of a world which we would have known nothing of," as one respondent put it.

Television was seen as one of the main means of disseminating Western values and behaviour in music and fashion, in habits, and in its value system. The negative impacts were seen strongly in the lives of young people, especially in their loss of respect for older people and for the advice older people can provide. TV also brings with it sexual depravity, debauchery, pornography, violence, and crime. The lack of censorship of programmes was an obvious worry, and the effect was even described as "freedom going too far."

> "Many of the folks of my generation see a definite breakthrough in our cultural values since cable TV hit our homes back in the '80s. The MTV culture dominates our youth. Local TV programmes many times imitate the format of talk shows, magazines, and news communication that is seen in foreign TV. I personally believe it is the number one influence in cultural change we have experienced in the last 20 years." *(Latin America)*

> "Whatever the film and TV programmes are espousing is seen as worth emulating." *(Asia)*
>
> Some of the words used to describe how people respond to television: copying, emulating, modifying, adopting, promoting, changing, embracing, imitating, identifying, sensitising, influencing, affecting, broadening.

Travelling abroad

An overwhelming majority of both youths and adults want to visit the United States, as Figures 4 and 5 illustrate. The reasons cited were various and include the high standard of living, the tranquillity and peace, the freedom and opportunities, the abundance, and the fact that the USA is a model of democracy.

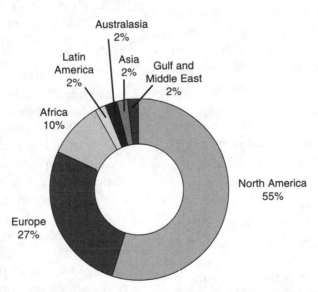

Figure 4. Which country do young people in your country most want to visit?

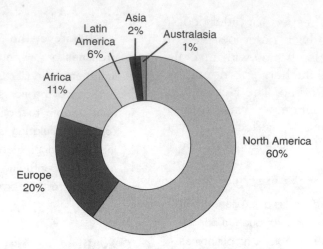

Figure 5. Which country do adults most want to visit?

"Those with money want to go to the USA with the goal of having security. Adults without money don't expect to leave the country." *(Latin America)*

"USA—because we are told that it is a country of freedom and abundance, with a low level of unemployment." *(Francophone Africa)*

"USA—more money, more attractions, more fun, more freedom, more opportunities, etc. At least that's what they perceive from here. It is another story when they finally move there." *(Latin America)*

"USA—because for them it is a land of opportunity and most of their relatives are in the USA." *(Asia)*

Some people mentioned wanting to visit neighbouring countries due to their proximity and because of knowing about what is available there, and perhaps even to use them as a stepping-stone. This is especially true for South Africa.

After North America, Europe is the next most popular destination, because of the ease of communication for those who speak Spanish, Portuguese, French, or English, as well as the possibilities to work, study, and travel. The high standard of living in Europe is also a drawing card. People want to visit Canada because it is seen as a country of peace and as highly developed. One person mentioned Israel as a popular destination for Christians, because of its biblical connections.

Family life

The way that globalisation affects family life was already touched upon in the first question in the cultural section, but this question enabled a deeper look at whether and how globalisation affects people's family lives. Nine people said it didn't, or didn't yet, and one spoke about taking great care to engender his/her own cultural identity so that globalisation does not dominate family life.

Television and technology are the two main means through which family life is affected. Television lessens the amount of time that families spend together. It is more popular than books or comics and is imitated by children.

It exposes young people to new value systems, makes them grow up faster, and gives them a thirst for consumer goods.

Other technology items, especially the Internet and telecommunications, are seen in a more positive light. Technology helps to connect families not living in the same place, brings new information on different topics, and allows fast communication by email. Work is made easier in the house through new gadgets and electrical appliances.

On the negative side, both television and technology lead to materialism, and they create a growing need for luxuries.

> "It is creating a false need for new and luxury articles." *(Latin America)*
>
> "We are exposed to products that certainly make life easier, but sometimes we are not able to afford them. There is tension in the family when there is a mismatch between wants and what we can afford. But when one can afford a certain product and it makes things easier, there is a degree of comfort too." *(Asia)*
>
> "Greater spending in areas that weren't well known, such as being presented with holidays as you see on IV with the advertisements." *(Francophone Africa)*

Within the life of the family, there are also changes. There is less time spent as a family, parents feel they have less control, and the extended family system is gradually becoming a nuclear family system. Globalisation is causing stress in some families as they fight to spend time together.

> "There is pressure for more work and less time to see each other and be together as a family. We are not caring for the family, and we worship work. We are putting our children into other people's hands because both parents have to work." *(Latin America)*

This is not the whole story, though. Others spoke of globalisation having a positive effect within the family, of improved family health, of being able to share with more people, and of feeling their children are global citizens and able to appreciate different cultures.

> "Parents spend better time with their children. They listen to them and very often decide things with them." *(Francophone Africa)*
>
> "In one way, our children are citizens of the world. Through my husband's work and mine, both have visited at least 10 countries, and neither is yet 15. This gives them a wider appreciation of the world and the different cultural forms than we had in my generation." *(Latin America)*

Foods and products

Some respondents said that the food that they eat is grown or produced locally, but they could still think of new foods that have appeared over the last 5-10 years. The majority of people said that some produce is grown locally, and some is imported. There seems to be no trend about where food comes from. The only food item that was mentioned as being imported into every continent was rice from Thailand.

> "Rice from Thailand being sold three times as cheaply as locally grown rice leads to loss of local production, because to eat local rice is a luxury because of its high price." *(Francophone Africa)*

New foods over the last 10 years include tinned produce reaching virtually every corner of the globe, fruit, rice, milk, cheese, cold meats, and junk food such as fast food outlets, hamburgers, and pizzas. Fruit juice and fizzy drinks are also widely available. GM products and seeds were also mentioned.

New products noted include electronic and electrical equipment, computers, cars, mobile phones, and gadgets. Other items include clothes, toys, medicines, and furniture.

Changes in the origin of products were also noticed, especially in Africa.

> "Origin of products has changed, especially in electrical appliances, cars, toys, and food. In the 'good old days,' they mainly came from Europe and the West, and to a lesser extent from the North and East. Now they increasingly come from Asia and to a lesser extent from the Americas." *(Francophone Africa)*

Products imported from Taiwan, China, Korea, Hong Kong, and Japan were mentioned most frequently. The USA was also mentioned as a common exporter.

A trend that seemed to be worrying some people is the decline in their own countries' production and a heavier reliance on imported goods.

> "Loss of our own crops, like coffee, because of depressed prices in the international arena. Less area sown with basic grains, because of the unfair competition from the US, who sells us products at low prices, because they subsidise the production, and they become the base of our food security." *(Latin America)*
>
> "Large quantity of shiny, cheap items available, discouraging domestic products and affecting the country's economy." *(English-speaking Africa)*
>
> "Nowadays we find the market flooded with products manufactured in China, Korea, and the like with local products being crowded out." *(Asia)*

The diversity of available products was noted. As an Asian respondent so eloquently phrased it, there is a "proliferation of choices … which inevitably affects time."

Computers and the Internet

Over half of computer use is for email correspondence, with another third being for research or information gathering. Some people use the Internet for news, and a very small minority use it for buying items or for business (see Figure 6).

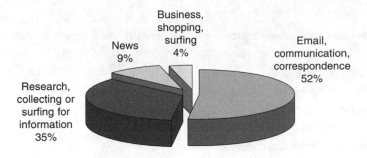

Figure 6. Computer and Internet use.

Spiritual Life

The questionnaire asked about the changes that respondents have seen in their churches over the last 5-10 years. Then it asked whether they thought these changes had anything to do with globalisation and, if so, how they are linked.

The biggest change that was noted is in the style of worship in church. New ways of worshipping are being introduced. Modern instruments and more of them are being used in some places. Some people mentioned a rock band style replacing a piano and hymns, along with new rhythms. One person said the mode of worship has been adopted from television and is more American in its style.

> "Change in worship—modern songs as well as traditional." *(Asia)*
>
> "We are importing music and theology." *(Latin America)*

Technological advances have also affected the church. Videos are being shown. There is easier communication via email, allowing more sharing between churches. In addition, the Internet, CDs, and multimedia equipment are being used. One Francophone African respondent talked about the fact that having an electricity generator means that power cuts can be overcome during services. Another person, in spite of saying that globalisation is not responsible for the changes seen in his church, did mention that mobile phones go off in the middle of the sermon!

Once again, the influence of television is strong, with imported programmes affecting worship styles and preaching; in one case, this was said to be a "performance."

> "It is what one sees in other countries (ways of doing something, rigour, materials, techniques, etc.), that you then apply to your own context." *(Francophone Africa)*

It is interesting to observe the effect that seeing Christians from another country on television had on one respondent:

> "New techniques of communication through evangelistic campaigns and sports show us that Jesus is the crux of all success. As a consequence, the majority of young people accept Jesus into their hearts. For example, in the 2002 World Cup, Brazilian Christians showed the supremacy of Jesus over all things."
> *(Francophone Africa)*

The increase in materialism and the change of dress were said to have entered the church, with "the rules and habits of the secular world ... taking hold more and more in the church." New trends and ideas are entering from overseas, with mega-churches and the prosperity gospel especially affecting Latin America.

> "Success is not measured by faithfulness to God, but by the results that movements have. There is a strong emphasis on idolising numbers." *(Latin America)*

Mainly Latin American respondents also cited televangelists such as Benny Hinn, the Toronto blessing, spiritual warfare, and the neo-Pentecostal movement as influences upon the church. African respondents mentioned better quality being demanded and more accountability.

Most people felt that the changes are linked to globalisation, but 12 respondents thought that globalisation was not involved at all. The communications revolution was cited as the reason for the vast majority of changes, either through television or through rapid communications systems. The other two main ways that globalisation is involved in changes in the church are through overseas travel and through education and training.

> "[The changes are linked to globalisation] primarily due to increased communications that globalisation has facilitated, yet whoever controls the media controls the culture." *(Latin America)*
>
> "We tend to think and believe that what comes from outside is better."
> *(Francophone Africa)*

The questionnaire then asked people whether they receive church materials such as Bibles, songs, study materials, or Sunday school materials from abroad. Many receive materials from the USA; far fewer people mentioned the UK. Countries that share languages provide some materials for one another: Brazil and Portugal send materials to Portuguese-speaking African countries, and Spain and Argentina supply other Latin American countries.

The final question was about which countries have the most influence upon the church in the respondent's country. Figure 7 displays the results by continent.

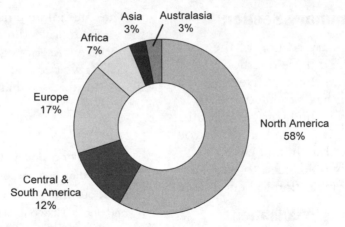

Figure 7. Regions exerting the most influence upon the church.

By far, the greatest influence is from North America, and this is mainly the influence of the USA, as can be seen from the breakdown of the results into countries (Figure 8).

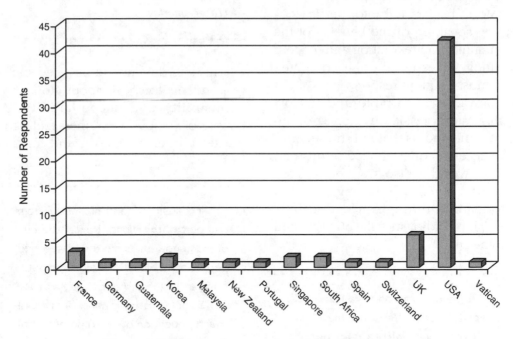

Figure 8. Which foreign country has the most influence upon the church in your country?

Summary Section

The summary section of the questionnaire asked three questions:

1. Can you think of five ways that globalisation has benefited you?

2. Can you think of five ways that globalisation has been harmful to you, your family, church, and culture?

3. What would need to happen in order for globalisation to benefit you?

Benefits of globalisation

The benefits of globalisation as listed by the respondents can be grouped into three main categories: communication and technology, the interlinking and opening up of the world, and benefits from products and services.

Most answers fell into the first category, speaking of the benefits of the communication revolution and modern technology, especially the computer. The most frequent response was about the advantages of rapid and flexible communication, although one respondent reminded us that in Latin America "the access is quite limited in this part of the world." Also frequently cited were the benefits of having access to information, through media such as television, radio, mobile phones, and the Internet.

> "To be at home and live like a citizen of the world." (*Francophone Africa*)
>
> "I can communicate with people around the world." (*Asia*)
>
> "Ease of exchange of knowledge and scientific and cultural experiences." (*Latin America*)

The interlinking and opening up of the world follows directly on from the technology. As our identity becomes global, so we become more interdependent and able to share with one another.

> "Breaking down cultural barriers means that human beings can share, conscious that we are under one sun and one sky like one big family." (*Latin America*)
>
> "Better understanding and cooperation between nationalities." (*Asia*)
>
> "Greater resource pool that can benefit many: networking, relationships, logistical and economic resources, etc." (*Latin America*)

This interdependence also led some respondents to speak about global responsibility and accountability. A couple of people mentioned feeling a greater burden for prayer and for the lost.

> "It is easier to send information from any part of the world. Hence, the evil of many nations is more exposed and people are a bit more afraid of perpetuating evil." (*English-speaking Africa*)
>
> "Social injustice is not an individual country question but an area of global concern." (*Portuguese-speaking Africa*)
>
> "Scope for the weakest to express themselves in a world where the richest make the laws." (*Francophone Africa*)

The idea of being interlinked—of being able to share knowledge and to have a wider view of life and the world—was definitely seen as a benefit of globalisation, along with being able to be part of and contribute to global networks. Interlinking also gives more opportunities for evangelising. Leading on from this are benefits that globalisation brings in the form of education and training, with new educational materials for distance education and for improving technical skills.

> "The ability for the individual to get personal training and benefit from the reality and experiences from other far-off countries." *(Francophone Africa)*
>
> "More preference for upgraded skill sets and lesser need to have the right contacts. Merit is valued, as is productivity, although having the right contacts does help a lot." *(Asia)*

Friendships and improved social relations with those from overseas, together with the possibilities that those relationships bring and the ease of staying in touch, were all suggested as positive results of globalisation. These things were mentioned in conjunction with people's faith and the unity to be found in diversity as Christians.

> "Christianity—in God's Spirit we can speak one universal language wherever we are." *(English-speaking Africa)*
>
> "I realise more and more the wonderful diversity of the church that Jesus has established as his now and future bride." *(Asia)*

Access to world markets in goods and services brings a variety of benefits—diversity and consumer choice, cheaper goods, foreign products, and the availability of good-quality goods. Some respondents suggested that stiffer competition raises standards, with healthy competition being seen as a good thing. The areas of health and food/agriculture were especially noted as having benefited from globalisation. Better health delivery and surgery (such as heart transplants and laser surgery) can be found, as well as more sophisticated agricultural equipment and means of production.

Harms of globalisation

Respondents' answers for this section were fuller than for the benefits section, and they were more difficult to group under broad headings. The negative aspects seem to be much more far-reaching, so I have gathered them under different levels—firstly, the global or international level; secondly, the national or cultural level; and thirdly, the family and church level.

Global level

The power and the injustice at the global level were pointed out in various ways. The lack of justice and equity, exploitation, the plundering of primary commodities, and the feeling that globalisation is out of people's control came across, especially in the responses from Francophone Africa. Respondents noted that the poor suffer, countries are unable to compete in the global markets, and inequality exists. The poor feel dominated by the rich, as the harmful effects of globalisation "advance at the pace of the giants."

> "It is the law of the jungle: the strongest impose their laws upon the weakest." *(Francophone Africa)*
>
> "The rules of the game are dictated by the great/powerful for their own interests." *(Francophone Africa)*
>
> "We are becoming a more and more dependent society on the powers of the North—our country is being sold out!" *(Latin America)*
>
> "My country is too poor, and I do not see how globalisation could bring good to my people. We are trailing behind the rich countries." *(Francophone Africa)*
>
> "It homogenises choices so that a counter to it in any realm is difficult to forge—most successful majoritarian rule ever." *(Asia)*
>
> "It promotes the survival of the fittest." *(Francophone Africa)*
>
> "Domination by the West and the North over the East and the South, mainly because of the bias of the multinationals and the Bretton Woods institutions (IMF, World Bank)." *(Francophone Africa)*
>
> "The powerful have more and better tools to impose their opinions upon the poor." *(Latin America)*

The neo-liberal economic system also caused a strong reaction among respondents. From all around the South, there were emotive cries as people spoke of being **strangled** under the economic plan, businesses being **sunk** by multinationals, entrepreneurs being **driven from** the markets, local markets being **invaded** by small arms, and local industrial initiatives being **killed**.

In the agricultural sector, feelings also ran high, with reports of agriculture being **abandoned**, farmers being **impoverished** due to the drop in agricultural commodity prices, and the environment being **degraded**.

> "The loss of food sovereignty and the massive influx of GM foods at lower prices because of their subsidy by rich countries." *(Latin America)*
>
> "The plundering of primary commodities in poor countries." *(Francophone Africa)*

National and cultural level

The blind imitation of the West and the bad influences from other cultures were also commonly cited as harmful effects of globalisation. Various respondents talked about how their native culture is not being valued, and people are abandoning it. Many of the negative changes mentioned in the first questions under culture and customs were repeated here; once again, the strength of feeling is evident. The loss of cultural identity was frequently mentioned, along with the adoption of foreign or imported values. It was noted that good aspects are eroded, and foreign styles and behaviour are imitated.

The decline in moral standards was seen in two main ways: in the rise in crime and in the growth of individualism. Violence and crime include prostitution, armed robbery, juvenile crime, drugs, corruption, underage sex, pornography, and robbery. Individualism includes lack of respect for others, living an immoral lifestyle, consumerism, and greed.

> "Materialistic and consumerist values replacing humane values; people are valued more by what they can produce, external looks, etc., than character (that's what we are sold and bombarded with)." *(Latin America)*
>
> "The search for non-essential material well-being." *(Francophone Africa)*
>
> "Dissatisfaction with the simple." *(Latin America)*
>
> "Develops self-centredness and disunity." *(Asia)*

Family and church level

The decline in moral values spreads into the family and church domains. Respondents talked of family disintegration, including distancing and breakdown in relationships as the family also becomes more individualistic. The extended family system was seen to have declined. Children's behaviour was spoken of in a negative way, with children demanding what they want, being impolite, and lacking patience with their parents. Television was seen to encroach on family time.

> "Understanding of the family structures and norms shaped by Western nuclear and individualistic models." *(Asia)*
>
> "Free lifestyle with no accountability towards society, friends, and family. Immorality is equivalent to 'open-mindedness.'" *(Latin America)*

> "Young people more than anyone do not have any points of reference because of the conflict between the education they receive and what they hear and see around them." *(Francophone Africa)*

Within the church, the harm of globalisation is also clearly seen. The importing of all kinds of foreign teaching and styles of worship means that churches are conforming to non-traditional values and imported behaviour and are not valuing their own cultural church heritage. There is a lack of understanding in the church about sects and the New Age coming in, especially in Africa. The secular world also has influence upon the church, and mention was made of Christians "cooling off" as the church conforms to consumerist values.

> "Tendency to reject Jesus as THE WAY." *(Portuguese-speaking Africa)*
>
> "There is a loss of identity in church, especially in the local church. There is a tendency to belong to all congregations and not one in particular. Especially in Latin America, the movement of believers from one congregation to another is common." *(Latin America)*
>
> "Loss of value in having a typically African service." *(Portuguese-speaking Africa)*
>
> "Tendency to build the tower of Babel once again." *(Portuguese-speaking Africa)*

Changes necessary to benefit people

The final question asked what would need to happen in order for globalisation to be a benefit. Respondents answered in different capacities—as global citizens, as the poor, as national citizens, as consumers, as individuals, and as Christians. I will group their answers under these different capacities.

Global citizens and the poor

Following on from the expression in the previous section about people feeling helpless in the face of globalisation, comments grouped in this section were all about people feeling that they cannot do anything in the face of global forces. There were various comments about globalisation needing to take the poor into account. The system should not be imposed upon the poor.

> "It is necessary that the rich become more aware of the solidarity between the rich and the weak (not only in their actions, but in their words). That they realise that within the existing rules of the game, the world is inescapably heading towards a catastrophe in which no one will be spared. They alone will be responsible for it, because they obstinately refuse to modify fixed rules because it is in their interests to continue to dominate the rest of the world (cf. the composition of the Security Council of the UN, with its permanent members who impose their own laws upon the other members and the rest of the world)." *(Francophone Africa)*

It should empower the poor rather than dominating them with hedonism, individualism, and materialism. The sentiments expressed were that globalisation is an unfair and unjust system that needs to be corrected.

Various other measures were suggested, including forgiving debt, providing information about globalisation, censoring unsuitable television programmes, using the global institutions to bring world history into the new generation, untying aid, and using networks to have more impact. Only a few people talked about the need for Christians to be involved in decision making and politics.

> "We would need more justice, more equity, and less selfishness by the great/big/rich in creating the rules of the game and in the running of international institutions and the big multinationals. For example, rules regarding the running of the WTO do not take very much account of the situation and the interests of the poor countries. How can you have a fair discussion when you don't start from the same point?" *(Francophone Africa)*
>
> "Correct the inequalities and injustices between the West and Africa. The Africans were the price paid for the development of the West." *(Francophone Africa)*
>
> "More involvement of Christians in politics—national and international. More involvement of Christians in advocacy—national and international." *(Asia)*

Citizens and consumers

The role of governments was both challenged and encouraged. Corruption must end, and governments must take their part in sharing risks and helping to contextualise and acculturate globalisation. Respondents felt that the role of governments is to legislate on behalf of the people—to allow only good-quality products into the country, to control broadcasts, to provide a social security net, to raise social protection measures, to respect common people, and to guarantee basic human rights.

> "Changes must be adapted to the context of each country. It is necessary to analyse each change, weigh up the pros and cons against the reality and mentality of the people of each country before applying them. The mission of each government." *(Francophone Africa)*

As consumers, respondents suggested that the quality and nature of products must be presented to reassure them. They felt that aggressive advertising should not be allowed, but that consumers should be allowed to make up their own minds. National products should be valued over imported ones. In addition, there was a call for the laws of international commerce to be changed so as to be equitable, and the neo-liberal economic model should be made more sensitive.

> "The rich countries forbid the poor countries to subsidise certain sectors (agriculture, for example) at the same time as they award subsidies to their sectors (CAP and EU, for example). The whole world knows that the American farmers are the most subsidised in the world, and the USA is the leading defender of economic liberalism!!!!" *(Francophone Africa)*
>
> "That the transnational corporations rid themselves of their miserly interests." *(Latin America)*
>
> "Support international politics to favour fair markets." *(Latin America)*

Individuals and Christians

There was a feeling of individual responsibility by a number of respondents. Above all, they indicated that they would like to learn about and be informed about globalisation. They want to be wise and not remain indifferent to globalisation. They desire to promote development and the benefits of globalisation rather than the harms. They want to accommodate one another and share technology. A few people spoke of spreading networks, linking into them, and taking advantage of what they have to offer.

> "Use only information that is useful and edifying. Use it for educative purposes. Use the Internet to connect people positively." *(Francophone Africa)*

> "Educate the people to understand to what extent they are being manipulated and only considered as consumers." (*Latin America*)
>
> "Ask questions and learn the 'why's' behind poverty and oppression. Look for examples of where differences are being made by communities." (*Portuguese-speaking Africa*)

People's response to globalisation is also seen in their individual behaviour. People do not want to remain indifferent to globalisation, nor to be dominated by it; rather, they want to be wise and selective, in order that they can tap into the benefits of globalisation.

> "Frankly speaking, globalisation is already benefiting me. It is just that it has side effects. Just as any drug has therapeutic as well as adverse effects, so with globalisation." (*Asia*)
>
> "Families need to be wise in order to use the things that globalisation offers, especially in the areas of information and communication but with the necessary spiritual and moral control." (*Latin America*)

With regard to how Christians and the church need to respond in order for globalisation to be a benefit, there was a feeling that both the church and Christians have a role to play and that Christians need to get involved in globalisation.

> "That Christians get involved in decision and policy making, struggle against corruption in order to inspire really good choices for the development of our countries." (*Francophone Africa*)
>
> "That the church becomes aware of its historic role (and ceases to be naïve and indifferent)." (*Latin America*)
>
> "A great Christian campaign to inform poor countries and communities about what globalisation is and its consequences, so that we can decide how to behave or accept, and not only react." (*Latin America*)
>
> "Reorient the total concept/policy of globalisation on the basis of 'divine love' as stated in the Bible.... The Kingdom of God should be the bedrock over which the globalisation should be planned." (*Asia*)

Conclusion

There is a lot of valid criticism that could be made about this small snapshot! The time period during which it was done was short, and in spite of my best intentions to get an equal number of questionnaires from around the Two-Thirds World, this did not transpire. The bias is towards Africa, and there is no voice from Central Asia at all. There is also a gender imbalance, in that less than a quarter of respondents were women. The number of questionnaires returned means that this analysis cannot in any way be a comprehensive overview of how globalisation is affecting the Two-Thirds World.

I have found it a daunting task to write this chapter. Translating and collating the responses and then representing those individuals who responded to the questionnaire have been significant challenges! I take full responsibility for any errors in the translations.

I have learned a lot from the information that has come in. The consistency across the world about how globalisation is affecting people's cultures and customs is striking. The strength of the media and especially the power of television were strongly expressed again and again. The comments challenge me to wonder how we as Christians should get involved in these areas.

The power that the USA holds over the Two-Thirds World is incredible. This power is linked to the control over a lot of television and media. Surprising to me was the fact that the USA has a tremendous pull even in countries that are not English speaking.

The influence of the USA over the church is also huge. Without further questioning, it is hard to draw any conclusions from the data, but the influence is certainly food for thought.

As a Westerner, I found that the greatest challenge was to read comments that told me that I was responsible for some of globalisation's harms. Respondents talked of Westerners as the rich dominating the poor. Some explicitly said that we need to act; others implied it. Part of me wanted to reject the notion that I could do anything more than pray and give, but the challenge to me was that I am one of the trampling "giants" and am part of the domination and the unfair globalisation system.

As a member of the interconnected Christian family, I was challenged to think about what my response should be. I hope that this snapshot will serve to inform Two-Thirds World Christians

about what others are thinking. In addition, I hope it will challenge other Westerners to respond in a way that helps alleviate the negative aspects of globalisation for the Two-Thirds World.

It is appropriate that the last word on this questionnaire be given by a respondent from the Two-Thirds World:

"First, I need to be more reflective on the matter: really stop and think through all that is being offered and filter stuff big time. I need to take advantage in order to network with the family of God worldwide and help channel appropriate resources to needs around the globe. I need to learn how to use all this information available to live and present the gospel in ever increasingly opportune ways. I need to constantly revisit my commitment to Christ to make sure I am not bowing down to the powers that are, and I'm being faithful to his calling of me as a Christian. I now have more resources available to enhance my local Christian ministry. But most importantly, networking with the family of God worldwide as a source of strength and accountability that improves Christian testimony and serving opportunities." (Latin America)

References

Giddens, A. (1999). *The third way: The renewal of social democracy.* Malden, MA: Polity Press.

Skillen, J. W. (Ed.). (2001). *Globalization and the kingdom of God.* Grand Rapids, MI: Baker Books.

Fiona Wilson *is Executive Assistant to the General Director of Tearfund UK, an evangelical relief and development agency that believes in professional excellence and spiritual passion. She recently graduated with a Masters in Social Policy and Planning in Developing Countries from the London School of Economics. Her focus was on poverty and social exclusion, education, and disability. Before studying, she spent three years with Latin Link in Bolivia. She traveled widely, working with Bolivian pastors and churches on building projects and with short-term teams from the UK and Ireland. Email: fiona.wilson@tearfund.org.*

Photo: Geoff Crawford / Tearfund

Part 3
Mission

11

Religion and the future of Christianity in the global village

BULUS GALADIMA

Nothing brings into focus the intersection of globalization and religion in the "global village" more clearly than the events of September 11, 2001 ("nine-eleven"). Although powerful, isolated, and "non-religious," or at least privatized in religious matters, the United States is not immune from the effects of the events planned in the remote caves of underdeveloped and religious Afghanistan. The two regions are unavoidably bound to each other.

All of the hijackers and their leader Osama bin Laden believed that their acts were the highest form of devotion to Allah. The slaughter of the "other" was a higher duty (Barber, 2001, p. 9). Todd Beamer, one of the passengers on the plane that crashed in Pennsylvania, said the Lord's Prayer before the ill-fated attempt to overpower the hijackers on the plane. Following "nine-eleven," "God bless America" signs were displayed everywhere, God-talk has been in vogue, and thousands of public and private prayers have been said in America and elsewhere in the West. In the wake of "nine-eleven," places of religious worship were full across America. In their most desperate hour of need, people turned to God. In many Arab countries and among Muslims around the world, there was jubilation and praise to Allah over the death of the thousands in New York and the Pentagon.

There is a stark contrast between the comforts of Osama bin Laden's cave office in Afghanistan and a corporate office in downtown Manhattan, New York. However, the two offices are similar in terms of the technological gadgets that fill them. They can be connected in a matter of seconds, thereby making them neighbors in the global village. Though globalization is thrusting people together and creating a "village," the inhabitants of this village are not cohering or connected the way neighbors are connected in a traditional village. The adhesive to bond people together is missing or at the very best is weak.

Globalization and religion are pervasive. We cannot escape their influence. The world is indeed a global village, and religion plays a very important role in understanding this village. It defines and shapes relationships between the individuals and nations making up the village.

In "Paradise": Life in a Village

I lived in a village. A village is small. Everyone knows everyone else. News spreads very fast. Life is slow and simple, though not necessarily easy. The safety of the community is of paramount concern and is the responsibility of one and all, because the members of the village share a common fate. Yet every member of the community retains his or her personal identity, along with specific and sometimes even unique roles. To fail to participate in the welfare of the community is to die slowly.

In the village, heroes are those who engage in self-sacrificial acts for the benefit of all, not those who promote themselves and look out only for their own interests. The security the village gives entails vulnerability. There is no anonymity. Religion is often homogeneous. Religion is tightly woven into the fabric of the village or community. Every event in life, from birth to death, is religious. These things are true for many communities around the world. Hopkins et al. (2001, p. 1) observe:

For the majority of cultures around the world, religion thoroughly permeates and decisively affects the everyday rituals of survival and hope. Reflected in diverse spiritual customs, sacred symbols, and indigenous worship styles, global religions are permanent constituents of human life. In fact, for most of the world's peoples, religion helps to construct the public life.

Today, globalization is mounting an assault on the centuries-old village lifestyle of many communities around the world.

"Paradise" Fragmented: Life in the Global Village

The characteristics of a village illuminate our understanding of the current global context. The global village is similar in size to the traditional village, but it is fundamentally different in value and composition. No nations or individuals have the option of isolating themselves from the emerging global community. Events halfway around the globe have an influence on people elsewhere. Failure to engage the global situation means a slow death. **Globalization**[1] refers to the phenomenon of interconnectedness of people and the world through technology, thereby facilitating the emergence of a common economic system and values.

Geographical barriers are overcome through technology. News spreads fast to and from every part of the world. However, life in the global village is quite complex. There are many options available, thereby undermining the security of an individual's identity. The way of constituting identity in the global village is defined by the values of globalization. Indigenous culture, although still powerful, is not the primary source of identity. A new form of human identity is emerging. This identity is shaped by the values of the global village as chiefly derived from economics. Yet for many, religion still plays a critical role in human integration and in helping make sense of the world.

Globalization is one of the logical consequences of modernity. Modernity has resulted in the spread of some vital institutions and ways of thinking, such as a capitalist economy, the nation-state, democracy, linear scientific reasoning, and modern technology, from the West to the rest of the world (Beyer, 1994, p. 8). Globalization means that "people, cultures, societies, and civilizations previously more or less isolated from one another are now in regular and almost unavoidable contact" (Beyer, 1994,

p. 2). Although globalization is viewed with suspicion by many non-Western cultures (NECF, 2001; Stackhouse, Dearborn, & Paeth, 2000, p. 2) and is seen as just another Western propaganda ploy for domination, those cultures cannot escape globalization's omnipresent influence. It is pervasive. Globalization is pulling the world together, revealing how interconnected we are. At the same time, it is also disrupting normalcy in many cultures so that, although they are unable to resist it, many cannot warmly embrace it (Stackhouse, Dearborn, & Paeth, 2000, p. 3). Globalization introduces crises not only at personal, tribal, and local village levels, but also at a national level (NECF Malaysia). Conflict between indigenous cultures and modernity/globalization can result in catastrophic crises, as in Chinua Achebe's *Things Fall Apart*,[2] in which the hero, Okonkwo, kills the symbol of the disruption and then kills himself because he cannot accommodate the changes.

Rapid change is a feature of globalization. There is a great concern about the direction in which the change is heading, who determines the change, and for what purpose. Beyer (1994, p. 3) says that power is more important than meaning in globalization. But for Christians, I believe that the primary concern ought not to be power but meaning. The ontological concern is of

---

[1] There are as many definitions of globalization as there are scholars. In this chapter, I have chosen to go with a descriptive definition.

[2] Chinua Achebe's *Things Fall Apart* is a classic African novel that captures the crisis that results when an African society comes in contact with modernity. Okonkwo, the hero, wants to stop this influence and save his village. He kills the court messenger, the symbol of this interruption of their peaceful society, but then he discovers he cannot stop the onslaught, so he commits suicide.

great import, because it addresses the question of who we are and what we are becoming.

Globalization has serious implications for human identity. The fast pace of life and the wide dissemination of news and information make us conscious of other people and religions around the world, even when we do not want to be. They increase the range of options of how individuals can constitute themselves in the global village. In fact, as Kurtz (1995, p. 12) notes, "Cultural and social diversity are the distinguishing characteristics of modern life. Individuals or groups in the 'global village' can choose their religious orientations from a variety of options rather than simply accepting the specific" one assigned to them by their family or their society. Unfortunately, the global systems do not tell us how to make the right and the best choice between the myriad of options available. At times, the subsystems may even lead in mutually contradictory directions. Beyer (1994, pp. 61-62) explains, "For instance, loyalties to one's career may conflict with health considerations, family ties, or political inclinations.... The result is often a problem of identity or self-description for individuals."

The fast pace of life in the global village is also creating a sense of disconnectedness, fragmentation, and homelessness—the "global soul," as Iyer (2000) phrases it. This person is everywhere but not at home anywhere. On the same day, the "global soul" could wake up in Bombay, have breakfast in Paris, lunch in Nairobi, dinner in the sky, catch a late night movie in Chicago, and attend the carnival in Rio

de Janeiro the next day. It gets all of these experiences without a proper context in which to integrate them or sufficient time to immerse itself fully in order to become a part of the various communities. It is always transient.

The fuel that drives globalization is economic profit. This is the prime value of this new world order. It creates a consumerism that it also seeks to satisfy (Netland, 2000, p. 3).[3] The impact of the new economic institutions reaches far and wide, resulting in new perspectives and even changes in families, tribes, and nations, changing their politics and culture forever. Schweiker (2000, p. 32) states, "The global economy is a contact between culture and society: the economy is one of the social spheres and yet it also generates and mediates cultural meanings in the global field. This is especially true of transnational corporations."

The global village is similar to the traditional village in that its members are close, yet it is very dissimilar in that they are not intimate but rather are growing apart. How can this condition be remedied?

In Search of a Lighthouse: Religion in the Global Village

Religion is a universal human phenomenon. There is a close relation between religion and culture. As Kurtz (1995, p. 20) articulates, religious traditions are central in "defining norms, values, and meaning; in providing the ethical underpinning for collective life; and in forging the cultural tools for cooperation and conflict."

---

[3] For a full discussion, see Netland (2001).

Religion is indispensable for understanding human beings and life in the global village. It is also critical for understanding the transition into the modern world and ultimately life in the new world global village. Globalization has greatly affected religion. Not only has it rearranged the environment within which religion operates; it has also affected the constitution of religion itself. In the one instance, it has created issues which religion must address; in the other, it has created values which it wants religion to adopt.

The modern and postmodern worlds challenge "religious traditional beliefs with scientific critiques and competing views of the world" (Kurtz, 1995, p. 19). This results in a relativistic and pluralistic environment. Pluralism in all things, including religion, is a common feature of the global village. Different religions are made "uneasy bedfellows" in the global village through the migration of people and the transmission of and access to information. In the village where I grew up, I was aware of just three religions—Christianity, Islam, and African Traditional Religions. But it is not unusual today for a child in elementary school in an urban area to have classmates belonging to all of the major world religions. Those in secondary school not only have classmates from these religions; they also have friends who are nice people who are agnostics and other friends who are atheists, elevating the problem to another level. Furthermore, they have access to information about the various religions on the Internet. They often ask questions that are intelligent and not easily dismissible regarding these different religions. At the university level, students are not only taught positions that are against traditional religious beliefs, but the traditional beliefs are disparaged and ridiculed. Young people today come in contact with religions and ideas about which their parents know little or nothing. This situation heightens the need for religious answers.

In the West, religion is considered a private matter rather than public. The global village structurally favors privatization of religion, but this does not imply that religion has no function in the public sphere. Although traditional religious forms in a secular state are no longer definitive for the whole society, they are powerful in the lives of individuals and groups who are often principal actors in the society.

Resurgence of fundamentalism in Islam, Hinduism, Christianity, and Buddhism is one of the strongest indicators of the various reactions to modernity and globalization. Some religious people want to conserve the gains made by their religion and prevent the intrusion of the "others" and the corruption that accompanies modernity. In their resentment of globalization and its "numbing and neutering uniformities" (Barber, 2001, p. 9), they call for a return to the basic or fundamental teaching of their religion. Robertson and Garrett (1991, pp. xix-xx) argue that the "universalizing tendencies of globalization" often lead individuals and groups to take "extreme actions in order to demonstrate their particularistic 'place' amid the empirical pluralism of the international arena."

Unlike in the global village, anonymity was impossible in the traditional village. In the village, each person was an open book. It was impossible to be private. This was one of the prices of belonging to the community. Members of the village saw through hypocrisy. One's walk and talk had to be in harmony. This virtue is seriously challenged in the modern context by the possibility of anonymity and privatization of religion.

Not only does globalization affect the expression of religion; in its extreme case, it posits itself as a form of religion to replace other religions. Hopkins et al. (2001, p. 8) maintain that globalization and its driving force constitute a religion. The challenge for Christianity in the global village is the myriad of "lighthouses" presenting themselves as legitimate. How can Christianity gain a voice in the midst of all these contenders?

In Search of a Platform: Christianity in the Global Village

The church is and has always been global in character, composition, and mission. At its inception at Pentecost, the church instantaneously became a global community (Acts 2), comprised of people from different nations. It is still a global community, although the demography is changing. At the beginning of the 20th century, 80% of Christians were in the West. Today, more than 60% of Christians live in the non-Western world (Kurtz, 1995, p. 22).

The new global environment and its structures encourage materialism and disrupt traditional ways of life, quickly eroding cultural structures. The primary drive of globalization is economics, and the goal of economics is profit. Morality is considered only if it has a bearing on profit-making. Thus, companies will often engage in charity work, because it is good publicity for the company, and the publicity will ultimately translate into more business.[4] Globalization feels no remorse over this situation. Barber (2001, pp. 7-8) says global economics is not committed to rescuing civic virtues, nor is it pursuing equality and justice. However, it is clear that economics without morality is empty and culminates in chaos. The recent Enron and WorldCom financial mismanagement scandals proved this.

Ethics and moral values are now admissible concepts and worthy of mention openly. Tolson (2002, p. 56) in *US News & World Report* states that scholars believe that "the market-dominant minorities" must be modest and generous towards the "ethnic majorities." Business schools now take the teaching of ethics seriously.

Barber (2001, pp. xxviii, xxx) does not think that the global economic system has the capability "to support the values and institutions associated with civic culture, religion, and the family." He suggests that this can be accomplished only through the general will of global citizens. This is similar to the aim of the United Nations, which has met with limited success.

Beyer's (1994, p. 71) proposal that globalization also provides fertile ground for the renewed public influ-

---

[4] Toshiba, the General Electric of Japan, boasted in its 1992 annual report that "as good corporate citizens" they "do [their] part to ensure that progress continues within the world community," but citizenship in that community—whether Japanese or global—is hemmed in on every side by limits set by the demands of profitability. Profitability, in turn, is driven by sales, which in 1992 totaled $25 billion (Barber, 2001, p. 24).

Equipping the Church

1. How ought the church to teach its members to respond to the new global environment?

2. How should the church carry out its responsibility of evangelization or mission in such a context?

3. How should the church go about equipping its members, who are sometimes major players/participants in the global economic context, to make morally sound decisions in an environment bereft of moral and spiritual convictions?

ence of religion holds more promise. Though in the West this might seem like a novel idea, in most parts of the world, religion is vital for public life (Hopkins et al., 2001, p. 1). Christians in the West, along with other religious people, can encourage the restoration of prayer in schools. In non-Western cultures, Christians need to become united and provide the necessary funds to hire qualified teachers. Society cannot cohere without a strong moral conviction. Thus the idea of religion in the society should be welcome.

Authentic Christian response

Beyer's suggestion on how religion can be useful in the global village is instructive. He says the usefulness comes not in active individuals, but in religious institutions. The church, then, ought to find a service which it alone provides. Beyer (1994, p. 80) asserts, "If 'pure' religion is at a disadvantage in modern global society, if there is pressure toward the increasing privatization of religion, then the solution lies in finding effective religious 'applications,' not in more religious commitment and practice." He states further,

"What is required for publicly influential religion is, at minimum, that religious leaders have control over a service that is clearly indispensable in today's world as do, for instance, health professionals, political leaders, scientific or business experts" (Beyer, 1994, p. 71).

We must move from religious function to religious performance. Religious function deals with aspects of devotion, worship, the cure of souls, and the search for salvation. Religious performance deals with the application of religion to problems generated but not solved in other systems, such as the economic, political, and social systems. Such application provides validation of the Christian message. James addresses this issue in chapter 2 of his epistle, in the well-known passage on the dichotomy between faith and works. Religious function is the basis of religious performance.

There are numerous issues to which the church must find ways of responding, including poverty, HIV/AIDS, racism, sexism, political and economic instability, war, care for the aged and destitute, building a strong moral society, responding to the moral poverty created by wealth around the world, economic poverty, political oppression, family estrangement, environmental degradation, and personal identity. In addition, the changes in biotechnology dealing with genetic engineering or re-engineering, the environment, and the boundaries of life and death deserve an informed Christian response in order for the church to be an effective witness to the gospel. Responding compassionately and authentically to these issues is one of the major tests for Christianity in the world. Authentic response comes at a high price, though: sacrificial Christian living.

According to Kurtz (1995, p. xii), "Religious pluralism will be a necessary precondition of the 'global village' for the seeable future." Many children today grow up in pluralistic religious contexts. They hear competing accounts of creation and salvation. This was rare or even unheard of in most places half a century ago. But today it is taken for granted. How can we coexist peacefully with other religions? What ought to be the basis of interreligious dialogue and cooperation? The church must develop an adequate response to many of the other major world religions, such as Islam, Hinduism, Buddhism, and Confucianism. The church no longer mediates these religions to its members; rather, the followers of these religions interact directly with Christians.

This is not merely a description of a pluralistic context but a new way of perceiving truth. It calls to question the validity of absolute standards. These competing voices are going to affect the worldviews and ethics of all peoples. What type of effect is there going to be? How can the church participate effectively in shaping the emerging worldviews, global morality, social ideals, or patterns? At the very least, it must participate in shaping what Christians come to believe in the global village.

What should be our responsibility as a church to the social evils in societies? How can we strive for justice and peace when laws of men conflict with the law of God? What is the Christian response to the conflicts that exist in the world and the violation of human rights? The United Nations is doing something, but it is obvious that it is impotent because it is plagued by the major ideological differences of its member nations. How do we cooperate across faiths on these issues? This is an important issue in a world rife with interreligious conflicts.

Identity issues

Apart from the quest for food, shelter, and clothing, probably the next greatest human need is that of belonging. Human beings have a dire need for identity. Failure to resolve this matter could undermine all the other needs, suggesting that the need for identity and belonging is more fundamental than easily meets the eye. Globalization appears to hold great promise in its desire to spread a universal human culture and brotherhood. It appears to transcend the various other forms of identity such as nation, religion, and tribe.

Challenges confronting the church come both from the society and within. The church's encounter with globalization reveals some of its unbiblical assumptions and practices. The church is still highly homogeneous in a world that is becoming increasingly heterogeneous. We need to learn to live as a global church, but race, ethnicity, class, sex, and nation still divide us. The divisions within the church are a stumbling block to many unbelievers. Many Christians find their primary identity in their culture, ethnicity, or class rather than in their commitment to Christ. Racism and ethnicity are the greatest tragedies in the church today. Many African Americans turn away from Christianity because of racism. In many Two-Thirds World countries, churches are segregated along tribal, ethnic, or caste lines. The church must find ways of defining Christian identity that will transcend these competing forms of identity that command primary allegiance.

Globalization and missions

The church is called not only to endure hardship for Christ, but also to propagate the good news of the gospel to a lost world. How can the church use globalization to advance missions? The face of mission is changing very fast. "Cross-cultural" is no longer geographically defined. In most urban areas, the mission field is only a 15-minute drive away. Many corporations are multicultural. The mission field has been brought to our doorsteps. It is in many workplaces. How can Christians be equipped to carry their faith into their workplaces in a society that claims that religion is a private matter?

Particularly in the West, there is a resurgence of a new type of skepticism with which Christian mission will need to contend. In the non-Western world, there is a resurgence of indigenous faiths, even in places where Christian-

ity is present and strong. This pluralistic religious context has led to a universal awareness being combined with an interest in spirituality, to create a unique situation. However, the type of spirituality emerging is individualistic and private rather than communal and public, and it is greatly influenced by the Eastern religions. How can Christianity be a party to this new spirituality without losing its distinctiveness? The global values of pluralism, tolerance, and inclusivism pose a serious challenge to the Christian message. To preach an exclusive gospel is considered as intolerance.

The task of missions is daunting. Only through cross-cultural cooperation will it be accomplished. Increasingly, missionaries are from the non-Western world rather than from the West. In fact, by 2000, missionaries from the Two-Thirds World outnumbered Western missionaries. In keeping with this shift, Christian mission in the global village must be characterized by partnership rather than paternalism.

Harmony, equality, and partnership are needed in Christian mission today. All hands must be on deck to reach the world. There are more people today who have not heard the gospel message than there were at the beginning of the last century. We must have a global vision. This is God's intention. It is only as a global church that we can effectively evangelize the world. To do this, the church needs to explore the multinational corporations' method of doing business, in order to cooperate to reach the whole world.

The Church and TNCs

1. What is the role of the local church in the face of the mighty transnational corporations (TNCs)?

2. TNCs are powerful, and they control economy. They are more powerful than some developing nations.[5] Although these corporations are faceless, they are controlled by people. How can the church influence the leaders of TNCs to make God-honoring (not Christian) decisions?

3. Many leaders of TNCs do not go to church. How can the church reach them?

4. How can churches cooperate cross-culturally, both locally and internationally?

Recovering "Paradise": New Christianity in the Global Village

Globalization gives us tremendous opportunities for advancing the cause of the gospel. The church must take advantage of the new technologies in order to take the gospel into places still unreached.

The pluralistic environment in which we live affords us the exciting privilege of reaching the whole world with the gospel. Some Christians might be intimidated; others might despair in light of the magnitude of the task. But the story of the church in Acts 2 should serve as an encouragement. Through the enablement of the Holy Spirit, when Peter spoke, each of the peoples heard him speak their language. Human ingenuity is not going to accomplish the purpose of God. Besides, this task is daunting. Human tactics and mechanics might give the illusion of success, but the product will lack the power and fruit that characterize faith in Christ. Only through the Holy Spirit can we speak the gospel in the "language" of the people around us and bring forth fruit that will remain. Dearborn (2000, p. 213) reminds us, "Only in Christ can a path to unity be found that transcends ethnicity, economics, social status, and class—without suppressing differences in a linguistic or social conformity. Only in Christ can diversity enhance unity—without furthering fragmentation."

Christianity is growing fast in the non-Western world—Africa, Asia, and Latin America. In these regions, it has a unique opportunity to participate in reconstituting society. Christianity has an appeal to the majority of the people.

---

[5] The UNDP report of 1992 stated, "The richest 20% of the world's population receives 82.7% of the total world income, while the poorest 20% receives only 1.4%.... The richest 225 individuals in the world constitute a combined wealth of more than $1 trillion. This is equal to the annual income of the poorest 47% of the world's population. And the three richest people on earth own assets surpassing the combined gross domestic product of the 48 least developed countries" (Hopkins et al., 2001, pp. 10-11).

Believers in these regions should be encouraged and empowered to develop a new spirituality that is not Western but biblical. Western spirituality is not fitting for them, because it does not respond adequately to their context. Instead of recreating and forcing Western spirituality upon the church in other parts of the world,[6] Western missionaries ought to encourage new believers to trust the leading of the Holy Spirit in their lives to respond to the needs in their context. Through the enablement of the Holy Spirit, the new non-Western churches will refresh those from the West.

The church can choose to respond to globalization in one of three ways. First, it can sharply reject all aspects of globalization as a worldly phenomenon (a fundamentalist type of response). Second, the church can accept globalization's relativism and pluralism, leading to a fundamental transformation of religious beliefs (a liberal type of response). Third, there can be an honest engagement of globalization's challenges in the light of the eternal truths of the Christian message. In order for this last possibility to happen, we must identify the core of the gospel. The seeming facile nature of this task is deceptive. It requires tact, creativity, and especially the enablement of the Holy Spirit.

References

Barber, B. R. (2001). *Jihad vs. McWorld*. New York, NY: Ballantine Books.

Barrett, D. (Ed.). (1982). *World Christian encyclopedia: A comparative study of churches and religions in the modern world, AD 1900-2000*. New York, NY: Oxford University Press.

Beyer, P. (1994). *Religion and globalization*. Thousand Oaks, CA: Sage Publications.

Evans, A. F., Evans, R. A., & Roozen, D. A. (Eds.). (1993). *The globalization of theological education*. Maryknoll, NY: Orbis Books.

Dearborn, T. (2000). A global future for local churches. In M. L. Stackhouse, T. Dearborn, & S. Paeth (Eds.), *The local church in a global era: reflections for a new century*. Grand Rapids, MI: Wm. B. Eerdmans.

Featherstone, M. (Ed.). (1990). *Global culture: Nationalism, globalization and modernity*. Newbury Park, CA: Sage Publications.

Hopkins, D. N., Lorentzen, L. A., Mendieta, E., & Batstone, D. (Eds.). (2001). *Religions/globalizations: Theories and cases*. Durham, NC and London, UK: Duke University Press.

Iyer, P. (2000, February/March). The global soul: Jet lag, shopping malls, and the search for home. *Civilization*, pp. 72-77.

---

[6] Seminaries, Western theological books, and Western funds are all ways that the Western church uses to advance and even force its views upon the emergent non-Western church, thus stifling the creativity of the Holy Spirit. Often the Western church assumes that its financial strength places it in the position to play the role of the Holy Spirit in the emerging churches, determining which projects are good for churches and which ones are bad. In the early church, some of the creative ideas came from the non-Jewish church. In Acts 11:19-21, the Gentile believers reached the Greeks. In Acts 13, Paul and Barnabas—Jewish believers—were sent out by a Gentile church. These incidents show what the Holy Spirit is able to accomplish if we listen to him.

Kurtz, L. (1995). *Gods in the global village: The world's religions in sociological perspective.* Thousand Oaks, CA: Pine Forge Press.

NECF Malaysia. (2001). *Engagement or isolation? A Malaysian Christian perspective on globalisation.* Selangor Darul Ehsan, Malaysia: National Evangelical Christian Fellowship.

Netland, H. (2000, Fall). Missions and the culture of modernity. *Trinity World Forum.* Deerfield, IL: Trinity Evangelical Divinity School.

———. (2001). *Encountering religious pluralism: The challenge to Christian faith and mission.* Downers Grove, IL: InterVarsity Press.

Pittman, D. A., Habito, R. L. F., & Muck, T. C. (Eds.). (1996). *Ministry and theology in global perspective: Contemporary challenges for the church.* Grand Rapids, MI: Wm. B. Eerdmans.

Robertson, R., & Garrett, W. R. (1991). *Religion and global order.* New York, NY: Paragon House.

Schreiter, R. (1997). *The new catholicity: Theology between the global and the local.* Maryknoll, NY: Orbis Books.

Schweiker, W. (2000). The church as an academy of justice: Moral responsibility in the world of mammon. In M. L. Stackhouse, T. Dearborn, & S. Paeth (Eds.), *The local church in a global era: reflections for a new century.* Grand Rapids, MI: Wm. B. Eerdmans.

Stackhouse, M. L., Dearborn, T., & Paeth, S. (Eds.). (2000). *The local church in a global era: reflections for a new century.* Grand Rapids, MI: Wm. B. Eerdmans.

Tolson, J. (2002, October 21). World disorder? Rethinking globalism and the need for modesty. *US News & World Report,* pp. 56-57.

Tomilson, S. (1999). *Globalization and culture.* Chicago, IL: University of Chicago Press.

Wilson, B. (1976). Aspects of secularization in the West. *Japanese Journal of Studies, 3/4,* pp. 259-276.

Bulus Y. Galadima, Ph.D., *is a lecturer in historical and African theology. He was former Dean at Jos ECWA Theological Seminary, Nigeria. He has served as a pastor in Nigeria and USA. He is currently with BEE International and is also an adjunct Professor at Trinity Evangelical Divinity School, Deerfield, Illinois. He is married with four children. Email: brgaladima@ earthlink.net.*

12

Can the global replace the local? Globalization and contextualization

Marcelo Vargas

What is globalization? For Sabina, an indigenous vegetable seller in an open-air market in the Bolivian capital, globalization means using a mobile telephone for her sales pitch, while sitting on the floor speaking a mixture of Spanish and Aymará, her mother tongue. For her, globalization also means having a son at university who daily surfs the Internet to be informed, to communicate, and to investigate. Further, globalization means being part of an extended family that has members who have gone in search of a "better life" in the United States, Brazil, and Argentina. And it means doing trade with a businessman who plans to take his products beyond national borders. For Sabina's neighbour, who also sells vegetables in the market, globalization has a different form and content. Each person imagines globalization in his or her own way (Garcia Canclini, 1999, p. 12). How one imagines globalization is one thing, though; how it affects each individual is another.

There are good things in globalization, of course. Globalization has intensified the interchange between societies by way of technological advances and communications. It has lessened distances and has caused the fall of seemingly insurmountable barriers that separated the human race. There exists in globalization a liberating character. While it is true that the benefits of globalization cannot be neglected, globalization's oppressive character is what has the most impact on the vast majority of the world, because the law of globalization is the law of the strongest.

Globalization is not a scientific nor an economic paradigm; neither is it a political or a cultural paradigm (Garcia Canclini, 1999, p. 47). Globalization is not a unique process; it is a result of many movements—some harmonious, others contradictory. Globalization invites integration, but this invitation has not been beneficial for all. When global economic liberalization is submitted to private interests, the problems and conflicts are aggravated—unemployment, violence, poverty, drug trafficking, pollution, etc. Globalization has caused the growth of social and economic inequality. Each year, reports from international organizations that fight against poverty say that the battle is being lost. The policies of the IMF (International Monetary Fund) have achieved destructive results, producing unemployment, misery, and death. An identical packet of imposed economic measures that is applied to all nations, without taking into account the history, culture, and context of each of them, is degrading and unworthy (Ramachandra, 1996, p. 123).

To refer to globalization is to say, for example, that the market economy dominates the world economy (Paredes, 2000, p. 195). This capitalist economy has been formed, developed, and promoted by the petty interests of people who hold unstoppable and devastating political and economic power. Globalization is the invasion of something foreign into local lifestyles, which are essentially different. In the beginning, globalization appeared to be a blessing, but it is a blessing that has been transformed into a curse. It offers very attractive and convincing advantages, but in the background it brings with it forms of domination and oppression.

The forces of today's system are destructive for all. What prevails in First World countries today is the ephemeral. In these societies, people live under the empire of the ephemeral (Lipovetsky, 1987), and the paradox is that the more that these societies turn towards the spectacular and the frivolous, the more their anxiety, worry, and depression increase. The cult of the body, consumerism, and well-being in these places is possible, thanks to the economic rules that in other places bring poverty. It is evident that there has not been democratisation of access to consumerism, but that there has been a manifestation of an ideology of consumption that has invaded cultures.

In Latin America, 12 multinational corporations, in conjunction with their governments, control much of the economy, perpetuating global economic injustice and consequently provoking and increasing social problems. Worse yet, the multinationals don't give account to anybody as to their true motives or the inhuman results of their policies in the lives of the poor majority. Bolivia, for example, is a country extremely rich in natural resources per square kilometre. In spite of this wealth, 70% of the population is poor, and of this percentage, half live below the bread line. Here the policy is to submit to the economic interests of the richest, whether they are nationals or foreigners. For example, recently the richest man in Bolivia was elected president of the country; this is the second time that he has assumed "the throne."

In Bolivia, the geographic heart of South America, the basic services of water and electricity, as well as the telephone system, modes of mass communication, petroleum, natural gas, and a large part of the agricultural production, are at present in the hands of British, German, Spanish, Italian, French, and North American multinational corporations. What is the principal motivation of these companies? It is the profit of easy money. The Bolivian economy, politics, and society are totally vulnerable to the will of the international market.

The vast majority of people who live on the earth are not conscious of the historic processes or the philosophy from which the globalization phenomenon originated and has expanded. There have been processes similar to globalization in the past, but these have been localized cases with a speed much slower than that of the present phenomenon. Today's civilisation is different from that of the past, because it is the first to have a truly global range.

The essence of globalization is contrary to the biblical mandate. The gospel of Jesus Christ must be proclaimed and lived in a unique way in each historical moment and in each cultural situation. The expansion of God's kingdom should be global, but its incarnation should be local. Christian mission should reach all the corners of the earth, but the application and living out of the gospel of Jesus Christ must be according to the context.

In Accordance With the Context

The seed and the plant pot

An illustration that helps us to understand the practice of contextualization is that of the seed and the plant pot. The gospel is like a seed that must and can be sown everywhere. When the seed of the gospel is sown in Palestine, the plant that grows has the identity and character of Palestine. If the gospel is sown in Rome, London, or Mexico, similar plants are obtained, but they are peculiar to these places. The sower who takes the seed from one place to the other doesn't have to take the pot as well. This precious seed is not permitted to be transported along with the soil; it travels alone, because it can conserve all of its essence but can also contextualize itself completely.

Contextualization badly done could convert itself into accommodation, acculturation, domestication, or syncretism. This is why the Uruguayan Mortimer Arias affirms:

> The relation between the gospel and culture has to be dynamic and dialectic, just the same as the seed that grows, taking of the soil and choosing those nutritive elements that are compatible with the life of the plant without losing its own nature.

The incarnation

In 1974, René Padilla (1986, p. 91), at the International Congress on World Evangelization held in Lausanne, Switzerland, raised the following questions:

> In what measure has the geographical extension of the gospel been accompanied by the

same type of incarnation in the multiplicity of human cultures? Can we affirm that Christians around the world are demonstrating that the gospel is a universal message, whose relevance is not limited to the Western world?

Meditating on these questions takes us to a paradigm that is even more complete: the incarnation. The infinite love of God for creation, especially for human beings, man and woman, led to the incarnation of God himself in Jesus Christ and his solution, his salvation. The content of God's love was love incarnate. This aspect was very important, but of equal importance to the content was the inseparable way in which God did it. He became man and lived like the common Jews of the first century. He dressed in the same clothes, spoke the same language, ate the same foods, and worked in the same jobs. He was a well-contextualized missionary, and he continues to be our best model. This is how the Peruvian anthropologist Tito Paredes (2000, p. 204) expresses it:

> Jesus assumed a language, a system of beliefs and values, a way of relating with himself and with others, and a way of living day to day in human space and time. Jesus affirmed and valued the Jewish culture as a living space and mission; we can deduce from this that the gospel affirms the diverse cultures of the earth. Therefore the gospel must convert all the culture for Christ.

Jesus' disciples

Following the example of Jesus, his disciples need to incarnate the gospel in all the peoples and cultures of the earth. Nuances of Christianity would be not only Jewish, Greek, Anglo-Saxon, or North American, but also Quechua, Aymará, and Mestizo. Christian workers or missionaries must not be mistakenly presenting their culture as if it were the gospel or as if it were like the identical packages of measures from the IMF for countries in debt. A photocopy of theological thought and missionary methods, originally created and thought out in North America, does not achieve relevance in other parts of the world, because the elements are out of context—they have another culture and history.

The Holy Spirit

How can Jesus' disciples incarnate the gospel? What makes contextualization possible? It is the manifestation of the Holy Spirit in the midst of the people of God. Culture is transformed when the gospel is incarnated by the church through the action of the Holy Spirit. What God wants is for the gospel to be incarnated in the church and, through the church, in every cultural-historic context. If we look at what God has done throughout the Bible, we find that the Spirit of God has always sought out man in his own particular reality in time and space.

Authentic and false contextualization

Can each of us distinguish between authentic and false contextualization? Have we made the proclamation and the living out of the gospel an encounter between God and his creation? From the Third World, Dr. Shoki Coe from Taiwan (as cited in Anderson, 1993) writes:

> A careful distinction must be made between authentic and false forms of contextualization.

False contextualization is a step towards uncritical accommodation, a type of cultural faith. Authentic contextualization is always prophetic, which invariably arises from a genuine encounter between the word of God and his world, and advances towards the goal of challenging and changing the situation through being deeply enrooted in, and in agreement with, a given historical moment.

Unity in diversity

Globalization has expanded with giant steps and has created a spirit contrary to authentic contextualization. Now that believers are from all parts of the world and the church has been converted into a world community, now is the time that the universality of the gospel must show itself to be free of ties to any culture or subculture in particular. We must work so that the multiform knowledge of God will manifest itself, allowing for the growth of unity in the diversity that is represented by all of the disciples of Jesus Christ. We must make Christ incarnate in our situations. We must be full of the Holy Spirit and obedient to the word of God and must free ourselves from imperialisms and ethnocentrisms.

The local and global together

To write from Bolivia, a country as culturally and socially diverse as is Latin America as a whole, is to live with a strong indigenous culture, together with a society that marches to the beat of the giddy changes (capitalism, industry, technology) that modernism has provoked throughout the world. Bolivia is representative of what Latin America

is as a continent. Social, political, and economic injustice abound, in part due to selfishness and internal corruption, but also because of the tremendous global inequalities, injustice, and moral degradation.

Poverty

If there is something that springs to mind in my context, it is the poverty that exists in the midst of most Latin American people. It is not a problem to recognize that poverty exists. Neither is it difficult to accept the idea that as followers of Jesus Christ, we must have a simple lifestyle. What is often lacking is the ability to evaluate regularly what we really do have. And it is difficult to accept and recognize that poverty, to a large extent, is a consequence of the injustice of the global system. At the heart of the current world system is the free market, which is characterized by the continuous accumulation of wealth as an end in itself (Ramachandra, 2000, p. 10). The idolatrous love of money is the beginning of all the evils that bind not only humanity but the whole of creation. Now is an opportune moment to free the prophetic voice, echoing what the Bible teaches. Westernised postmodernism, emphatically relativist and consumerist, is a process that in recent decades has already started its own self-destruction. The Bible warns us that every unjust system is consumed by its own corruption and evil.

Ethical challenges

It is crucial for the models of Christian mission that are practiced today that we are conscious of this injustice and the ethical challenges it implies. What can be done by those involved in mission? First, there has to be a turning of one's eyes to oneself, with a sincere desire to make changes in one's attitude and one's conduct. Second, time needs to be set aside to dialogue with members of national churches and with those who are reflecting on the mission of the church in relation to political, social, and economic realities. Third, one should read the best evangelical and non-evangelical authors, especially those from the Third World. Finally, it is necessary to find those points where the theory leads us to themes that are real and true.

Christian mission and globalization

How does Christian mission question globalization? We can see this questioning from two points of view. Firstly, the oppression of the poor by rich nationals and foreigners is advancing without an honest and sincere concern for the situation or for the real and integral needs of the people and their particular way of life. This type of situation is reaching a head now in every one of the politically, socially, and economically weak countries. Secondly, national and multinational corporations practice their actions of exploitation with the consent and help of the national governments, which are both dependent and corrupt. Through what eyes and with what attitude do we see the activities of the multinational corporations? How do we evaluate and condemn them? It is necessary to fulfil the role of the prophet—and not just with words—against the unmeasured expansion of the Western neoliberal economic system.

Previous ways of doing mission must be abandoned and new forms assumed with creativity, faith, and courage. What has been the relationship between the expansion of Western capitalism and today's missionary work in the Third World? To what extent can this relationship be evaluated and changed? What is the role of the church? Who defines this role and carries it out? Up to what point does this role have to be in agreement with the demands of the gospel and with the whole message of the Bible?

Is it possible to have a critical rapprochement based on a biblical and historical vision and not in a given economic, political, and sociological system? An honest review of more than 150 years of missionary work in Latin America affirms with pain that the missionaries and the church have moulded their work more to Western identity than from biblical foundations and the lessons learnt from history. Blessed is the day that the European and North American missionary pioneers came to the Latin American continent to sacrifice their lives for the kingdom of God. What is increasingly evident, though, thanks to historical analysis and evaluation, is that they did it (and some are still doing it) without adaptation to the context and while keeping their Western character. Their missionary task, their work here, brings with it the marks of a worldview foreign to the native.

The Anabaptist model

How strong and knowledgeable was the Anabaptist model of mission at the beginning of the 17th century! These humble pioneers held to a simple way of living. Whatever social system existed, the more they were against giving it the name "Christian." This firm position was accompanied by a conviction with regard to the uniqueness of the people of God and the single nature of their mission. They presupposed the formation of true disciples of Christ and of a church consciously given to him. The church that would conceive itself in this way, whether it is in Latin America or elsewhere, could confront every type of situation with a missionary mind and calling.

Parallels between mission and Western expansion

A careful analysis of history and the current situation under the light of the gospel would help us not to repeat the mistakes of the past, e.g., of responding to the demands of each generation with the resources and the spirit of the world, in place of the overabundant resources of the Word of God. Various authors from the Northern and Southern hemispheres have observed both direct and indirect parallels between missionary development and the expansion of Western modernism, as much in concept as in method.

What will happen to the Third World church that continues to be dependent on Western culture? It will separate from its own culture, reducing faith and Christian experience to concepts and categories foreign to their reality. Their mission is not an extension of the kingdom of God in the mould of the paradigm of the incarnation, but the expansion of a homogenizing cultural Christianity.

Consequences for Mission

We have already given some guidelines regarding the mission of the church in times of globalization, and points of extreme urgency have already been raised. We will now consider missionary work on the field inside changing world structures and international relations. The speed of these changes is great. Often the changes parallel the conflicts that arise and the ways that countries, especially the strong ones, make reforms and confront their crises. The changes that happen are always submitted to the hegemonic strategy of globalization.

Frequently, even with the best intentions of foreign missionaries, their mere presence in our lands is taken as justification of the existing world order. If missionaries accept the existing order passively, or if they reject it and are critical of it, either way their presence is interpreted as active cooperation with the perpetration of the system. The revolutionary aspect of missionary activity is in service embodied in local and national realities, necessities, and interests.

Acceptance and separation

The world of the missionary Paul and that of the early church was the world of Roman dominance. The context that conditioned and influenced the missionary advance was that of the Roman Empire. However, the New Testament does not identify mission with Roman rule. To present himself as a Roman citizen at times brought advantages to Paul—advantages similar to those, in our time, of holding North American, British, or Swiss passports. But the New Testament did not bless or consecrate the Roman Empire and its attempts to globalize; neither was the church put at the disposition of its interests. We should follow the example and principles of this combination of acceptance and separation. Globalization has created a world of opportunities and challenges, but it is at the same time oppressive and dominant. In its character and in its foundation, today's missionary work has to develop a truly biblical attitude in the face of the dominance of the West.

Politics and missionary strategy

How many missionary movements are simply a reflection of the practices of Western dominion? This weakness is not peculiar to the Anglo-Saxon character but to all imperialist practice. The Latin American church has been a witness to the difficulties of missionaries from all parts of the world who come to rural or urban Latin America and do mission that has been moulded by a foreign culture. What needs drastic revision is the uncritical acceptance of a foreign system of thought and behaviour (their dichotomized worldview, the way they organize people, their concept of ownership, their approach to interpersonal relationships, their views on sharing, etc.). These things need to be taken from those who are not only missionaries involved in the day-to-day practices, but who are also involved in forming missionary policies and strategies.

The special nature of mission

It is necessary to discover the special nature of missionary strategies and practice for each place and for each time, as is taught in the Scriptures and in the incarnational model of Jesus. It is necessary that missionary vision and strategies reflect the autochthonous situation according to the will of God, the individual in Christ, and life in community. Something important in mission is the conviction that the presence of the people of God with their culture, their structures, and their practices already

is, in itself, the presence of the new, the presence of the kingdom of God.

The Western church

To be sensitive to the realities of globalization should not mean that the churches of the West should be discouraged or less committed to mission. In the face of the temptation to dominance and intervention from the politically and economically strong countries, believers need to renew their understanding of mission. The possibilities to help are many; they range from facilitating international help to the continuation of sending missionaries who are serious about contextualization.

Selfless service

Another way of doing mission that goes against the presuppositions of Western dominance is for missionaries to serve and invest their lives without expecting any type of personal or institutional gain. "Foreign help" has been converted into a euphemism that covers a multitude of sins in the international relations of today. The truth is that the practice of charity is not synonymous with justice, and to dispense justice would mean that much of the time charity would be unnecessary. The time is now favourable for the Christian community to apply the justice of the kingdom of God within universal dimensions.

Eschatology

Another important aspect is that of eschatology. Biblical eschatology should shape mission in the age of globalization. Jesus' life was not shaped by the categories of success as understood by the world. He was content to fail from a human point of view, when this required testifying to the truth and following the way of obedience to God. Through obedience, Jesus' mission was successful and came to be universal. The mission of the church is similar. Many times, the church seems to be a total failure in human eyes, but in this way it is being faithful and obedient. Until Christ returns, his church, as in all past generations, will continue to be rejected, persecuted, and suffering, because it will not be shaped by the spirit of the current system.

Western values and the kingdom of God

The gospel should be contextualized. We must avoid falling into the subtle trap of equating Western values with the reign of God. With a prophetic voice of renouncement and with a life of austerity, we must make it clear that we don't think that material prosperity, according to Western models, is a "sign" of the kingdom of God. If we believe that prosperity is important, we will be committing a grave error and will be limiting our understanding of the mission of the church in the world.

An example of a prosperity mindset is seen in the Latin American cities preferred by missionaries. These are Cochabamba in Bolivia, Quito in Ecuador, and San José in Costa Rica. In these beautiful cities, there exists such a concentration of foreign evangelicals that it has brought the attention of social scientists, who have studied the case with much interest. Why have these places been converted into places of preference, as opposed to others? Missionaries opt to live in Cochabamba, Quito, and San José for the advantages they offer: comfort, climate, and accessibility. These values are analysed from the optic of a Western lifestyle: shopping centres, tarmac roads, supermarkets, airports, bilingual schools, large houses, etc., are all very attractive. Missionaries come with religious motives, but the effects of their stay are cultural, economic, and social. Without exaggeration, the presence of large numbers of missionaries in these cities has caused a rise in prices for things such as house rentals, buildings, and private school fees.

Contemporary missiology

Obedience to the Bible should come to shape our understanding and praxis of social justice. If we do not obey the Bible, we will make the Christian movement equivalent to capitalist theory and practice. Without any real reference to social justice, we will only end up distorting good theology and the missionary task. In view of the fact that modernism has already arrived in practically every corner of the earth, contemporary missiology should pay much attention to how the church brings to a head its mission in places where the utopia of capitalism is generating antisocial changes that are a production line of misery.

False gods

Our beloved lands, as much in the secular world as in the religious, are found to be heavily impregnated with false gods that have enslaved their followers and caused suffering and misery everywhere. Many of these gods have infiltrated the church, weakening its testimony. Christian mission is constantly accompanied by antichristian elements—idols with weak foundations that should be recognised and brought to the light of an obedience centred on the cross. Everywhere the cross should be preached and imitated, unmasking the rich, the proud, the powerful, and the religious.

The Lordship of Christ

True mission implies living under the Lordship of Christ and also implies preaching against idols. No missionaries are true missionaries if they do not live and announce the gospel in such a way that leaves it clear that they do not worship Mammon or Caesar. Mission is based in the uniqueness of the gospel, in the model of mission of Jesus and in his victory. Christians, perhaps, should be a scandal as much to the right as to the left. But we should assure ourselves that the scandal is the scandal of the cross and not the scandal of the Western or American dominance or any other human political system.

The spirit of globalization

As in the first century, when Paul was involved in mission within the context of the Roman Empire, Christians should use the opportunities provided by globalization, without falling into the spirit of the global age. The spirit of globalization is contrary to the values of the kingdom of God, which are justice, peace, and love, in every time and place. As servants of God, we should be respecting and promoting the many autochthonous expressions of faith that are being developed in all parts of the Third World.

References

Anderson, G. H. (Ed.). (1993). *Asian voices in Christian theology*. Maryknoll, NY: Orbis Books.

Arias, M. (n.d.). Evangelización contextual en América Latina: entre la acomodación y la confrontación. *APOYO*, 79, Buenos Aires, Argentina.

Escobar, S. (1998). *De la misión a la teología*. Buenos Aires, Argentina: Ediciones Kairos.

García Canclini Néstor. (1999). *La globalización imaginada*. México DF: Editorial Piados.

González, J. L. (2001). *Mapas para la historia futura de la iglesia*. Buenos Aires, Argentina: Ediciones Kairos.

Lipovetsky, G. (1987). *L'empire de l'ephemere: la mode et son destin dans les societes modernes*. Paris, France: Gallinard.

Míguez Bonino, J. (1995). *Rostros del Protestantismo Latinoamericano*. Buenos Aires, Argentina: Nueva Creación.

Padilla, R. C. (1986). *Misión integral: Ensayos sobre el reino y la iglesia*. Buenos Aires, Argentina.

Paredes, T. (2000). *El evangelio: un tesoro en vasijas de barro*. Buenos Aires, Argentina: Ediciones Kairos.

Ramachandra, V. (1996). *Gods that fail: Modern idolatry and Christian mission*. Cumbria, UK: Paternoster Press.

Marcelo Vargas *is a Bolivian and a staff worker in IFES movements in Brazil and Bolivia. He was a pioneer and founder of the IFES movement in Bolivia and has served as the General Secretary of the Comunidad Cristiana Universitaria de Bolivia. He completed postgraduate studies in mission in Brazil and was Dean of Students and Professor of the Training Centre for Mission in Brazil. He is married with a daughter and a son who is leading the Training Centre for Mission in La Paz, Bolivia. Email: ccm@ceibo.entelnet.bo.*

13

Mission possible or impossible? Learning lessons from theology's engagement with globalization

WARREN BEATTIE

Globalization influences the way theologians reflect about theology. This in turn is affecting mission, and we need to be aware of these changes if we are going to engage in mission in ways that are relevant in the 21st century.

Contemporary study of globalization involves an extensive literature, as does material on theology and globalization, so I have tried to choose works in this chapter that I feel are both significant and representative. The selection aims, first of all, to give a flavour of the directions in which theology and globalization are moving. Second, it seeks to stimulate reflection both on what is happening in theology and on how we constantly need to modify our own thinking about mission.

By way of background, I have been involved in ministry and mission in Scotland, Europe, and Asia, initially in South Korea and latterly in Singapore, working with Reformed and Presbyterian churches and also with many other Christian churches and organisations. I studied theology in Scotland in the Western Reformed tradition, and this tradition defines my own "universal theology," in the terminology I will use later in this chapter. I write "universal theology," because my experiences in Asia constantly challenge me to think about the importance of local context and the limits of any one theological tradition.

Wandering in the Botanic Gardens in Singapore, I have often gone past the Reflexology Path, which is made of upturned pebbles set in concrete. The pebbles fiercely impact the feet and hence the bodies of those walking along the path. Every time I walk by this path, I am reminded that Chinese society traditionally views health and medicine differently from Western society. Very few days pass at the college where I teach in Singapore without some discussion of topics associated with Chinese health practices. The perspectives of the Chinese diaspora on health are evidently influenced by the worldviews of the Chinese traditional religions. Not surprisingly, there is little discussion of these matters in the works of Reformed Scottish divines, nor do they talk much of how Christianity relates to the Taoist, Buddhist, or Confucian worldviews that lie behind Chinese perspectives on health.

Such an example, however inconsequential it may seem to some readers, is not incidental or frivolous in Singapore, and it reminds us of the way in which culture influences what is thought to be important and effective in everyday life. In a global world, we are forced to come to terms with the implications of other ways of thinking, not just in the area of practical theology but in every realm of theology. This chapter will focus on the implications of this diversity for mission and on how mission is shaped by globalization.

Globalization

The term "globalization" has historical roots dating back to the 1960s, and its application varies from the late 20th century back to the Bronze Age, depending on scholars' perspectives. What I shall refer to as globalization dates to the early 1990s. By this, I mean the contemporary usage of the term as typified by Held and McGrew (2000, p. 1) in their benchmark survey:

> In an epoch of profound and unsettling global change … the discourse of globalization seems to offer a convincing analysis of the contemporary human predicament … the notion of globalization has become the leitmotif of our age.

This "discourse of globalization" is an attempt to make sense of reality and is based on a wide-ranging analysis of contemporary society. Social scientists have identified several key dimensions of the process of globalization. The **economic** context of market capitalism is connected with **technological** changes, particularly in the area of telecommunications, and these have an impact on **political** interactions and on **cultural** influences. Beyond these things, there are several key characteristics of globalization that are important—**extension**, **compression**, and **reflexivity** (Schreiter, 1997, pp. 8-14). Extension and compression refer to the ways in which the effects of globalization are extended and intensified across time and space. Reflexivity refers to the fact that not only do the external dimensions of globalization impact our global world in new ways—as, for example, with the Internet—but because of globalization, our understanding, as well as our experience of the world, is irrevocably changed (Beck, 2000, pp. 8-13).

It is in this context of reflexivity that we can look for connections between globalization and theology. In this chapter, we shall consider the impact of globalization on theological method and on specific theological issues. We will then conclude with some implications for mission.[1]

Globalization and Theological Method

The global context: its importance for the theology and globalization debate

Globalization forces us to become aware of the world as our context as we do theology and think about mission. One of the most sustained engagements between theology and globalization has come from the Association of Theological Schools (ATS) through editions of their journal *Theological Education*.[2] The ATS decided to study globalization because they felt it was an important dimension of contemporary society. As the ATS engaged with globalization, they discovered that its impact went beyond their early expectations and that it did offer fresh insights into the study of theology. This suggests the importance for theologians and missiologists both to engage with globalization and to keep an open mind as to its potential impact and ramifications.

In the early stages, the discussion of globalization and theological education could be characterised as the search for multicultural perspectives or global awareness within North American theological education. By 1999, the ATS members were offering a more sustained attempt to look at the dynamics of globalization and its theological significance. Globalization in theological education was seen to mean "recognising the entire world as the context for our curricula" (Lesher, 1993, p. 36). By this, they meant that globalization forces an awareness of the importance of the global world as a "context" in itself, rather than the global world simply offering a diversity of new "contents" to theology. We are challenged in globalization to have a wider perspective.

If "the world" is the context for mission, then we need to involve "the world" in the way we think and reflect about mission. A good example of what this means in practice is given by the Sri Lankan, Vinoth Ramachandra (1994). He points out that often when global mission is discussed in evangelical circles, the approaches to and breakdown and analysis of the problem often seem to reflect Western value systems and Western organisational thinking. It can seem that a blueprint has been drawn up from one part of the world that poses as a "global scheme," but it has not really embraced the perspectives of those from other regions. Globalization challenges this way of thinking. A proper understanding of the global context forces us to allow repre-

---

[1] This chapter will draw on a wide range of theological perspectives, but it will look primarily at the implications of globalization for evangelical missiology.

[2] The ATS is an association that relates to major educational institutions teaching theology in the United States. See especially the volumes of the journal *Theological Education* in 1986, 1993, and 1999.

sentatives from the wider world to be involved. In practice, this means that local or national perspectives need to be a major part of determining our whole approach to and ethos of mission. We need to listen carefully to the perspectives of "the world" as to what constitutes mission, at both a missiological and a practical level.

The global-local polarity: its relevance for theology and missiology

Globalization forces us to look closely at the relationship between the wider world and the specific parts of it. This interaction between the global and the local is one of the most discussed aspects of globalization.

One theologian, Robert Schreiter,[3] who has worked with many international students in a seminary and university context in Chicago since the late 1970s, became interested in the way in which local theologies are formed and shaped. This interest led to a consideration of the relationship of local theology to global theology. Schreiter has made a sustained attempt to link globalization and theology and to examine particularly theology's interaction with globalization in his work *The New Catholicity: Theology Between the Global and the Local*. His book discusses the way in which the context of globalization involves the interplay of global and local dynamics and how this inter-

action affects theological formulation. Schreiter argues that because of globalization, any discussion of theology "will be pursued under the overarching idea of theology being refashioned between the global and the local realities in which it finds itself today" (Schreiter, 1997). Theology under globalization is shaped by this global-local interaction. Schreiter describes this interaction as "glocalization" and suggests, "Some of the most salient features of religion and theology today can best be described from the vantage point of the glocal." (Schreiter, 1997, pp. 1-4, 12).[4]

It has been suggested that "glocalization" is part of local culture's engagement with globalization. Hoedemaker (2000, p. 174) states, "Glocalization means that local constructions of common life ... can only maintain their identity and impact if they enter the arena of competition with the forces of globalization and accept the accompanying risk of redefinition and reconstruction." The theological parallel can be seen in discussion of concepts of local theology and global theology— where the term "contextual theology" is often used synonymously with "local theology," and "universal theology" has frequently been substituted for "global theology."[5] In terms of global theology as a concept, there has been some previous discussion, but contemporary interest is more limited. This would suggest that there is currently some un-

---

[3] Schreiter is an expert in the area of culture and theology and has written a widely used book on local theology (Schreiter, 1999).

[4] Schreiter is drawing on the sociological ideas of a respected commentator on globalization, Roland Robertson.

[5] Schreiter and others also consider to what extent "universal theologies" such as the Reformed tradition, the Catholic tradition, and so on, which have been largely developed in the West, really do function "universally."

certainty about whether writing global theology is really a feasible endeavour.[6]

Conversely, the place of local/contextual theology seems to be of growing importance. In his writing in 1993, Schreiter describes contextualization as "the co-relate of globalization." In this sense, contextualization is an example of glocalization within the theological community.[7]

Contextualization, as a manifestation of glocalization, is what happens when local people try to deal with issues that they encounter locally which are not satisfactorily dealt with in the theological framework that they have inherited. This is not necessarily because the theological framework is essentially inadequate but simply that it has not had to deal with these specific issues at a previous stage.

In Chinese culture, there are aspects of the Chinese mindset—non-linear thinking, a high view of the wisdom of antiquity, a leaning to pragmatism, and the concrete expression of concepts—which affect how preaching is done. This mindset leads to the choice of appropriate sermon forms, a willingness to draw on quotations from biblical sources (supplemented by examples of Chinese wisdom traditions), and the need to make a strong connection between spirituality and practical ethical teaching. We can also find theological treatments of local festivals, which consider, for example, what sort of activities Chinese Christians might do during the lunar New Year festival.

It could be argued that it was not necessary to have a debate on globalization to make these efforts realities, and that is true. For example, Paul's description of issues connected with Gentile conversions to Christianity in Acts 15 is an early example of contextual theology. However, globalization has made people more conscious of the imperative to shape their own identities or to be shaped by default by the outside world. The pressure of globalization in the modern world is pushing theologians in non-Western regions to want to deal in relevant ways with issues of local importance. These theologians wonder if the universal theologies that they are taught at seminary are really the best way to do theology. In the same way, these theologians query whether the models of mission that are used in their society—and often imported from outside—are the most appropriate or effective ways to do mission.[8] Hwa Yung (1997), in his book *Mangoes or Bananas*, looks at this issue both in terms of the content of theology and in the way in which Enlightenment ways of thinking (i.e., Western thinking) and Western approaches to theology can still dominate how Asians approach theology. As Hwa points out, mangoes and bananas are both yellow on the outside, but only mangoes are yellow on the inside—do read his book to pursue the implications for non-Western theology!

---

[6] See the section on global missiology for some contrasts between "global theology" and "global missiology."

[7] See further chapter 12 on contextualization in this volume.

[8] Within evangelicalism, a good understanding of what is meant by this is given in Paul Hiebert's discussions of "self-theologizing."

Non-Western Christianity in an era of globalization: its impact on theology and missiology

Globalization makes us look at different parts of the world in a new way. It has created a forum for different forms of local theology that can shape and influence our theological discussions. It has also forged a context in which people in the West have become more conscious of the non-Western world.

Non-Western Christianity and theology

In an essay on theological education, Thistlewaite (1993) states, "Globalization in theological education is the uncentering of the intellectual hegemony of the West." She suggests that at the beginning of the debate, globalization was thought to influence theological education by being seen as "one more dish on the intellectual potluck table of modern culture." Looking back, she suggests that people were unaware of "the more profound epistemological implications of the project." She would prefer to see the real implications of globalization as follows: "The development of critical consciousness in theological education means letting go of the assumption of the universal validity and priority of the intellectual traditions of the West."

Thistlewaite notes parallels here with Schreiter's themes in *Constructing Local Theologies*, and she sees negative reactions from the Western theological establishment to globalization as a more realistic response than simply indifference. This is because reflection on globalization would have a real impact and would challenge the idea that Western perspectives in theology and missiology are dominant simply because they are Western.

Non-Western Christianity and missiology

Globalization has prompted deeper reflection on theological thinking across the world. This has happened due to the impact of globalization on the church and missionary movements worldwide. Hiebert (1993, p. 72) sees the church as benefiting from globalization by becoming a worldwide body. In his opinion, the hegemony of the West is decreasing with the shift of the centre of gravity of the church towards the non-West. He also notes the simultaneous rise of the non-Western world missionary movement.[9] This shift of the church towards the non-West is an important phenomenon which has been studied at a statistical level by David Barrett and whose theological significance has been noted by missiologists such as Andrew Walls and Walter Bühlmann. The rise and recognition of non-Western mission movements has had significant impact on missiology, in showing that the history of missionary activity has had more input from non-Western cultures than had previously been realised and appreciated. The Korean missiologist Timothy Kiho Park surveys Christian outreach starting from Korea from 1907 onwards and shows how Korean Christians were part of the larger picture of mission, particularly in a northeastern province of

---

[9] For consistency, I am using the term "non-Western." "Two-Thirds World" missionary movement is more common elsewhere.

China and also in Siberia, Japan, and Hawaii.[10] Most histories of mission written in the West would not include the activities of such non-Western personnel, especially in the early part of the 20th century or before. The full implications of the connections between these movements and globalization are also largely unexplored at the present time.

David Tai-Woong Lee is a missiologist in South Korea who is directly connected with the Korean missionary movement. Lee has been teaching for several years on the rise of non-Western missionary movements, in terms of their history and practice, as well as their theological and missiological connections with conciliar, evangelical, and Catholic conferences in the 20th century. He has recently turned his attention to the ways in which these movements are now in turn influencing what he calls "the formulation of a global missiology." He sees some evidence for this in the representative and collaborative approaches to missiology adopted by organisations such as the World Evangelical Alliance (WEA).[11] By this, he means that efforts are being made within WEA circles, for example, where

groups of theologians from different sectors of the world have met to discuss in collaborative ways specific aspects of missiology. Since they are coming together as representatives of several of the world's continents, they can offer, to some extent, a global perspective—hence, a global missiology. Lee also recognises the earlier roots of such endeavour within the writings of conciliar and evangelical congresses during the 20th century.[12]

It is interesting that such an analysis has originated from within the circle of non-Western missionary movements. It is likely that non-Western missionary movements (like the church in the non-Western world) will continue to have a major impact on missiology. The impact of non-Western missionary movements and non-Western missiology in the 20th century under globalization will be a fruitful study, both to uncover their influence on global missiology and as a source of untapped creativity for missiology.

There are two implications here. First, if we are engaged in global mission and are not part of networks in which we are sharing with others from around the world, then we are prob-

---

[10] See Park (1993) for an interesting Asian example.

[11] Lee gave a series of lectures on this topic at the Centre for the Study of Christianity in Asia at Trinity Theological College, Singapore, in March 2002. Unfortunately, his works are not widely available in English. Readers of Korean can visit the GMTC website, www.gmtc.or.kr. See below for his contribution to the WEF conference at Iguassu in Brazil in 1999. Lee sees the Iguassu Affirmation as a helpful example of theological reflection that could help shape the quest for a more global missiology.

[12] We might wonder why there seems to be growing interest in global missiology when discussion of global theology is temporarily diminishing. It may be that the search for global theology has emphasised the whole field of theology—a theology of reference to the whole globe. This is a far-reaching task. By contrast, global missiology has emphasised debate on more specific topics but from a range of global perspectives—a missiology which tries to be *representative* of the global church. This is a more limited and, in some senses, a more manageable endeavour.

ably not engaging in mission that truly reflects today's global realities. Where possible, we need to engage with those of other backgrounds in the same area of mission. My own organisation, OMF International, has greatly benefited not just from its partnership with local Christians in Asian churches, but also from the diverse range of Asian members who have joined over the years (mostly since 1965, but there was one Chinese woman who joined in 1880). Their presence and contributions allow the organisation to gain input from a variety of perspectives on Asian missiology and mission. In an era of globalization, those involved in international organisations and projects must be ready to involve a wide diversity of voices in this way.

Second, if we are doing missiology and are not learning from perspectives outside our own cultural or denominational backgrounds, then we are probably too limited in our reading and thinking about mission. If we are dealing with specific topics, such as mission and the church, then we should make efforts to include some missiological reading that comes from outside our own theological or cultural circle. The same approach could apply to theological topics, including preaching, worship, and so on.

Globalization and Theological Issues

Globalization has impacted theological method, but it has also brought about considerable theological discussion on two particular topics of wide interest: the place of religious resurgence in a global world and, second, the role of the global economy and global responsibility.

Religious resurgence and globalization

The relationship between Christian mission and religious traditions of the world, especially the global faiths, is receiving increasing attention within evangelicalism. It is important in a global world that the church be more informed about religious differences. Non-Western writers in particular are urging a better understanding of other faiths—in terms of both apologetics and dialogue.

The renaissance of religion in global society is attracting renewed interest. While scholars offer "divergent views on this [religious] resurgence," all appear to be in "agreement that we are in the midst of one" (Stackhouse, 2000, p. 32). In his book *Religion and Globalization*, Beyer (1994, pp. 111-113) discusses how this resurgence affects both the Abrahamic faiths and Eastern religions. He gives case studies on groups as different as the "New Christian right in the United States," the "Islamic revolution in Iran," and "religious environmentalism."

Proof of the impact of this religious resurgence can be seen in the responses given by theologians. Bliese (1997, p. 177) suggests that "religions are not dying out in global culture; they are pervasive, powerful, influential, and growing." For Bliese, this will put pressure on Christian claims that salvation is possible "in no other name," especially in the context of Christianity seeking to be "globally inclusive." "The naming of God in global culture will certainly be linked to the theological discourse about soteriology.... The power of salvation will be tied together with the power of God's name." Bliese envisages a world of multiple claims to salvation with intense scrutiny of the Christian trinitarian doctrines of God—both in terms of how God is named and conceived in terms of these doctrines and the relationship of these doctrines to the process of Christian mission.

Tan Kang San (2002, pp. 8-9) writes:

We need to accept the reality that our modern world demands deeper engagements with both secular and other religious belief systems.… The challenge of raising a new generation of scholars in Islam, Buddhism, and Hinduism is an urgent task within the evangelising church in a multicultural setting.

In terms of other Christian perspectives, two volumes produced by the Council of World Mission (CWM) look at the potential impact of religion on mission. These collections of essays argue that people are more conscious of religious and cultural plurality, because multicultural social interactions have increased under globalization.

One of the important things to note in this debate is the way in which the consequences of globalization are interpreted. Some Christian writers see the emerging pluralist experience in a globalized world as leading inevitably to a pluralist ideology.[13] There is a tendency in both theological and sociological literature in the West to suggest that people who hold strong religious beliefs, such as conservative Christians or Muslims, and who live in communities where other beliefs are not present, react negatively to the "other."

This is no doubt often true, but Moonjang Lee, a South Korean, writing on religious pluralism in his country, points out that many other parts of the world have experienced pluralism rather differently. In Asia, the hub of many of the world's major faiths, there has been coexistence of different religions and, at various times of history, coexistence with Christianity. Religious plurality is not a new phenomenon of the globalizing era in Asia; it is part of a common and enduring process. Many Asian Christians are used to being in a relative minority in their own countries (M. Lee, 2000).

In this context, non-Western evangelical theologians such as Moonjang Lee and Tan Kang San, who are accustomed to religious plurality, are adopting different responses from theologians in the West. They would say that the appropriate response to increased religious resurgence is to take stock of one's own religious faith, its scriptures, and its community, and to seek to live with, dialogue with, and witness in appropriate ways to one's faith with others in the wider community, whilst at the same time becoming more informed about other religious traditions. It will be important to consider in the future how such theologians, who are emerging from religiously plural contexts and who engage with academic theological discourse on pluralism and dialogue, might offer alternative perspectives on theological method and content to other strands of the academic community.

There are complex issues surrounding religion in today's global world. The West can include regions such as Bosnia and the Faroe Islands. Places asso-

---

[13] Paul Hiebert (1993) has a brief and useful discussion of the implications of postmodernity and its intrinsic subjectivity in terms of religious belief.

ciated with resurgent religious nationalism include countries that are increasingly restrictive, such as Brunei (with an Islamic ideology) and India (with a Hindu ideology), but Asia also embraces countries such as Vietnam, where "economic ideology" restricts religious belief. By contrast, a religiously homogenous country such as Thailand, which has a strong and resurgent Buddhist ideology, is relatively free. However, whether due to religious resurgence or simply to a new awareness of pluralism, religious change puts pressure on Christians to think about how they understand religion and mission. There is a special sensitivity about Christian mission and religion in a post-colonial world, and it may be that theologians from the non-Western world can offer a more neutral lead in these areas.

Tan's call for a greater understanding of other religions, both in terms of their social implications and to further dialogue, is understandable. This has serious implications for Christian mission today. Websites with a selection of English materials on Hinduism or Buddhism may be a starting point for understanding other faiths, but it often takes a much longer and deeper engagement with a culture to really make sense of what is happening.

Insider perspectives are also crucial. It is important that the opinions of local people be canvassed to make sense of other religious contexts and perspectives. This will have relevance too when it comes to producing audio-visual productions and literature on religious themes and mission. If these are developed without reference to local understanding, including local Christian perspectives, they risk not just offering limited perspectives on religions in today's world, but also causing unnecessary offence. I well remember an Indian Christian from a Hindu background once saying to me that a particular book on Hinduism was in many respects a good introduction—given its limitations as being written by someone outside of Hinduism. Carelessness in this respect will inhibit dialogue and witness and will hinder the work of the Christian church.

Global responsibility and globalization

Contrasting perspectives

Another important theme is the way in which Christians respond to the impact of the global economy and the apparently increasing economic disparity in today's world. In an introduction to volume 1 of the project in the series entitled *God and Globalization*, Max Stackhouse (2000), a professor of theological ethics at the University of Princeton, offers a searching and wide-ranging theological overview of globalization and its relevance to societies in the world. He sees the effects of globalization as impinging on many areas of social life—traditional religion, ethics, culture, economics, politics, and society. For Stackhouse, the idea that religion is "the locus at which questions of truth, justice, and holiness take their most intense forms" is very important. He sees religion as a key discourse for ethical discussion, although he acknowledges that religious claims to truth must be verified in a critical and independent way.

The ATS theologians mentioned above, including Stackhouse although representing a range of traditions, are archetypal proponents of what has been termed "theology from above"—a theology for and by those who represent authority structures in the world and church. A rather different perspective is found in the Association of Third World Theologians (EATWOT).[14] These theologians espouse, in methodological terms, a "theology from below"—a theology for the people and by the people, in that they also actively encourage the contributions of non-professional theologians. This is significant for a discussion on globalization. The ATS represents Western-based academics whose societies reap the benefits of globalization. Non-Western academics look with a more critical eye on globalization as a phenomenon whose impact on their societies is somewhat mixed, and this has a bearing on the discourse.[15]

One of the most striking differences between EATWOT and the above discussion is the language associated with globalization. The overall consensus in ATS circles appears to be that globalization is an inevitable process bringing "promising as well as threatening possibilities" (Stackhouse, 2000, p. 5).[16] In EATWOT writings, the language is both more loaded and more negative. Abraham (1997) reminds us that "globalization is not a neutral process ... —an alliance forged by the forces of

domination for profit is the driving force of much of globalization." Using more guarded language, Mananzam (1998) paints an equally bleak picture of the impact of globalization on the poor in the Philippines, speaking of the "death-dealing forces of globalization." The underlying concern that links the EATWOT authors is "an inadequate capitalist world economy" (Irranazaval, 1998).[17] There is generally less ambivalence to globalization in the analyses of the EATWOT theologians than there is in the writings of the ATS members.

Implications for missiology

The new emphasis of global responsibility, articulated by Stackhouse, emphasizes the need for the church both to scrutinise the ethical orientation of its activities and to be involved in the world. This theme of global responsibility is an important one in the theological literature.[18] It is clear that theologians across the spectrum are ready to address globalisation's impact on society, irrespective of whether globalization is seen as a positive or negative force. "Globalization will certainly foster global protests ... however, it must also foster an acceptance by churches of global responsibility" (Bliese, 1997).

---

[14] EATWOT is an association of theologians from the Two-Thirds World who publish conference proceedings and a journal to disseminate their views.

[15] This is not to overlook the fact that some ATS members are from a diversity of ethnic backgrounds.

[16] See also Stackhouse's comments on pages 4-7 of his book for a generally positive, if guarded, perspective on globalization.

[17] In saying this, Irranazaval specifically stresses that globalization does not mean "an evil and demonic reality."

[18] An excellent summary of how liberation theology is a response to "the residual problems of the global system" is given in Beyer (1994), pages 140-141, and in chapter 6 of his book.

Within evangelicalism, global responsibility finds expression in "developmental" and "transformational" dimensions of mission. Missiologists with an interest in economics and development recognised that the disintegration of the Soviet Union and the collapse of the controlled economies in Eastern Europe constituted a significant shift of economic power and one that was likely to lead to a new era. Sugden (1997, pp. 324-325), a commentator on the missiology of Vinay Samuel, suggests that this shift forced an examination of the implications of the new market culture in Samuel's missiological writing. Sugden says that Samuel's continuing interest in making sense of mission in the light of changing world economic realities is an attempt to engage with globalization. Samuel was also conscious that the new dimensions of the shifts of power evident in globalization were factors that Christians needed to address, noting perceptively that even Christian views on those issues were shaped "from the perspective of those who attempt to manage the world" (Sugden, 1997, p. 333; see also pp. 327, 331).

"Developmental" and "transformational" forms of missiology are dimensions of mission that are attracting interest within missionary movements and evangelical Christian communities around the world, especially in the West.

The international scope of the journal *Transformation* and the recent publication of *Mission as Transformation* show that considerable reflection has gone into the thinking on transformation at both a developmental and a theological level. It also suggests that a range of international missiologists are conscious that we need to respond to the world in mission, both with a theological message and with practical help.[19] It would seem that the rise in this type of missiological thinking has coincided with more discourse on global responsibility in an increasingly global world. Unfortunately, it is also a world in which economic disparity is increasingly a problem, and this remains a stimulus to engage in multi-dimensional forms of mission.

On a practical note, we should be grateful for the rise of evangelical agencies such as Tearfund in the UK, both for the expertise that such agencies bring to a discussion of economic issues and for the ability to target impoverished communities across the world. However, we need to be careful that a focus on developmental issues and mission does not obscure the need for churches and missionary organisations to integrate more extensive thinking on transformation and holistic mission into their understanding of mission—this, I think, is an urgent need for the 21st century.

Globalization and Theology: Missiological Implications

This chapter has looked at how globalization interacts with theology. We have considered the place of context in influencing theological formulation, recognised the influence of alternative networks from within the non-Western world, and considered key theological themes such as religion and global re-

---

[19] A fuller survey can be found in Sugden (1997).

sponsibility. We can see points of contact with these themes and the "fourfold typology" of globalization given by Browning (as cited in Lesher, 1993, pp. 33-35), at an early stage in the ATS debates on globalization:

The word globalization has at least four rather distinct meanings … For some, globalization means the church's universal mission to evangelize the world…. Second, there is the idea of globalization as ecumenical cooperation…. Third, globalization sometimes refers to a dialogue between Christianity and the religions. Finally, globalization refers to the mission of the church to the world, not only to convert and to evangelize, but also to improve and develop the lives of the millions of poor, starving, and politically disadvantaged people.

One detail of Browning's schema is omitted in much of the recent discussion on globalization, when he writes, "For some, globalization means the church's universal mission to evangelize the world." It is worth turning our attention to globalization and evangelization as we draw our survey to a close.

Global mission as evangelization

The global nature of the church, global missionary movements, and global theology all imply a universal dimension to the church—a dimension which has resulted from an historical process of evangelization and Christian expansion. This raises questions as to how global mission as "evangelization" relates to the contemporary debate of globalization and to what extent mission is still conceived as evangelization, as opposed to other categories or modes of mission.

Non-Western perspectives on mission and evangelization

In an article written for the Iguassu consultation, David Tai-Woong Lee (2000), who identifies with the outward-looking Korean missionary movement, offers an alternative perspective from the non-Western world.[20] He envisages a world in which non-Western Christian communities develop their own theological and missiological style and are involved in mission, but he maintains a close interest in evangelization. His perspective is representative of other non-Western missionary movements.

We are at an early stage in the analysis of material about non-Western world missionary movements, but certainly countries in Asia and the Pacific, such as India, Korea, Japan, the Southern Pacific islands, and Myanmar, have had internal cross-cultural missionary activity for decades; South-East Asia has seen growing movements in recent years. At moments in history, these movements have crossed national boundaries.[21] My point in drawing attention to these movements is to show that movements not directly identified with classical Protestant and evangelical missionary

---

[20] Lee also gave a series of lectures at the Centre for the Study of Christianity in Asia at Trinity Theological College, Singapore, in March 2002.

[21] An excellent introduction to these movements can be found in Wong et al. (1973). Unfortunately, no up-to-date summary of the whole phenomenon really exists at present.

movements of the 19th and 20th centuries and located in a wide range of religiously diverse nations have, somewhat independently, kept mission as evangelization firmly on the church's agenda.

The relevance of theology for global mission

Theological methodology

The discourse on religious resurgence illustrates how globalization impacts both theological formulation as well as its content. We have seen that the phenomenon of religious resurgence and the experience of plurality, particularly in the West, have created new sensitivities in this respect. Those critical of Christianity's failure to move in this direction bluntly express their feelings about "Christianity's poor record in the area of interreligious and cross-cultural dialogue. Too many Christian theologians still tend to discourse in naïve supremacist and exclusivist terms, e.g., by sticking to some unnuanced account of Jesus as Saviour of the world" (Lipner, 2000, p. 87). Given that around a billion people across the world do recognise Jesus of Nazareth as their Saviour, we can see from such loaded writing the degree of challenge which Christians face and the need for clarity and boldness as well as appropriate dialogical styles.

The impact of globalization on theological method in the wider church may well surface in theological language connected to religious diversity and plurality, and it will have an especial impact on Christology, with some pushing away from what they see as Christo-centric models of theology.[22] It is important, as the ATS writers have suggested, that we keep sight of the global context and the range of global contributors who can help us reflect on these topics. This includes those from the non-Western world who continue to offer a range of alternative perspectives and methodological approaches to theology that promote mission.

Theological themes

We have seen that theological foundations are important to the discussion of mission and globalization. We have also suggested that debates about important issues in a global world raise questions not just about traditional theological categories, but also about other questions of Christian relationship to society. Christian identity is challenged in a world where ethnic, national, and religious pluralism are all increasingly important. The Christian contribution to global responsibility becomes acute in a context where Christians, particularly in the West and parts of Asia, are often personally wealthy and affluent, and their relatively rich economies make a huge impact on the economies of the non-Western world (though the Christian church is neither directly responsible nor even well-placed to effect change—and even national governments claim that economic influence goes beyond their powers at times). Nonetheless, Christians rightly see the challenge and responsibility of working for good in the global context and look for missiological approaches that are creative and allow for integrity.

---

[22] See, for example, Lipner (2000) and the volumes of *Voices From the Third World* mentioned above.

Missiological implications

Globalization has allowed, in a new way, an exchange of theological and missiological opinion and interaction, which has permitted the non-Western segment of the church to make a real contribution to the life of the world church and to mission in a global era. It will continue to be important for non-Western strands of the global church to demonstrate alternative approaches to theology and mission, both through new missionary movements and through their own emerging approaches to missiology.

Conclusion

This survey has tried to make sense of the influences of globalization on theology, has considered theological responses to globalization, has presented some of the ways in which these two fields influence mission, and has discussed the implications for evangelical missiology. It remains to be seen what the shape of mission in an era of globalization will be. Whatever the outcomes, the global church will need to take cognisance of changing currents in theology and to embrace the contribution of the non-Western church to the ongoing mission of the church and its theological formulation.

References

Abraham, K. C. (1997, December). Editorial. *Voices From the Third World, 20*(2), p. 7.

Beck, U. (2000). *What is globalization?* London, UK: Polity Press.

Beyer, P. (1994). *Religion and globalization.* London, UK: Sage Publications.

Bliese, R. (1997). Globalization. In K. T. Muller, T. Sundermeier, & S. B. Evans (Eds.), *Dictionary of mission: Theological, historical perspectives.* Maryknoll, NY: Orbis Books.

Held, D., & McGrew, A. (Eds.). (2000). *The global transformations reader: An introduction to the globalization debate.* Cambridge, UK: Polity Press.

Hiebert, P. G. (1993). Globalization as evangelism. In A. F. Evans (Ed.), *The globalization of theological education* (pp. 64-89). Maryknoll, NY: Orbis Books.

Hoedemaker, B. (2000). Religion beyond modernity. In P. L. Wickeri, J. K. Wickeri, & D. M. A. Niles (Eds.), *Plurality, power and mission: Intercontextual theological explorations on the role of religion in the new millennium.* London, UK: Council of World Mission.

Hwa Yung. (1997). *Mangoes or bananas: The quest for an authentic Asian Christian theology.* Oxford, UK: Regnum.

Irranazaval, D. (1998, June). Theology in the "other" globalization. *Voices From the Third World, 21*(1), p. 181.

Lee, D. T. W. (2000). A Two-Thirds World evaluation of contemporary evangelical missiology. In W. D. Taylor (Ed.), *Global missiology for the 21st century: The Iguassu dialogue* (pp. 133-148). Grand Rapids, MI: Baker Academic.

Lee, M. (2000). Experience of religious plurality in Korea: Its theological implications. *International Review of Missions, 88*(351), pp. 399-413.

Lesher, W. E. (1993). Meanings of globalization. In A. F. Evans (Ed.), *The globalization of theological education.* Maryknoll, NY: Orbis Books.

Lipner, J. (2000). Religion and religious thinking in the new millennium. In P. L. Wickeri, J. K. Wickeri, & D. M. A. Niles (Eds.), *Plurality, power and mission: Intercontextual theological explorations on the role of religion in the new millennium.* London, UK: Council of World Mission.

Mananzam, M. J. (1998, June). Five hundred years of colonial history. *Voices From the Third World, 21*(1), p. 244.

Park, T. (1993). *A Two-Thirds World mission on the move.* Unpublished Ph.D. thesis from Fuller Seminary.

Ramachandra, V. (1994, October). The honor of listening: Indispensable for mission. One-sided nationalistic vision hinders global perspective and partnership in mission. *Evangelical Missions Quarterly, 30*, pp. 404-409.

Schreiter, R. (1997). *The new catholicity: Theology between the global and the local.* Maryknoll, NY: Orbis Books.

————. (1999). *Constructing local theologies.* Maryknoll, NY: Orbis Books.

Stackhouse, M. L. (2000). *God and globalization. Vol. 1. Religion and the powers of the common life.* Harrisburg, PA: Trinity Press International.

Sugden, C. (1997). *Seeking the Asian face of Jesus.* Oxford, UK: Regnum.

Tan Kang San. (2002, February). *Globalization and the church: Challenges to evangelization and discipleship.* Conference speech delivered in Malaysia.

Thistlewaite, S. (1993). An historical survey; Commentary. In A. F. Evans (Ed.), *The globalization of theological education.* Maryknoll, NY: Orbis Books.

Wong, J. Y. K. (1973). *Missions from the Third World.* Singapore: Church Growth Study Centre.

Warren Beattie *grew up in the Highlands of Scotland. He studied Mathematics and later Divinity before working as a minister in Edinburgh. He and his wife Stroma joined OMF International in 1991, working in South Korea with local churches and students, as well as in missionary training. Currently in Singapore, Warren lectures in Missions at the Discipleship Training Centre and is doing part-time doctoral studies at New College, Edinburgh. Stroma serves as the International Medical Adviser of OMF. Email: beattiewarren@omf.net.*

Globalization
and the church

Alex Araujo

I still remember with some excitement my trip to Southern Serbia during the Kosovo tensions. We traveled by car from Macedonia. Crossing the tense border checkpoint, we could see the blue tents on the hills, from which United Nations peacekeepers kept an eye on the valley below.

In Serbia, we spent the night in a town not far from the site where, days earlier, a NATO bomb had fallen by mistake. Our hosts were a Serb pastor and his wife, leaders of a new church which met in their home. One evening, we went to the Gypsy district, where a group of 200 believers received us for a special church meeting. I remember perspiring profusely in the small room, in which we crowded together in narrow bench rows, knees pressing on the person in front. It was a cold evening outside, but the crowded room was very warm, as was the welcome from the Gypsy believers.

My mind skips from Serbia to Bangladesh, where I met for worship with about 20 laborers. We met in the late afternoon, on the floor of their semi-private sleeping quarters within the makeshift factory where they worked. Even as I try to describe this scene, another image begins to form, this time in West Kalimantan, in a Dayak village where, some months earlier, Dayaks had killed and beheaded immigrant Madurese in a flurry of racial tension. We met in a church building and then went to the pastor's house nearby for a meal.

The Global Church

I can roll out similar stories from more than 50 countries in which I have seen the church in a variety of local forms and conditions. The church is global, by God's intent and through the obedience of missions. It is a spiritual entity **not of this world**, but it exists **in this world** and ministers to the world through the physical, social, and economic vehicles available. By virtue of its ability to emerge and thrive anywhere on earth, the expanding church displays some characteristics similar to other global structures. However, it would be a mistake to read too much similarity into the comparison.

Globalization

There are many helpful definitions of globalization. For the purpose of this chapter, I will select R. Robertson's definition cited by Malcolm Waters (1995) in his book *Globalization*:

Globalization as a concept refers to both the compression of the world and the intensification of consciousness of the world as a whole … both concrete global interdependence and consciousness of the global whole.

At its most basic level, globalization means at least two things. First, it is the dynamic expansion of a local phenomenon to the rest of the world. The local phenomenon could be a product (e.g., Coca-Cola), an idea (e.g., human rights), or a system of social interaction (e.g., banking). Secondly, globalization means the global influence exerted on otherwise local phenomena, such as the pervasive insertion of English idiomatic expressions into the daily life of non-English-speaking societies because of the computer revolution.

In the realm of ideas—and more fundamentally, of worldviews—globalization means greater exposure to and less protective isolation from alien worldviews in local communities. This exposure generates pressure toward relativism concerning ultimate things. It may be said that relativism is a foundational mindset of globalization. In order to succeed, globalization must not only discard rigid geopolitical borders; it must also weaken localized worldviews. A very simple but very real illustration is the conflict between globalized clothing fashion and local Islamic convictions about female modesty. On a recent trip to Lebanon, I could observe the contrast between pervasive fashion marketing, with the public display of "immodest" fashions by some women, and affirmations of Islamic modesty values by others.

Globalization pressures us into withholding our convictions in order to coexist with other value systems, for the sake of peace. It is in this realm of worldviews that the interaction of the church with the globalization phenomenon becomes particularly relevant. While the church can legitimately assume different forms of expression in different social and cultural contexts, it cannot legitimately hold to more than one worldview, without denying its very nature and purpose. Christians are generally quite clear about what distinguishes Christianity from other formal religions. We know that Hinduism (or Buddhism or Islam) is not Christianity. Attempts to integrate the Christian faith with any other religion are not likely to find wide acceptance nor to last very long.

The challenge for Christians (and presumably for Hindus and Buddhists and Muslims) comes from unexpected, subtler corners. We acquire our theology consciously through proposition statements. Our worldview, however, is acquired subconsciously, in small and imperceptible parts. Note, for instance, the consumerist lifestyle and dependency among conservative evangelicals in the West. Their theology is faultless, yet they practice daily surrender to a worldview that rationalizes and excuses consumption excesses. C. S. Lewis (2001, ch. 12) describes this process by placing in the mouth of his fictional character Screwtape the following words:

> We know that we have introduced a change of direction in his course which is already carrying him out of his orbit around the Enemy [God]; but he must be made to imagine that all the choices which have effected this change of course are trivial and revocable. He must not be allowed to suspect that he is now, however slowly, heading right away from the sun on a line which will carry him into the cold and dark of utmost space.

> For this reason, I am almost glad to hear that he is still a churchgoer and a communicant. I know there are dangers in this; but anything is better than that he should realise the break he has made.

In the World But Not of the World

According to Scripture, the church is the people of God in pilgrimage through this fallen world.

> By faith he [Abraham] made his home in the promised land like a stranger in a foreign country; he lived in tents, as did Isaac and Jacob, who were heirs with him of the same promise. For he was looking forward to the city with foundations, whose architect and builder is God (Heb. 11:9-10).

Christ himself declared that his followers are in the world but not of the world:

> I have given them your word and the world has hated them, for they are not of the world any more than I am of the world. My prayer is not that you take them out of the world but that you protect them from the evil one. They are not of the world, even as I am not of it (John 17:14-16).

Redemption from sin and a whole new birth bring a person into a new community, marked by a new fellowship with God the creator. This understanding is fundamental to our grasp of how the church relates to the globalizing process that so shapes current human life. This question of being **in** but **not of** the world is at the root of how we understand the church's relation to the world's globalizing process.

Parallels With Globalization

We acknowledge the parallels, at a secondary level, between the world-wide spread of the church, with its biblical values, and the secular globalization of social values, goods, and structures. Both phenomena propagate core values that transcend geographical and cultural borders. Both offer the potential for community when people of different countries meet. There are common concerns, vocabulary, and themes. There is also a sense of identification that comes from the similarity of forms of social interaction, tools, and instruments. For example, in the church, music and instrumental arrangements resemble each other across cultural borders; outside the church, young business managers have been steeped in Druckerisms and One Minute Manager concepts and language.

These similarities are often readily visible, and they may deceive us as to the utterly different essential natures of the church and the global world order. The deception is particularly strong in societies that manifest the more positive characteristics of globalization. In affluent countries and among the affluent segments of poorer societies, the benefits of globalization are more clearly seen and appreciated. For Christians in these places, it is easy to believe that globalization is useful in the pursuit of Christian ideals. For instance, since computer technology has generated wealth and material benefits in these societies, it seems reasonable to assume that technology will have a similarly beneficial impact on the remaining task of world evangelization. Unfortunately, the visible and awe-inspiring achievements of globalized technology often mask any shortcomings. Affluent Christians may not realize that believers living in places under the unfavorable effects of globalization are less likely to share their enthusiasm for channeling globalization for Christian purposes.

We acknowledge that the church manifests itself in the world through the various means of human social expression that are available. We eat, drink, sleep, and work in the same way other people do, and we all use the same tools. We share communal conditions with our neighbors and fellow citizens. In addition, we propagate the gospel through communication, transportation, and other technical means that are shared by everyone else.

Radical Differences

In spite of the similarities between the church and the global world order, the fact remains that the church differs radically from the world with regard to the fundamental meaning of human existence. While we live in and make use of the same created environment, we attribute crucially different meanings to all things. As the Apostle Paul puts it:

Though we once regarded Christ in this way, we do so no longer. Therefore, if anyone is in Christ, he is a new creation; the old has gone, the new has come! (2 Cor. 5:16-17).

Further:

You did not learn Christ in this way, if indeed you have heard of him and have been taught in him, just as truth is in Jesus, that, in reference to your former manner of life, you lay aside the old self, which is being corrupted in accordance with the lusts of deceit, and that you be renewed in the spirit of your mind, and put on the new self, which in the likeness of God has been created in righteousness and holiness of the truth (Eph. 4:20-24).

This difference in perspective—in the fundamental way in which we relate to the world and in our understanding of ourselves and everything else—is further clarified in Paul's instructions to Christ's followers:

Do not conform any longer to the pattern of this world, but be transformed by the renewing of your mind. Then you will be able to test and approve what God's will is—his good, pleasing, and perfect will (Rom. 12:2).

Though once we were fully part of this world, sharing with it not only the externals of life on earth, but also its very spiritual condition and worldview, now as Christians, we no longer share anything except the externals.

At this point, it is fair to ask the question: Is the above statement really true? Note the contrast between the two passages above. 2 Corinthians 5:16-17 states it as a fact that we have been radically changed and no longer share the world's view. Romans 12:1-2 calls us to intentionally avoid being conformed to the world's pattern, implying that we are not yet sufficiently different from the world. Ajith Fernando (2000, pp. 254-255) observes:

Biblical community is an area in which the church will have to present a prophetic alternative in today's society. Yet I fear that this is an area in which we have conformed greatly to the pattern of this world .... I fear that many of our structures of community life

are derived more from the business world than from the Bible.

What does conforming or not conforming to the world have to do with globalization? Globalization is more than a way of organizing how humans relate to each other as individuals and as societies; it is a framework for making sense of the universe and of our existence in it. In this sense, globalization is another version of previous human frameworks for making sense of life without God. This should not surprise us, since a world that does not have God as its point of reference inevitably develops a God-less worldview. This does not mean that globalization is without virtue in any of its parts. It does mean, however, that to the extent that it is a worldview—a way of making sense of God's world without reference to God—it is unable to meet fundamental human aspirations. It is here that the church, the only effective alternative, needs to exercise its prophetic role. To quote Ajith Fernando (2000, p. 255) once more, "We have to be prophetic in the way we practice biblical community, because biblical community is so different from what we see in the world."

The Power of Globalization

The danger of globalization for Christians today is in its power to shape not only how we live, but also how we think and how we place ultimate value on things. This danger is not new, of course. Earlier historical manifestations of worldly patterns have had similar effects, and often the church has fallen into them unwittingly. Notable among them is the attempt to propagate the gospel by military force in the era of the Crusades, or in more recent history, ideas of racial superiority that Western Christians shared with their unbelieving compatriots. Globalization, at the level of worldviews, is today's dominant manifestation of the "pattern of this world" to which the Apostle Paul refers, and it is aided by new and powerful instruments of technology.

Technological development strengthens globalization's power to shape our thinking in two ways. First, technology accelerates the propagation of products and ideas around the world, so that we are bombarded by information at a rate impossible to control. Technological development generates sweeping changes very quickly, affording Christians little time to consider and prepare a biblically sound response. The sheer volume of information dulls our senses and our ability to discern. Our best efforts at resisting the pressure drive us either to give in and choose to see only the products of technology and the immediate benefits, or else to withdraw from taking part in anything that technology offers (Zengotita, 2002).

Globalization facilitates ethical accommodations—as some might say, "If you can't beat it, join it." Some colleagues in the missions movement argue hopefully that we can control the effects of globalization, so that they serve our purposes and advance the gospel. If globalization represents a worldview antithetical to the gospel, though, how can we integrate it into Christian purposes? Serious reflection is needed in this area.

The second way that technology affects us is through sophisticated marketing language. Such language is dominant worldwide in this globalizing age and is capable of creating artificial impressions, or pseudo-realities, that offer persuasive arguments against every reservation raised by our overwhelmed but still struggling minds. Marketing entices us by suggesting that we take advantage of its help to accomplish our ends, even though with the means comes also the meaning, and with the use of the tools comes also a new pattern of thinking.

The Pattern of the World

Here lies the major challenge to the church. Are we able to see beyond the immediate and isolated parts to the pattern that lies behind the whole system? In every age, the church has had the same challenge. In this generation, the challenge takes the form of the globalizing process. Globalization can be particularly deceitful, in that it can present its fantasies in full color and with movement. The evolution of highly developed marketing techniques, supported by special-effects technology, promises the church amazing results from a simple and inoffensive starting point.

In this respect, globalization reveals the character of the one the Scriptures call the prince of this world, who shapes the pattern of this world's thinking. The lure of globalization harks back to the simple, enticing promise made to our first mother and later to our Savior. What can be wrong with a bite of fruit when you consider what you will accomplish with it? How can the transformation of stones into bread to allay legitimate hunger be anything but good? Eve did not see through the ruse. As a result, she introduced herself and her descendants to a world of distortions and death. Jesus saw through Satan's deception clearly and did not even entertain a discussion on the merits of the offer. He discerned the pattern of the prince of this world and responded accordingly. He can give us new eyes so we can see through the deceptions of the world as well.

History is clear: the pattern of this world will always seem enticing and sensible. Resisting may at times look foolish. After all, we reason, we can reach the world with the gospel a lot faster and more effectively by making full use of the instruments of globalization. Perhaps so, but do we see the pattern behind the technology? Can we discern the truth? Is the church equipped to see, or have we spent all our energies trying to capitalize on the bounty offered by the world, at the expense of the spiritual edification of believers? Have we failed to sharpen the eyes of believers to see through the ruse?

Implementing a New Pattern

As I said before, we live in this world, using the means available in the natural and social environment that constitutes earthly existence today. How else can we bear witness of the new world in Christ, if not within the context of this world? Yet we must not diminish in any way the fact that we are no longer of this world. Christ gives us a new pattern of thinking that guides us, even as we live in and minister to this world. It is the calling of the church today to equip believers so that they will be able to avoid being conformed to this world's pattern and instead will be transformed by the renewal of their minds.

Since we are talking about a way of thinking, practical action must involve changes in those places and mechanisms by which Christians are taught to think about their faith. Seminaries must do more than churn out preachers and local church administrators. They need to develop Christian thinkers—people who are competent to engage the issues of the day in light of the uniqueness of the gospel. Local churches must no longer be a weekly detour from our real, secular life. Rather, they need to be a place where we are reminded of our distinct calling. Sunday school curricula need to go beyond teaching fact and behavior. They must also help children, youth, and adults to think about our unique, distinctive nature as people of God and about how we must speak to the world.

There needs to be an energetic literary critique of what passes for Christian literature today. So-called Christian publishing has become largely part of the system of this world. As such, it has a vested interest in maintaining that system, even if it contains small-scale messages to the contrary. It has embraced conspicuous, superfluous consumption as its necessary operational base. But it is precisely against such things that the Christian worldview stands. The gospel does away with the need to buy, the need to have, because it fulfills our deepest longings with the love of Christ. We need to rebuild Christian literature around the pattern of the gospel, so that the new generation of Christians will be transformed by the renewal of their minds.

Implications for Missions

So, what does the preceding discussion have to do with missions? I would like to highlight several areas.

The church and its role

The evangelical missions movement today places great significance on church planting, yet I hear very little in missions circles about the nature of the church. Typically, the approach seeks primarily to answer the question of quantifiable church presence—a church for X number of people, a church for each village, a church comprised of X number of adult believers, and so on. There seems to exist an understandable fear of artificial and unhelpful disunity between various denominational views of church structure, which may in part explain the silence on the subject of what a church is. Another probable reason for the silence is the absence of serious ecclesiology in our current missions workforce. I have detected no significant discussion on this subject in missions circles in the last 25 years. The emphasis has been on evangelism. Where church planting is specified as a goal, it seems to be conceived as a necessary collection of evangelized individuals, rather than a clearly developed spiritual community along the lines of Ephesians 4. The local church seems to be validated by its mere numerical existence, rather than by its spiritual essence and nature.

The modern missions movement may be propagating a truncated model of the church, i.e., one that is incapable of judging the spirit of the age. More likely, the local church becomes merely another player in the world's game, rather than presenting an alternative. If I am correct in this assessment, it becomes vital to reintroduce in our missions movement the discussion of what the church is and what its role is in the face of globalizing trends that shape so much of how we live and think today. The missions movement needs to rethink itself, not simply as a promoter of a truth statement, but as a propagator of a people of God. Evangelical missions have, for the most part, abandoned a conscious intention to expand the religious structure of Christendom, yet in practice that seems to be precisely what we continue to do. We are caught up in methodologies and structures, in visible and quantifiable entities, when what we need is a living, spiritual body that manifests itself in a diversity of ways, because it is not bound to any one form but rather transcends form.

A new way of thinking

Christian missions must display an alternative way of thinking about ourselves and the world, not simply a formal change of religious allegiance and behavior. Globalization has been casting the church as "Christianity," meaning just another religion that needs to be recognized among all the other competing religions. This is a trend of enormous power, and it is difficult to resist, because it offers us benefits if we conform to this identity. We will be allowed a vending stall in the globalized marketplace, if we play by the rules and don't challenge the arrangement. Yet the church must follow its head, Jesus Christ, and must be willing to overturn the market stalls and scatter the profits on the ground. I do not mean this in the literal sense of vandalizing material objects and structures. More traumatic than such acts, we need to shatter a whole way of thinking, since God has rejected it, and we need to offer the gospel of God's love in Christ as a new determiner of what matters in this world.

The power of projection

Globalization has a definite Western flavor to it. This is not surprising, because when globalization breaks down national barriers, those societies with greater power of projection will be in a better position to take advantage of it. There is a flow of people and information in all directions today. However, the rules of engagement are mostly defined by the West. The ubiquitous presence of CNN and the BBC wherever there are television sets by far outweighs the token foreign TV programs that find occasional presence in Western living rooms. Joseph Stiglitz (2002), formerly senior vice president and chief economist of the World Bank, puts it bluntly:

> The Western countries have pushed poor countries to eliminate trade barriers, but kept up their own barriers, preventing developing countries from exporting their agricultural products and so depriving them of desperately needed export income…. But even when not guilty of hypocrisy, the West has driven the globalization agenda, ensuring that it garners a disproportionate share of the benefits, at the expense of the developing world.

The Western missions movement also shares in the West's power of projection. Western mission agencies have the capacity to mobilize resources and establish a presence among the new mission frontiers of the world sooner and more solidly than most other agencies. Where the West cannot literally establish a permanent presence, it can provide resources to locals and others, so that its influence is felt even where its personnel can't be physically present. The church established under this influence will reflect both the benefits and the problems of the West.

When Jimmy Swaggart lost much of his visibility in the United States as a result of his public embarrassment, his ministry had already established solid enough activities in Brazil, for example, to sustain his enterprise. Another case in point is the question of what the appropriate form of worship is. This question has been a primary concern for church leaders in North America in recent years. It is amazing to see the same question becoming central to churches in Brazil today. This area was not a concern at all while I was growing up in Brazil.

Social interest groups

Globalization is in great part the Westernization or even the Americanization of the world. The world missions movement undeniably reflects this reality. In North America, the church exists to a great extent as one of the many interest groups competing to gain benefits from the established social structures. It sacrifices its claim as a beacon pointing to a different world, in order to become one more player in the competition for advantages within the existing world system.

In countries where the work of missions has led to a well established church, this same phenomenon is taking shape. Thus, we see the evangelical presence in South Korea, Malaysia, Chile, and Brazil, among others, assuming the form of social interest groups seeking power and influence with the political and social structures, as has happened in North America.

Recovering a "mustard seed perspective"

It is important to recognize that the mechanisms of globalization have an inherent power to shape not only how people in general think, but also how we, the church, think. It is in this sense that the church may become a vehicle for the globalization of a new pattern of this world, of which Paul warns us in Romans 12:2. There is no need for the existence of intentional human agents for this to happen. There is no need to see some dark conspiracy of dominant societies that shape how everyone else lives or thinks. Globalization is like a well paved highway open to everyone, but it is a highway in which those with the most automobiles are the primary and preferential users, for the simple reason that they have the greater means to use the road. Unless we intentionally heed Paul's admonition, we become simply part of the system, with nothing significant to contribute to it. The salt loses its flavor.

We must heed Paul's command by recovering a "mustard seed perspective," remembering the small band of 12 with which Jesus changed the world. The system of this world is caught up in largeness, loudness, and overwhelming clutter, which impairs thinking and encourages consumption. We need to break this mindset, not just as individuals, but as the church and as a missions movement. We need to rediscover the power of smallness and of low visibility. Like salt, we release our flavor by emptying ourselves, not by gathering ourselves in ever bigger saltshakers with great spires for everyone to see.

References

Fernando, A. (2000). The church: The mirror of the Trinity. In W. D. Taylor (Ed.), *Global missiology for the 21st century* (pp. 239-256). Grand Rapids, MI: Baker Academic.

Lewis, C. S. (2001). *The Screwtape letters.* New York, NY: HarperCollins.

Stiglitz, J. (2002). *Globalization and its discontents.* New York, NY: W. W. Norton.

Waters, M. (1995). *Globalization.* London, UK: Routledge.

Zengotita, T. (2002, April). The numbing of the American mind: Culture as anesthetic. *Harper's Magazine.*

Alex Araujo is Interdev's Director of International Operations, as well as a consultant in intercultural partnership relations and contextualization issues. Previously, he was Director of International Operations for Partners International. Born and raised in Brazil, Alex was the Brazil National Director of COMIBAM 87, the first continent-wide missions conference in Latin America. His missions work has given him the opportunity to help establish cooperative relationships with Christians in 54 countries in all continents. Email: aaraujo@interdev .org.

15

Cutting out the middleman: mission and the local church in a globalised postmodern world

Ros Johnson

Altrincham Baptist Church (ABC) has around 1,000 attenders and is situated in a middle-class suburb of Manchester, UK. During a church service in 1998, Roger Sutton, the senior pastor, heard God say to him, "Go to Uganda and take a team." He had no desire to go to Uganda and promptly forgot about the injunction, but some 18 months later God said to him, "Why haven't you gone?" He felt rebuked, and he knew he had to respond.

Roger and several members of his church already knew members of an Ugandan dance team who had visited the UK. They liked and trusted the team's leader, who led a church in Jinja, the second city of Uganda, so Roger decided they should go there. He took advice from members of his congregation who knew Uganda and from the African Pastors Fellowship, and he paid a preliminary visit before returning with a team in early 2000. At that stage, they were still unclear about what they should be doing, but to start with, they offered ministry and teaching to pastors. Gradually and through subsequent visits, specific projects and activities were identified with which members and contacts of ABC wanted to get involved. These included support for vocational training of AIDS orphans, financial support for a local church, and involvement by a number of individuals in medical projects.

The link spread spontaneously well beyond the church walls and led directly to a "twinning" arrangement between the city of Jinja and the Metropolitan Borough of Trafford (part of Greater Manchester). There are plans to set up links between businesses in the two cities, and schools are also starting to establish links. Local residents of Altrincham are joining church members in sponsoring Ugandan orphans. Further spin-offs are in prospect.

At a spiritual level, the links have had a significant impact on those ABC members who have become directly involved. Personal contact with Ugandan Christians, who had few material goods and many problems yet were happy and dignified, prompted many to recognise the extent of materialism and selfishness in Western society and to reassess their own attitudes and goals. They realised, in particular, the importance of relationships. Moreover, the link and the associated publicity raised the profile of ABC in its local area, and those who went to Jinja found that their mission trip gave them good opportunities to talk about their faith to non-Christian friends when they returned.

BMS, the UK Baptist mission agency, did not operate in Uganda. However, it found itself in the novel position of being asked by ABC and some other Baptist churches to start working there. This would mean BMS could be the sending agency of church members who (as a result of going with a church

team to Jinja) felt called to full-time mission work in Uganda. BMS agreed to this arrangement.

Despite these positive outcomes, the development of the ABC/Jinja relationship has not been a straightforward process. On the contrary, it has been untidy, laborious, and at times hurtful to both sides. Roger and his congregation had sought informed advice, but they still had to grapple at the Ugandan end with denominational differences and inter-church jealousies; unrealistic (to Western eyes) expectations, leading to disappointment and hurt feelings; and problems in identifying projects to fund which would be genuinely worthwhile, as opposed to those which some Ugandans thought important. They were constantly feeling their way. Yet the attitude in ABC towards the link is overwhelmingly positive, and they are looking to expand and consolidate the link.

This story of a Western church engaging directly in mission-related activities is far from unusual at the beginning of the 21st century. A survey of 157 active evangelical churches in the UK in 2001 conducted by Global Connections, the UK Evangelical Missionary Network, showed that 31% had a direct link with a church in another country, and 24% had already started their own mission projects overseas. Such a development would have been almost unheard of 50 or even 30 years ago. The factors which make it logistically possible can be summed up in one word: globalisation.

But globalisation alone would not be enough to prompt local churches to do mission directly. An additional factor is the growth of the global church (arguably itself a by-product of globalisation), which means that there are Christians in many countries of the world with whom partnerships can be formed. And finally, attitudinal changes linked to postmodernity mean that professing Western Christians, if they engage with global mission at all, will increasingly want to do so on their own terms and in their own way.

In the traditional mission model which has stood for around 200 years, agencies were the main players, and churches provided the support in terms of candidates, money, and prayer. We are now moving to a new model, in which local churches are becoming active participants in mission and mission agencies will increasingly be required to justify their existence. This raises serious questions for agencies. Will they ignore the trend, attempt to oppose it, or embrace it and adjust their approach so that they can cooperate with churches in new ways?

The evidence cited here is very largely from the UK, but missiological journals and books published in North America indicate that a similar trend towards disintermediation in mission has been evident there for some years (e.g., Borthwick, 1999). This is not surprising, since North American churches are often far larger than the average UK congregation of around 100-400 members, and so they have the resources to develop their own mission programmes. Churches as large as ABC are rarely found outside big cities in the UK, and here too the longest established mission ventures by local churches tend to be in such big churches. However, more recently even small congregations in the UK are getting directly involved.

Providing the Means

Globalisation makes different parts of the world and peoples increasingly interconnected. This interconnectedness makes it practically possible for local churches to undertake their own mission activities. The connections are of many kinds. For example, the huge advances in communications and technology in the 19th and 20th centuries, from the telegraph to the Internet and satellite technology, have transformed both the volume of information that can be transmitted around the world and the speed of transmission. We are bombarded with data of all kinds through the media, and the Internet provides instant access to huge amounts of information that might previously have been available only to specialists.

Developments in transport, in particular the aeroplane, make it practically possible to undertake mission activities on the other side of the world, even during a two-week summer holiday. The growth of international tourism and business travel means many ordinary people have experience of coping in a foreign culture and so are more ready to contemplate dipping their toes in global mission than they would have been a generation earlier. Cultural diversity is now a reality in most cities of the Western world and often in smaller towns and villages too. Moslems, Hindus, or Sikhs may live down the street, meaning that many people have acquaintances or colleagues of very diverse ethnic and religious backgrounds. The development of globally dominant cultural phenomena, whether we are talking about the English language, McDonald's, or Madonna, has provided commonly understood reference points in almost any part of the world, however superficial some of them may be.

Global communications, transport, medical and scientific advances, and the dissemination of knowledge have also helped to ensure that mission is generally, in physical terms, neither as taxing nor as dangerous as it was in the 19th or early 20th century, and therefore it is easier for the non-professional to contemplate. The general availability of information through the media means that we can now be better informed than was ever possible in the past about what is happening in other parts of the world and about the material and spiritual needs. Journeys to and from a prospective "mission field" now take hours rather than weeks. Communications with home take minutes by telephone or email and not weeks or months by letter. In the event of illness or accident, there will usually be either an adequate hospital within striking distance or an aeroplane or helicopter to ferry the patient to a suitable medical centre. Doctors in most corners of the world will have at least some knowledge of recent advances in most areas of medical science through attendance at international conferences and access to the Internet. The media provide up-to-date news on areas of tension, and a speedy withdrawal from a danger zone will usually be possible by a variety of forms of transport.

This is a very different world from that in which the "modern" era of mission was launched some 200 years ago. Nowadays, a lifelong commitment no longer seems necessary, mission work

From Peru to London

Samuel Cueva, a pastor in Peru, believed that Peru should begin sending missionaries beyond its borders. He and his family put this belief into practice by coming to London in the late 1990s, with the aim of starting a Spanish-speaking church to minister to some of the many Spanish speakers living and working in the city. Soon after his arrival, he called at St. James Muswell Hill, an Anglican church in North London, to ask for directions to one of the internationally known churches in Central London. He received such a friendly welcome that after attending a Sunday service at St. James, he and his wife felt God saying to them that this was the church where they should start their ministry. The vicar of St. James, Alex Ross, and the church council agreed to this proposal.

The Spanish-speaking church meets at separate times from the British congregation, but Samuel is part of the St. James' ministry team, and the two congregations cooperate in local evangelism and ministry. Two teams from St. James have also gone to Samuel's home church in Peru, with the aim of strengthening mutual support and fellowship and undertaking joint outreach there. Samuel has organised two international conferences on global mission which have been hosted by St. James.

need not be pioneering, the mission field is seldom unknown or uncharted, knowledge of English will get you a long way, and you can go for as long or as short as you want.

Providing Opportunities

The emergence of the global church in the last two centuries—in one sense itself a product of globalisation—has helped to make mission from the local church more feasible than ever and has ensured that mission will also be multi-directional and multifaceted. This means that old categorisations, such as that of "sending" and "receiving" countries, have not just ceased to be relevant but become a barrier to understanding the diversity of what is now happening, sometimes as much by apparent chance as by any human design.

60% of all Christians now live outside the West. There is a Christian presence on every continent, with thriving evangelical churches in many places, frequently Pentecostal or charismatic in character. This worldwide Christian presence has created new opportunities for Christians from different nationalities to work together in serving God's kingdom. Almost as many missionaries from the South are now working cross-culturally as from the North. Encounters with Christians from the South are helping congregations in the West to realise that although they may have much materially, they are often spiritually impoverished in comparison.

Go to the Nations

Go to the Nations (GTTN; www.gonations.org) was set up in the early 1990s by a network of Brazilian churches with a passion for evangelism. They believed God was challenging them to world mission and that he was saying that it should be done through partnerships and shared resources. Their vision is to build relationships with churches in the UK and Europe, sharing their own enthusiasm for relationships, prayer, and worship, but also benefiting from the European church's maturity and experience; and then jointly to undertake mission in other countries, especially Eastern Europe and the 10/40 Window. A view of the local church being at the heart of mission is central to this vision.

Christian Life Church (CLC) in Hereford in the west of England, with about 150 members, has had a relationship with GTTN since the mid-1990s. A series of Brazilians have come to live in their community for a year or two at a time, and members of the church have also gone to Brazil. According to the minister of CLC, the impact of the Brazilians has opened the congregation's eyes to the need and call of missions. They are realising that as a body they are called to mission, and they are developing joint teams to go on short-term missions to Brazil, Africa, and other parts of Europe.

The likelihood is that as contacts of all kinds grow between Christians of different cultures, there will be a parallel growth in understanding that, as Charles Van Engen (2001, p. 27) has argued, drawing on Ephesians 4:7, Christians around the world need each other. More can be achieved by working together, with each group of believers offering their gifts to the others, than by working individually. This is no longer an arena just for the professionals in mission.

Impact of Postmodernity

The final major factor contributing to the new climate for mission is the emerging worldview described as postmodernity, which is affecting Christians as much as non-Christians. Its course and implications have been brilliantly mapped by Gerard Kelly (1999), amongst others. Here are some features of a postmodern society which are influencing attitudes to mission:

- **Cynicism**, especially about authority, hierarchy, and "experts." This translates into a lack of interest in or support for traditional mission agencies among many individuals born after about 1960 ("Generation Xers").
- A strong emphasis on **personal relationships** and contacts, rather than organisational structures, to provide the networks for getting things done. People—both collectively and individually—respond to situations with which they can empathise directly.
- An emphasis on **reality**, rather than truth. One implication of this is that the individual's motivation for mission may often be less spiritual ("to save the lost") than practical (to help others "find fullness of life").

- Desire for **hands-on involvement** and for **adventure**, which can in part be met by short-term mission experiences.
- **Insecurity** about the future. This makes individuals reluctant to commit for the long term and helps explain the popularity of short-term and gap-year mission experiences.
- **Consumerism** and **customisation.** People want to choose for themselves where and how they get involved in mission.
- **Materialism.** The seduction of material wealth can blunt Christian commitment. It does, however, mean that many Western Christians have material resources which could help the work and witness of Christians in countries where the church is struggling financially, although a relationship focused on one-way financial transfers poses particular risks.

In short, postmodern Christians—essentially those born after about 1960—are likely to be interested in mission only when it is relationship-based, seems relevant, gives them a chance to get directly involved, and where their involvement can be on their own terms rather than dictated by an organisation.

Local Churches and Mission

All these factors taken together create conditions for doing mission in ways very different from the familiar patterns of the past. Of course, things will not change overnight, in a year, or even in a decade. The situation is an evolving one. Much depends on the denomination (if any), age range, and leadership of individual churches.

Bruce Camp (1994) identified three paradigms of local church involvement in missions:

■ **Supporting.** This is broadly the traditional approach and involves trusting agencies to know best, supporting them in prayer and giving, receiving visiting mission speakers, etc.

■ **Sending.** This approach was a development of the 1980s, in which churches began sending their own church members as missionaries and wanted a meaningful relationship with them. The services of mission agencies might be called on as required, but the partnership was expected to be an equal one.

■ **Synergistic.** In this approach, churches focus their mission efforts on a few items which they can do well and then partner with others to produce greater effectiveness. Church members are encouraged to visit the mission field to get a sense of ownership and are empowered to get involved. The approach is pragmatic and opportunistic, combining evangelism and social action. There is openness to working actively with non-Western churches to assist them in achieving common goals. Mission agencies may not be involved at all.

As Camp observed, few churches will operate in one paradigm only. But the synergistic approach is well suited to the effects of globalisation and post-modernity and is on the increase.

The "New Church" movements in the UK make an interesting case study in this respect. Typically their membership is young, often with a fair sprinkling of professionals. The levels of commitment and expectation tend to be high, and there is an emphasis on the gifts of the Spirit. Because these movements started from scratch within the last 30 years, their attitudes to mission are likely to be geared to what is relevant and appropriate today, rather than influenced by traditions of the past.

A 1998 survey into the overseas mission involvement of UK New Churches discovered, on the basis of 240 responses, that on average each church had four overseas mission interests and that these churches were working in partnership with mission agencies in 34% of their overseas interests. The report (Graham, 1998, pp. 15, 16, 18-19) also commented on "a seeming reluctance on the part of the majority of New Churches to engage in any kind of systematic planning of mission activities and advance. While the promptings and leading of the Holy Spirit are considered to be vital to the onward thrust of mission, nevertheless there is a reticence to strategise or affix time scales to mission activity." So far as mission agencies were concerned, the survey indicated that New Churches "were comfortable with the mission agencies acting in a consultancy role as and when required, but they were less happy about their participation in planning/ strategy and the supervision of specific projects." They expected agencies to show an attitude of service to the local church. In addition, they felt that agencies should demonstrate a flexible style, have a structure capable of accommodating the exceptional rather than insisting on conformity, emphasize quality relationships, and hold to a theology with a positive regard for the place of spiritual gifts in the church today.

In other words, New Churches generally do not see a need for mission agencies in their traditional role of professional intermediary. As far as they are concerned, the disintermediation of mission has already happened. The middleman has truly been cut out.

New Frontiers International

New Frontiers International is a dynamic "New Church" movement begun in the early 1980s. It currently has nearly 300 member churches, of which up to 70% are in the UK. The autonomy of the local church is a foundational principle, and considerable value is also attached to building strong relationships between churches within the movement for mutual support and networking. Individual churches will specialise and take a lead in specific areas of ministry, including mission, providing advice and training to members of other NFI churches. Both evangelism and social action are seen as essential elements of mission.

Bournemouth Family Church (BFC) was started as an NFI church plant in the early 1990s and currently has a membership of around 240. It is strongly mission oriented and gives around 40% of its annual budget to mission, but only to people or projects with which the church has a direct connection. It supports mission in several countries, and one of its major areas of involvement is rural Uganda. As a result of a personal link with a leading Ugandan Christian, BFC is supporting a network of pastors in remote rural locations who are struggling with poverty and lack of teaching and who are vulnerable to cults and the advance of Islam. They started by building relationships and giving training, but they have also assisted with health education, establishing schools, and setting up self-subsistence projects.

BFC approached Wycliffe Bible Translators (WBT), seeking to "adopt" an unreached people. With WBT's help, they established a strong personal link with the only Christian from a people group in a country bordering Uganda. Members of BFC plan to work under an Ugandan leadership team in church planting within Uganda and the unreached people group.

BFC typifies the New Church approach in several respects. Confident, compassionate, and committed to the spread of the gospel, they saw no need for mission agency support in their work within Uganda. But in the more difficult area of reaching an unreached people, they recognised the need for specialist assistance and found in WBT an agency willing to work in genuine partnership with them. All BFC's mission involvement is founded on strong personal relationships with teams of people that they trust.

Within the traditional denominations, missionary-minded churches usually have a greater proportion of older people in the congregation than the New Churches, and they are more likely to operate in the supporting or sending paradigms or a mixture of the two. Prayer and financial support for agencies remain a significant element of the global mission activities in many of these churches. Church-to-church or church-to-project partnerships are, however, increasing, often funded outside the traditional missionary budget. Mission support generally is becoming increasingly relational, with church members (especially those under 40) wanting to give to people or projects with which they have some personal connection.

The Role of Mission Agencies

Are the sorts of relationships and partnerships in which churches such as Altrincham Baptist are engaging actually mission? And if so, who are the missioners, and who is the mission field? This is where traditional terminology and concepts become inadequate. By giving money to the work in Jinja, ABC is supporting mission, and the impact of the links on members of the ABC congregation and the wider local community is also a form of mission. But it is not mission as we have known it. The relationship has evolved in a largely unplanned fashion, and so have the outcomes. It is in some respects a risky venture. The regular money transfers which ABC is sending to Jinja could create an attitude of dependency at the Ugandan end. And the arrival of what from the recipients' angle will be huge amounts of money may pose a temptation to corruption. But the relationship is clearly proving stimulating and rewarding for both sides.

The instinctive reaction of mission agencies to the direct involvement of churches in mission in this way is often one of disapproval and concern. This is understandable. After the col-lapse of Communism in Eastern Europe in 1989, many churches in the West rushed to take out aid and set up links to support churches there. Lack of understanding of the local culture and church scene meant that some of those initiatives were ill-advised or ineffectual. There are several potential pitfalls for the unwary who attempt to set up a relationship with those in a very different culture—in particular, difficulties of communication, differing expectations and, above all, money. Several relationships have foundered on these rocks.

Churches doing "mission direct" are also indirectly threatening mission agencies' role as the professionals in mission and thereby their very existence. Agencies have accumulated, often over decades, a store of knowledge and expertise in their areas of the world or specialist ministries, as well as in the practicalities of placing, managing, and supporting people who are sent overseas to do Christian work. It is naturally disturbing to them to see their expertise ignored, with the very real risk that churches will make avoidable mistakes.

Is the future for mission agencies, then, gloomy? Almost certainly yes, if they cling to the old ways and attempt to discourage churches from playing an active role in mission themselves. But if they can respond creatively to the changing situation and redefine their role by partnering with churches to provide advice, expertise, and specialist functions, the prospects will still be challenging but much more positive. Instead of seeing local church involvement as a threat to be opposed, agencies should accept it as an irreversible trend with which they need to work, so as to ensure that mission is done well, whoever is involved.

CMS

CMS is a large Anglican mission agency that recently celebrated its 200th anniversary. Its long and honourable history covers the whole course of the modern missionary movement, and in many ways it is a very traditional organisation with an ageing supporter base in churches. In recent years, however, CMS has done some hard thinking about its role and future, and it has brought in modernising leaders and innovative strategies. Its 10-year "Strategy for 2001–2010" recognises that "future studies" suggest that in the West "institutional forms of church (but not belief) are collapsing under the processes of globalisation.... New mission needs a new culture: one which is reorganised, enabling people to connect directly with wider cultural changes in an evangelistic way."

CMS is now working to create an agency culture capable of accommodating flexible local missionary responses to global changes, and it recognises the need for pioneering, non-bureaucratic mission.

Biblical Perspectives on the Local Church and Mission

The Bible, in particular the book of Acts, gives no clear guidance on who should be responsible for doing mission. The initial wave of missionary work outside Jerusalem occurred in an apparently haphazard and unplanned way as the result of persecution (Acts 8:1, 4; Acts 11:19). Acts 13 records that the first planned missionary journey took place when, by the prompting of the Holy Spirit, the church at Antioch sent out Saul and Barnabas with some others (Acts 13:3). This pattern of small missionary parties sent out by the Antioch church to plant churches is repeated in Acts 15:39, 40. See also Acts 16:3, 11, which indicates that both Timothy and Luke joined Paul and Silas on Paul's second missionary journey, but they split up when it seemed sensible to do so (Acts 17:14). Whether alone or with others, Paul evangelised and planted churches wherever he was.

On this evidence, it could be argued that, according to the biblical pattern, mission should emanate from the local church. But the evidence base for such a conclusion is slender. In the first century AD, the church consisted of small, scattered groups of believers. It appeared to use whatever means came to hand to spread the word. Moreover, if a view that mission is the function only of local churches had been rigidly enforced around 1800, it is questionable whether the modern mission movement would ever have got under way. As Andrew Walls (1988) has shown, the missionary society of the 19th century was a pragmatic response to the needs of the time and the task, and it was modelled on the trading companies of the period rather than on any clear biblical precedent. But the amazing fruit of missionary societies' work was the growth of the global church.

This necessarily brief survey suggests that from the evidence of the Bible and history, there is no "right" or divinely approved means for doing mission. God can and does use a variety of means to achieve his purposes.

Conclusions

Because of the changes attributable to globalisation, the global church, and postmodernity, it is already clear that the future of mission will be very different from its past. It will be diverse as to methods and models, multidirectional, increasingly disintermediated, often lacking any obvious strategic direction, and above all relational. The New Churches are mostly already there. In the traditional denominations, as those now aged under 40 move increasingly into positions of leadership, local churches may either lose interest in cross-cultural mission (if they see the traditional model as the only option), or they may want to be active in mission for themselves in ways already being modelled by the New Churches.

Mission agencies need to rethink their role in order to meet the new challenges. Above all, they need to start seeing themselves as servants and consultants, ready to offer advice and support to local churches. They can offer:

■ knowledge of life and mission around the world.

■ expertise in recruiting, sending, and supporting people for mission.

■ training facilities.

■ networks and contacts.

■ specialisms such as Bible translation, unreached peoples, working with street children, or medical mission work.

All of these would be of immeasurable assistance to churches in helping them to avoid mistakes or reinventing the wheel. But churches are unlikely to seek help from agencies that take a negative or patronising attitude or insist on calling the shots. The long-term future of many agencies may depend on how they react to the disintermediation challenge.

Writing in the 1920s, the British missionary Roland Allen (1962, pp. 96-97), who was ahead of his time on so many issues, spoke presciently of the need to distinguish between the organisation of the church as a missionary body and the "modern" missionary organisation. He pointed out that the results of missionary work done through organisations were due, not to the organisations, but to:

… that undying spirit of love for the souls of men which Christ inspires. The modern organisation is only the form in which we have expressed that spirit; and a time may come when organisation, which seems to us to be absolutely necessary, may cease to be necessary, or may take such different shape as to be hardly recognisable; for it has within it elements of weakness which betray its temporal character.

Allen (1962, p. 114) went on:

The societies have taught us from every pulpit that every Christian should be at heart a missionary, on the unshakeable ground that the spirit of Christ is given to all Christians…. That teaching has not been without effect. Many are beginning to believe it, and one day many will act on it. There is nothing in the teaching to convince anyone that to express his missionary zeal he need support, or belong to, any other society than the church to which he already belongs.

The time which Allen dimly foresaw—when missionary organisations would no longer be the only way of doing mission—is now upon us.

References

Allen, R. (1962). *The spontaneous expansion of the church*. Grand Rapids, MI: Wm. B. Eerdmans.

Borthwick, P. (1999, July). What local churches are saying to mission agencies. *Evangelical Missions Quarterly*, *35*(3), pp. 324-330.

Camp, B. K. (1994, July/August). Three ministry paradigms for local church involvement in missions. *International Journal of Frontier Mission, 11*(3).

Graham, E. (Ed.). (1998). *The body international: First ever survey of New Church ministry overseas*. Available from Global Connections, Whitefield Nouse, 186 Kennington Park Road, London SE11 4BT, England.

Kelly, G. (1999). *Get a grip on the future without losing your hold on the past*. London, UK: Monarch.

Van Engen, C. (2001, January). Towards a theology of mission partnerships. *Missiology, 29*, p. 27.

Walls, A. F. (1988, April). Missionary societies and the fortunate subversion of the church. *Evangelical Quarterly, 60*(2), pp. 141-155.

A civil servant by profession, in 2001–2003 **Ros Johnson** *was seconded by the British Government to the Oasis Trust, a Christian charity. Here she worked on the Connect! initiative, which highlights the way global mission has changed and which encourages local churches to get directly involved (see www.connect.nu). This chapter is based on that work and the research Ros did into UK local churches already active in global mission. Ros lives in South London, is married with two sons, and is an active member of her local Anglican church.*

Conclusion

16

Globalization, world evangelization, and global missiology

STEVE S. MOON
DAVID TAI-WOONG LEE

As we reflect on globalization and world evangelization, we need to mention two things at the outset. First, "globalization" is a slippery word whose meaning changes like a chameleon. In some ways, globalization is like a worldview. You are a part of it and cannot ignore it without facing a serious problem, yet you cannot readily pinpoint it. Globalization is, at one time, talking about cultural changes. At other times, it is a way of portraying socio-economic trends and developments.

The second point we should note is that globalization is like a wave or wind that flows or blows without any apparent cause(s). Nonetheless, there is usually a major player(s) behind it. In the Roman world of the New Testament times, the Romans were the major players politically. Philosophically, the Greeks were one of the key players. Fortunately, the early church was a key player in a globalization of its own kind. Christians sought to accomplish globalization through world evangelization, although no such terminology was used. Their aim was successful, as we read in the book of Acts and in later church history. In the colonial times, we all know who the main players were. During the days of internationalization after World War II, the North Americans were the ones who carried globalization out on their own terms (see Robert, 2002, p. 50).

If we were to lift the curtain up and look behind it, we would no doubt find that there are many forces competing to bring globalization on their own terms, with some fading away. Communism and similar forms of ideology are now off the scene. But it is obvious that the West, in one form or another, is very actively involved in globalization, as are the fundamentalist segments of the Islamic and Hindu worlds.

As we discuss globalization and world evangelization, we must not do it naïvely. On one hand, we will be very much aware of the complexities and competitions of globalization. On the other hand, to prevent the discussion from becoming too broad, some degree of simplification is inevitable. In most of the following discussion, globalization will be fleshed out primarily in relation to world evangelization. That is, the phrase "globalization by world evangelization" refers to the global extension of the gospel.

The term "world evangelization" is used in at least the following three ways among evangelicals:

1. It is similar to doing evangelism worldwide.

2. It has evangelism at the core but includes much more.

3. It encompasses both evangelism and social responsibility.[1]

In this chapter, "world evangelization" will be used in a general sense that includes items 2 and 3 above. When used in this manner, "world evangelization" can be synonymous with "world mission." Furthermore, unlike some tracks of missiology that emphasize the missional activities of missionary teams to the exclusion of the ministry of the church as the people of God engaged in missions, this chapter will not make a sharp distinction between the two.

It is hoped that this chapter, first of all, will show how world evangelization has ushered in the globalization of the church and missions and, second, will draw lessons for the present and future direction of world evangelization.

Biblical Perspective

Relationship between globalization and world evangelization

Even with just a cursory look through the Old Testament, one cannot but acknowledge the universal (or global) scale with which God deals with his creation. The writer of Genesis says, "In the beginning God created the heavens and the earth" (Gen. 1:1). It is no accident that God's initial mandate was

---

[1] Granted that the terms "world evangelization" and "mission(s)" are interchangeable, world evangelization traditionally has had the following three streams: (1) mission as evangelism (pre-Lausanne and AD 2000); (2) mission as both evangelism and social responsibility, with priority in evangelism (post-Lausanne); (3) mission as evangelism and social responsibility equally ("radical discipleship group"). See Moreau (2000) and Barrett (2000). We have regrouped and rephrased the definitions in accordance with the consensus of current evangelicals on world evangelization or mission, as we understand it.

given in accordance with this perspective, i.e., to the whole of humanity (Gen. 1:28ff.). It will be noted that not until Genesis chapters 10 and 11 do peoples or tribes come into focus. Nonetheless, God's original intention has never been altered. There are many records that prove this express universal focus ("globalism"). A few key texts are Genesis 12:1-3, Exodus 19:4-6, and Psalm 67 (see Kaiser, 1999).

It is not until we come to the New Testament, however, that these germinal thoughts on "globalism" come into clearer focus. See, for example, the so-called "Great Commission" passages, especially Matthew 28:18-20 and Luke 24:44-48. Also, the Apostle Paul succinctly expresses both continuity and discontinuity between the Old Testament and the New in his epistle to the Ephesians (see Eph. 3:1-8).

To sum up, both the Old Testament and the New Testament anticipate the globalization of the world through world evangelization. We can see at least one such attempt of an earlier process of globalization through evangelization of the known world in the book of Acts.

Common themes

The kingdom of God

When Jesus began his earthly ministry, his first proclamation was on the coming of the kingdom of God and people's preparation for it (Matt. 4:17; Mark 1:15; Luke 4:17-19). Without going into detail, we can see through the history of Christianity that the kingdom of God has implications for both globalization and world evangelization. Although the kingdom of God by nature is not territorial and is thus not to be equated with world evangelization automatically, neither can we deny that it exists in creative tension with world evangelization. It is therefore legitimate to say that there is interplay between the kingdom of God, world evangelization, and globalization. We anticipate the culmination of these three as portrayed by the Apostle John in Revelation 5:9-10 and 7:9-10.

The church and the people of God

The church presupposes both the local and the global. The Bible allows for pluralism of culture and thus the translatability of Christianity (see Sanneh, 1989). Nonetheless, there is also strong support for the catholicity of the church. The Apostle Paul therefore writes, "There is one body and one Spirit—just as you were called to one hope when you were called—one Lord, one faith, one baptism; one God and Father of all..." (Eph. 4:4-6). It is regrettable that the missiological literature of the 1970s through the 1990s emphasized the locality of the church at the cost of "globality" in world evangelization.[2] It is time that the "globality" or catholicity of the church receives its due attention in the formulation of global missiology for a global age.

---

[2] Since the concept of contextualization began in the 1970s, much of the missiological literature has focused on localness and the interplay of local culture with the gospel. It was during the 1990s that the "globalness" of churches began to receive due attention along with the "localness." See such books as Pittman, Habito, and Muck (1996) and Taylor (2000).

The gospel

Nowhere in the Bible is the idea mentioned that the gospel is for any one race or people. Throughout both the Old and New Testaments, whenever the gospel is described, it inevitably takes a global stance. Even when the whole context is particularistic, as in the prophetic literature, often when the Saviour is being portrayed, the prophecy crosses racial boundaries and takes on a universal stance. The global nature of the gospel as it is written in both the Old Testament and the New Testament is quite well summed up by Jesus himself in Luke 24:44-47:

> … Everything must be fulfilled that is written about me in the Law of Moses, the Prophets, and the Psalms…. This is what is written: The Christ will suffer and rise from the dead on the third day, and repentance and forgiveness of sins will be preached in his name to *all nations* (emphasis added).

We can, therefore, conclude that globalization and world evangelization are not new to the Bible. From the beginning of creation to the end of the world, God is concerned about the whole world. World evangelization and globalization are an inevitable outcome, according to the divine drama written by God. (We even have the final act mapped out for us to refer to in the book of Revelation.)

It is clear that the problem today is not globalization that results from world evangelization. On the contrary, the crux of the problem is the *lack* of genuine world evangelization, according to the Bible. This in turn results in the lack of globalization as it is portrayed in concepts such as the kingdom of God, the church/the people of God, and the gospel. Skillen (2001) has succinctly expressed the same thought in a different way:

> Globalization should not surprise Christians, who confess that God created one world and sent forth the first man and woman to populate and steward the entire earth. Nor are Christians shocked by the fact that much of the populating and "stewarding" has amounted to destruction, oppression, and unspeakable poverty. From Adam and Eve's first disobedience has sprung a history of multigenerational disobedience to the Creator, who entrusted us with so much. Christians may not wallow or lose hope in the darkness, for their very identity is marked by repentance, thanksgiving, and hope. God did not discard or depart from the creation so misused and fouled by the men and women who fill it and are supposed to steward it wisely. In Christ Jesus, God became human in order to reconcile and redeem the world—the whole earth.

What are we to do as Christians? We must not sit by idly and let globalization take effect, according to agendas mostly invented by unevangelized minds. Instead, as Goudzwaard (2001) recommends, our eyes must be opened to the following facts:

- We are being hypnotized and need to be awakened.
- We can engage in changing the direction of globalization.
- A Christian worldview will change the tide of globalization, however small our efforts may be.
- A $10 trillion global economy is transacted through global Christians

annually. Global Christians can use this as leverage for ushering in kingdom values in the global economy.

■ Globalization must be tackled holistically if we want to direct it towards the kingdom of God.

The effect of world evangelization on globalization could be enormous, provided that our theology of world evangelization has been updated from the old 19th century paradigm.[3] The fact that the church throughout the ages could have done much more is evident as we look at the current globalized world. It is a far cry from the ideals set by the kingdom of God, the church, and the gospel.

Historical Outline

The ideal of globalization by world evangelization began—even if it was only in an embryonic form as a so-called "proto-evangelism"—as early as the Garden of Eden, when God declared, "… I will put enmity between you and the woman, and between your offspring and hers; he will crush your head, and you will strike his heel" (Gen. 3:15). From the outset, it was clear that globalization through world evangelization would not come without severe struggle between the competing forces.

Globalization in the modern sense came much later. The apostles had an early start after Jesus to evangelize the

Roman world. During the Middle Ages, rather than the official Roman church taking the lead, small remnants such as Benedictine communes, Celtic *peregrini* (wandering evangelists), and other Monastic Orders spearheaded the efforts to evangelize the barbarian peoples of the North and other parts of Europe (Winter, 1999).

It was Europe—first the Roman Catholic Church and later the Protestants—that moved ahead and set their feet on the rest of the globe, including the New World. By this time, however, evangelization was synonymous with colonization—particularly to those who had been colonized by the West (Winter, 1999, p. 210).[4] Nonetheless, Christianity in various forms had reached other parts of the world besides Europe. In evaluating world evangelization as a globalizing force during this time period, we see an ever-widening sphere of expansion by "Christendom" to "non-Christendom" through colonialization and spreading their own civilization, sometimes using military force. The Spanish and Portuguese conquest of South America and Central America is one example. This is particularly true during the period of the Roman Catholic missionary advance from 1500 to the beginning of the 18th century. Latourette has called this period the "Three Centuries of Advance."[5] Protestants fol-

---

[3] There was a time when world evangelization in some camps meant solely personal evangelism in a cross-cultural context. There is a healthy holism that has been developing since the Lausanne Movement began in 1974.

[4] Winter claims that by 1945 Europeans had virtual control over 99.5% of the non-Western world.

[5] Luzbetak (1996, pp. 91-92) contends, "The extension of the Cross with the Crown seemed quite natural to the Spaniards and Portuguese … the Portuguese relied heavily on military might." He also admits that world evangelization was achieved through colonialism, although this was not the only factor.

lowed from the latter part of the 18th century. It was only during the last part of the 20th century that people in general began to acknowledge that so-called "Christendom" no longer exists, as the West has become equally a mission field.[6]

There were some religious orders, such as the Jesuits, who played a major role in world evangelization, particularly during the "Three Centuries of Advance." Yet it was the Roman Catholic Church together with the political powers that led the Christianization or globalization process during this period. However, it was not a true world evangelization process, at least not in the type modeled in the book of Acts. The beginning of the modern missionary movement was what spurred the globalization process through world evangelization from Protestant sectors. There is no doubt that colonialization had tremendous impact on the process of globalization through world evangelization in parts of Africa and Asia. It is unfortunate that world evangelization coincided with colonialization as a globalizing force during this period.

After two centuries of world evangelization attempts since the beginning of the modern missionary movement, Christianity was spread virtually all over the globe by the middle of the 20th century. Although some, such as Luzbetak (1996, p. 92), contend that by the 18th century Christianity had already become a *worldwide* religion,"[7] it was much later that Christianity became truly global, not only geographically, but also as a globalizing force, as the church participated in world evangelization.[8]

There are two aspects that are worth emphasizing as we discuss the historical perspective on the globalization of Christianity through world evangelization. One is the fact that the church has spread virtually all over the six continents. We have tried to sketch the historical scene thus far. The other aspect is how the missionary movement has become global as the result of world evangelization. Discussion from this point on will be focused on the global nature of the missionary movement.

There are a number of factors that have contributed to ushering in the global missionary movement. The following are some of the key causes:

---

[6] See books by writers such as Lesslie Newbigin and others. He and like-minded persons have awakened the West about the "myth of Christendom." The International Missionary Council (IMC) began to take this stance much earlier. At the Whitby IMC conference held in 1947, there was already a resolution for both the West and the non-West to become partners in world evangelization, with slogans such as, "From six continents to six continents." See such books as Newbigin (1986) and Hunsberger and Van Gelder (1996) for mission to the West.

[7] Luzbetak refers to Latourette as his source. However, he acknowledges that the spread of "Christendom" is meant when he said that Christianity has become a "worldwide religion."

[8] See Johnstone (1998). In this book, Johnstone portrays the global nature of Christianity as he describes the size and structure of the church worldwide. Pages 140-147 give the vision of world evangelization and how the global church is trying to accomplish this vision.

1. Success of the European/North American missionary force in world evangelization.

2. Globalization of churches and churches assuming their role in world evangelization.

3. Independence of nations formerly under colonial rule and their initiatives in the "global village." This spirit has permeated their churches as well.

4. Convening of international missionary conferences. These gatherings have helped the leaders from newly evangelized countries to catch the vision for world evangelization.

5. Internationalization of the missionary sending structures. As early as the mid-1960s, Western missionary organizations such as the Christian and Missionary Alliance (C&MA) and Overseas Missionary Fellowship (OMF) began to internationalize. By the end of the 20th century, virtually all of the major sending organizations from the West had taken on global characteristics.

6. The rise of the Two-Thirds World missionary movement in the mid-1970s. Perhaps this is the result of all of the above factors put together and more.

To single out one factor among many, perhaps the rise of the Two-Thirds World missionary movement has had the greatest ramifications for the global expansion of the missionary movement. In turn, there have been unprecedented effects on world evangelization. This influence did not grip the minds of the majority of Western missiologists until the mid-1970s, as we survey the missiological literature written during that period.[9]

Pate (1991) estimated that by the end of the 20th century there would be more missionaries from the Two-Thirds World than from the West.[10] Mission work is no longer confined to the older sending countries. The tide has now turned, and mission is truly global as we enter the 21st century. In fact, after the "September 11th" incident, many of the Western missionaries in the Middle East and, for that matter, in most of the ardent Islamic countries have been losing ground. The Two-Thirds World missionaries are filling in the vacuum left by the West, thanks to the global missionary force that consists of both the West and the Two-Thirds World. Thus, world evangelization goes on as a result of the globalization of missions in this 21st century, in spite of all of its shortcomings hinted at above. Once it was world evangelization that ushered in the globalization of the church. Now it is the globalization of mission that enhances world evangelization.

---

[9] Among a vast quantity of missiological literature, only bits and pieces were found that dealt with a vision for the Two-Thirds World missionary movement. Only one such example will be mentioned here. Warren Webster (1976) wrote, "The home base is everywhere in mission in time and space." There were fewer than a dozen statements or paragraphs that were found on this theme, as we gleaned missiological literature dating back to the 1970s.

[10] See also Johnstone (2002, p. 895). He claims, "Since almost all of the countries have missionaries, as well as have sent out missionaries, mission is truly globalized."

Missiological Developments

The global perspective in doing missiology began to take shape quite late, in comparison to the globalization of the world evangelization force.[11] It is only in the mid-1990s that we find some literature dealing with a wider perspective, flickering out from the missiological circles.[12] However, the literature is still largely Western missiological scholarship extending their horizon beyond the West. Missiology is still being done from the West, which inevitably means a continuation of what has been going on for a century. This is certainly advancement in comparison to the pre-Lausanne era. Nevertheless, considering the fact that more than half of the world evangelization forces today are from the Two-Thirds World, coupled with the fact that two-thirds of the evangelicals/churches are in the Two-Thirds World, there is an urgent need for missiology to be truly global.

It is now up to the Two-Thirds World churches to fill in the gap, rather than mourning over the current situation. Fortunately, a number of international missionary conferences organized by the World Evangelical Alliance Missions Commission,[13] the Lausanne Committee for World Evangelization, and the AD 2000 and Beyond Movement have contributed towards establishing a forum where parties can hammer out some of the pertinent issues, so that missiological literature dealing with world evangelization will not be parochial.

Existence of the global church

As we have already seen in the historical outline above, we now have a global church as a result of globalization through world evangelization. This is a radically different situation from when the modern missionary movement began in the late 18th century. At that time, missions, in the spirit of "volunteerism," were engaging in world evangelization. There was only meagre support from the church at the outset of the modern missionary movement. Now, in the 21st century, the global church with a global missionary force is engaged in world evangelization. In order to highlight the implications of the global church for globalization by world evangelization, it is necessary to deal briefly with the development of the relationship between ecclesiology and world evangelization.

The ecumenical movement

The first sign of a systematic study of the subject of the church and world evangelization on a global level was at the International Missionary Council (IMC) conference in 1952 in Willingen, Germany. There, delegates took a fresh look at who the major players were in world evangelization, and they focused on the church as the major player. The

---

[11] Dana Robert (2000) sees the shift of Christianity as having begun as early as 1945. See also Robert (2002).

[12] See, for example, Pittman, Habito, and Muck (1996) and Verstraelen (1995).

[13] Taylor (2000) is one of the typical examples of both the West and the Two-Thirds World working together to produce a globalized missiology. See also O'Donnell (2002).

conference did not stop there but went further "upstream" and found God as the initiator, the motivator, and the sustainer of the world evangelization effort. The study culminated at the 1961 New Delhi World Council of Churches (WCC) General Assembly. It was there that delegates took the step to combine the WCC with the IMC, in accordance with their conviction about the missionary nature of the church.

Unfortunately, just when the church was about to recover its rightful place, it quickly lost its role in world evangelization again. At that time, people such as J. Hoekendijk were emphasizing the theology of the apostolate. As a result, the church was soon forced to take a back seat as the theology of the church was replaced by the theology of the apostolate.[14]

The theology of the church in ecumenical circles has now become very vague, following Hoekendijk's argument that the locus of world evangelization is no longer the church but the world. Slowly, the theology of world evangelization has become captive to secularism, and the church has given her place to the kingdom of God on earth. There has been an inversion of the original order of God, the church, and the world in doing missions. The new order is God, the world, and then the church (Bosch, 1980, pp. 176-177). The church has become expendable in this scheme, contrary to what the Bible says about the place of the church in world evangelization. Now the church must look into the world in order to find out what God is doing. This was coined as Missio Dei (Bosch, 1980, pp. 189-190).

The evangelical missionary movement

When we look at the evangelical Protestant missionary movement, it is not much more encouraging. First, among Protestant circles, the church became prominent through the "three-self" indigenous church movement during the 19th and early 20th centuries. It again received attention through the church growth movement in the 1970s and 1980s. However, emphasis was usually placed on indigenization or numerical growth in the receiving countries, rather than on the Two-Thirds World churches actively engaging in world evangelization.

Second, there was a struggle over definitions, even among evangelicals who have been in the process of formulating a theology of world evangelization for the last 30 years. In the process, the kingdom of God received more attention than the church in some circles. In the AD 2000 and Beyond movement, it seemed as though there was a reversal of this trend. However, the emphasis of the church was narrowed down to planting churches for unreached people groups, rather than going to the core of the theology of the church in a global context and its implications for world evangelization.

---

[14] After the 1947 Whitby IMC conference, Dutch missiology opened the door to the "apostolate theology," which emphasized mission above church. Hoekendijk had enormous influence in leading the ecumenical community in this direction. For him, church was a "function," while mission was the essence. He believed that in due time, the church becomes a bystander, while mission becomes Missio Dei, "a universal humanization process." See Bosch (1980, pp. 176-180) and Scherer (1987, pp. 96-97).

In the global church era, we need to take a fresh look at the relationship between world evangelization and the global church. We need to examine this area theologically for two reasons. First, existentially we now have a global church that can engage in world evangelization. When the modern missionary movement began in the 18th century, there were no evangelical churches other than the Western churches. It is one thing to ignore the role of the church at a time when Christians had not yet awakened to the fact that the Great Commission was issued to the church. It is another thing to ignore the role of the global church in world evangelization when so much has now been written about the missionary nature of the church. The global church must have a greater role in world evangelization.

Second, Shenk (1996) contends:

Two centuries of worldwide missionary exertions sponsored by Western churches largely failed to effect a fundamental reorientation in their ecclesial consciousness.... What happened 'out there' was missions; what happened in the West was church.... Christendom assumptions and habits of mind furnished the conceptual framework even among those with an experience of global mission.

This trend continues to permeate missiological studies done by the West, while the missiologizing of the church in the Two-Thirds World is left undone. This is a great loss for the cause of world evangelization.

Meanwhile, the Two-Thirds World church has a unique opportunity to look at the Bible afresh, without the Western perspective on the relationship between missions and the church which has dominated missiology for the last century. It can now begin to missiologize the global church.

We face an unprecedented era in this 21st century, when the global church with a global missionary movement from both the West and the Two-Thirds World can move ahead in world evangelization. The world has certainly become much more complex and hazardous. But when we consider movements such as "Back to Jerusalem" by the coalition of the seven house church movements in China to send 100,000 missionaries,[15] and many more innovative efforts like this, even the recent setbacks in the Muslim sectors by Western missionary efforts seem insignificant. We must not give up our vision for globalization through world evangelization.

Global strategy of mission

Prior to the globalization of mission through world evangelization, strategizing for mission was mainly done by Western missiologists and mission organizations. The tide turned much ear-

---

[15] This information comes from a personal interview with Paul Haddaway on June 6, 2000. He has done extensive research on people groups in China and Southeast Asia for a number of years. He said 100,000 missionaries are merely a tithe of 100 million Chinese Christians.

lier for the ecumenical camp[16] and much later for the evangelicals. The 1974 International Congress on World Evangelization was a watershed for evangelicals. Since then, a number of global-level missionary consultations have been sponsored by global bodies, such as the Lausanne Committee for World Evangelization, the World Evangelical Alliance Missions Commission, and the AD 2000 and Beyond Movement, to formulate global strategies on world evangelization.[17]

For the ecumenical movement, the concept of partnership between the West and the non-Western world existed as early as the 1947 Whitby IMC conference. Evangelicals popularized the same concept only in the early 1990s. In the 1952 Willingen IMC conference, ecumenicals adopted the notion of the whole world being the mission field. As far as the evangelicals were concerned, it was at Lausanne II held in Manila in 1989 that "the whole world" began to be considered as the mission field. Ecumenicals, on the other hand, had already made this decision in 1961 at the World Council of Churches meeting in New Delhi, where

"the churches of the Third World began to play a dominant role in world mission so that the trend of Willingen and Ghana was reinforced" (see Wind, 1995). It was not until the 1970s that evangelical missiologists became aware of the Two-Thirds World mission, let alone joint strategizing in world evangelization.

As recently as the end of the 20th century, strategizing has been done mostly by the West, in particular by North Americans, except through occasional global consultations on world evangelization. This trend must be changed in order to keep in step with the globalization of the missionary force. In numerous consultations on strategy of world evangelization, there are inevitably voices from the Two-Thirds World. In addition, more and more strategizing done by the Two-Thirds World missionaries and churches fills the vacuum left by the West.

The global missionary movement

As has been already alluded to, long gone are the days of all missionaries coming from Western countries. It is no

---

[16] See Scherer (1987, pp. 94-95). Already by 1921, the International Missionary Council (IMC) was formed. Although the West dominated the IMC until World War II, the framework was established for the global task. Thus, by the 1947 Whitby IMC conference, participants were able to say that the foundation for future cooperation between the West and the Two-Thirds World had been laid. "In a remarkable way, Whitby anticipated almost every positive development in later ecumenical mission policy, including reevangelization and 'six-continent mission.'"

[17] While there was the World Congress on Evangelism held in Berlin in 1966, the 1974 Lausanne International Congress on World Evangelization was unique in that it was a working congress attended by wider constituencies from both the West and the Two-Thirds World. It marked the beginning of the global strategizing of world evangelization. Numerous global congresses and consultations on world evangelization have followed since then. Examples include GCOWE 95 in Seoul, GCOWE 97 in South Africa (AD 2000), the 1989 International Consultation on Missionary Training in Manila, and the 1994 Consultation on Interdependent Partnership in Manila (WEA Missions Commission).

longer strange to see non-Western missionaries on the field. In fact, in almost every mission field today there are missionaries from the Two-Thirds World. For example, the Korean church sends out missionaries to more than 162 countries (see Moon, 2001, p. 4). Not all of the Two-Thirds World sending countries have the same degree of mobility as the West. The Indian church sends more than 95% of their missionaries to different cultural groups within their own country. Less than 5% of their missionaries are sent to other countries. Nevertheless, they are filling in the gap that has been created by the visa restrictions set by their own government.

When we think of the Chinese church with more than 100 million members, we can truly anticipate world evangelization to be completed sooner than we thought, as the missionaries from that church fill the globe one day. There are also Latin American churches, African churches, European churches, and North American churches, if the Lord sends his Spirit to revive them again. The Lord admonished the disciples, "The harvest is plentiful but the workers are few. Ask the Lord of the harvest, therefore, to send out workers into his harvest field" (Matt. 9:37-38). We too must obey this command.

Global missiology

As has been suggested, there is a great need for formulating global missiology in the true sense of the word, since there is now a global missionary community. Mission literature such as *Global Missiology for the 21st Century: The Iguassu Dialogue* (Taylor, 2000) is a good example. Nevertheless, it is only the beginning of the task. In order for missiology to become truly global and thus affect world evangelization, there must be more active participation from the church and missionary community of the Two-Thirds World. Here is an excerpt from *Global Missiology*, concerning what one "think tank" has suggested for the future direction of the new missiology:

There is now a need for a new missiology to fit a new global context. The global missionary community needs to produce this new missiology. A remodeling of old missiology will not meet the needs of the ever-changing world in which we live. On the other hand, this resource team recognized the value of continuity and the regard for work completed in the past (Brynjolfson, 2000, pp. 487-488).

There must be a "creative tension" between "globality" and "contextuality" in relation to the different cultures that the gospel encounters. The concept of "glocalization" captures this sentiment well. Also, "missiology must be praxis-driven." In order for this to happen, missiology must strip off some of the older remnants of Western dichotomist thinking and strive for biblical wholeness. Finally, "missiology must be inclusive." For example, it must do justice to both "gender differences" and the generation gap (Brynjolfson, 2000, pp. 487-488).

We are grateful for the breakthrough in formulating global missiology that will further enrich the world evangelization efforts by both the West and the Two-Thirds World church. At the same time, we must admit that missiology by and large is still a Western construct that is extending its sphere to the global context. It is still burdened with a presupposition that missiological theories and strategies are mostly universals that fit all situations. It is still shackled with an older paradigm of world evangelization, in which Western Christendom moves out to a non-Christian world.

It is time for us to realize that there is no border in world evangelization. A brand new context has dawned upon us. What kind of missiology will reflect this trend? For one thing, it will not be the conventional missiology that has dominated the field for the last century. It has to be worked at from many angles. There must be a global outlook; there will be a need to approach missiology from the level of the grassroots. Global team efforts must continue to make their impact. But what that team will consist of and how it will operate must change continually to suit the context.

Equally important is the need for local churches to make a greater impact on world evangelization. This was largely left out of Western missiology, since churches were non-existent in the mission field when the modern missionary movement began. The scene has changed greatly since then. There is now a global church. Globalized missiology must include this aspect in the future missiologizing process. In this regard, globalization, world evangelization, and global missiologizing will continue to interplay in this global age.

We have examined the dynamics behind globalization and world evangelization through examining some of the key selective themes in missiology. We now need to take a final look at cultural interplays in globalization by world evangelization.

Cultural Implications

Effects of globalization on world evangelization

Discussion here will be limited to how a globalizing culture affects world evangelization, since other writers have already dealt with different aspects of culture. Globalization of culture has deep implications for world evangelization. When we go back to the world of the New Testament, for example, we can see that the globalization of Graeco-Roman culture was advantageous for the missionaries of that region. They did not have to spend time learning the language and culture. They were able to assemble into a mobile team and move in and out without delay. Homogeneity of the culture created an amiable contact point for the gospel, so that communicators could make the message relevant and understandable. This is not to imply that there was no further need for contextualization. We witness in Paul's message to the people of Athens in the book of Acts that he did contextualize his message according to his understanding of the Athenians, in spite of the facts that they all lived in the Roman world and spoke the Greek language, with Hellenism as their basic cultural make-up. There were certainly not many cultural barriers between the missionary team and the Jews of the Diaspora who had been spread throughout the known world. Thus we see that in spite of its disadvantages, globalization of culture has some advantages in terms of world evangelization.

On the other hand, the constant persecution of Christians by the global power of the time (the Romans) was no small matter. We can carry this dynamic over to the modern world. For example, colonialism is one kind of globalizing phenomenon. At first glance, colonization seems to have helped the progress of world evangelization, since it provided missionaries from colonizing countries with free access to the mission field. However, when we accumulate all of the evidence of resistance to the gospel that has resulted from the colonial period of the West, we must conclude that colonization was abhorrent.

The current trend of globalization is no less complicated when it comes to evaluating its worth in world evangelization. Travel, communication, greater degrees of common ground in communication, faster flow of information, and the greater degree of shared culture—these are all advantageous for world evangelization. At the same time, the Westernizing effect of globalization has presented the global church with unprecedented obstacles in many parts of the world. More recently, the interplay between globalization and Jihad makes it more and more difficult for Western missionaries to take part in world evangelization—especially in the Muslim world.

The problem is that like all of the preceding efforts of globalization, we can neither ignore nor stop the trend. As with modernization, if we ignore globalization we will be left lagging behind the changes that are taking place, thus losing the crowd that rides the crest of the wave. The situation is like throwing out the baby with the bath water. We have no choice but to ride the crest of globalization, but we must do it with critical mind and action. We must beat the secular globalization wave and usher in our own form of globalization by world evangelization through global missionary teams and the global church.

Effects of localization

The global Christian community cannot accept globalization efforts that do not respect local cultures. It is one thing to utilize globalization trends in world evangelization. It is another thing to be active in ushering in the modern secular concept of globalization. We have to guard against the homogenizing effects of the global culture. On the contrary, we need to seek local forms of missiology, the church, and Christian lifestyle, as well as their globalized expressions. Otherwise, our efforts will inevitably make the message and messenger foreign. In some cases, we could initiate a cultural change that is unfavorable to the people that we are trying to evangelize, without being aware of doing so. In other cases, we might find that people prefer the forms of foreign cultures introduced by missionaries, whether they are from the West or the Two-Thirds World, over the local forms. This can be equally counterproductive.

There will be continuous interplay between the global and the local—in this case, between the global church and the local churches. There will be constant flow of influence both ways—from local forms of Christianity to the global church, but probably more from the global to the local. Thus there will be lively interplay, and these interactions will make up the whole of the global body. This is what we call "glocalization." When we talk about globalization through world evangelization, it is more of "glocalization" than globalization as homogenization per se.[18]

We get a glimpse of this global/local interplay in the book of Revelation. The Apostle John describes it as follows:

> After this I looked and there before me was a great multitude that no one could count, from every nation, tribe, people and language, standing before the throne and in front of the Lamb. They were wearing white robes and were holding palm branches in their hands. And they cried out in a loud voice: "Salvation belongs to our God, who sits on the throne, and the Lamb" (Rev. 7:9-10).

The scene has global objects, such as the people of God, the throne, the Lamb, our God, and the common worship. There are also local objects such as nations, tribes, and languages. This is our model of true globalization as we participate in world evangelization.

Conclusion

As it was in the New Testament times and subsequently in the Middle Ages (particularly through the religious/political powers of the Roman Catholic Church), later in the colonial times, and more recently through modernization, globalization has proceeded as an apparently inevitable phenomenon. Globalization has at times enhanced world evangelization; at other times, it has brought more harm than good.

Globalization did not come only in secular forms. It also affected global Christianity through world evangelization. For one thing, it ushered in the global missionary movement and the global church as a new globalizing force. Both the West and the Two-Thirds World now make up the global missionary community. Moreover, there are now churches all over the globe. This is probably the greatest gain since the beginning of the modern missionary movement, as some believe that "in no time in the history of missions have more than 1% of the nationals been won to the Lord by missionaries."[19] As our missiology begins to missiologize the global church, world evangelization will speed up even more.

In this regard, globalization has enriched the global mission community and has had significant effect on world evangelization. It is for this reason and many more that we cannot ignore the impacts of globalization on world evangelization. As with modernity, if we ignore globalization, we will have to pay the consequences. But we dare not accept or follow it blindly. We need to pay close attention to the interplay between globalization and world evangelization and strive towards globalization on our own terms through world evangelization.

---

[18] See Robert (2000, p. 56). She has a helpful discussion on the interplay of "global" and "local."

[19] Lamin Sanneh mentioned this in a lecture at Trinity International University.

References

Barrett, D. B. (2000). Evangelization, measurement of. In A. S. Moreau (Ed.), *Evangelical dictionary of world missions* (pp. 346-347). Grand Rapids, MI: Baker.

Bosch, D. J. (1980). *Witness to the world: The Christian mission in theological perspective.* Atlanta, GA: John Knox Press.

Brynjolfson, R. (2000). From synthesis to synergy: The Iguassu think tanks. In W. D. Taylor (Ed.), *Global missiology for the 21st century: The Iguassu dialogue* (pp. 477-488). Grand Rapids, MI: Baker Academic.

Goudzwaard, B. (2001). *Globalization and the kingdom of God.* Grand Rapids, MI: Baker.

Hunsberger, G. R., & Van Gelder, C. (1996). *The church between gospel and culture: The emerging mission in North America.* Grand Rapids, MI: Wm. B. Eerdmans.

Johnstone, P. J. (1998). *The church is bigger than you think: Structures and strategies for the church in the 21st century.* Pasadena, CA: William Carey Library.

Johnstone, P. J., et al. (2002). *Operation world* (21st century Korean ed.). Seoul, Korea: Joy.

Kaiser, W. C., Jr. (1999). Israel's missionary call. In R. D. Winter & S. C. Hawthorne (Eds.), *Perspectives on the world Christian movement: A reader* (pp. 10-16). Pasadena, CA: William Carey Library.

Luzbetak, L. J. (1996). *The church and cultures.* Maryknoll, NY: Orbis Books.

Moon, S. S. C. (2001, October 1-5). *The Acs of Koreans: A research report on the Korean missionary movement.* Paper presented at the Global Congress on Church Ministry and Mission, Seoul, Korea.

Moreau, A. S. (2000). Mission and missions. In A. S. Moreau (Ed.), *Evangelical dictionary of world missions* (pp. 636-638). Grand Rapids, MI: Baker.

Newbigin, L. (1986). *Foolishness to the Greeks: The gospel and Western culture.* Grand Rapids, MI: Wm. B. Eerdmans.

O'Donnell, K. (Ed.). (2002). *Doing member care well: Perspectives and practices from around the world.* Pasadena, CA: William Carey Library.

Pate, L. D. (1991, April). The changing balance in global mission. *International Bulletin of Missionary Research, 15*(2), pp. 56-61.

Pittman, D. A., Habito, R. L. F., & Muck, T. C. (Eds.). (1996). *Ministry and theology in global perspective: Contemporary challenges for the church.* Grand Rapids, MI: Wm. B. Eerdmans.

Robert, D. L. (2000, April). Shifting southward: Global Christianity since 1945. *International Bulletin of Missionary Research, 24*(2), pp. 50-58.

———. (2002, April). The first globalization: The internationalization of the Protestant missionary movement between the world wars. *International Bulletin of Missionary Research, 26*(2), pp. 50-66.

Sanneh, L. (1989). *Translating the message: The missionary impact on culture.* Maryknoll, NY: Orbis Books.

Scherer, J. A. (1987). *Gospel, church, and kingdom: Comparative studies in world mission theology.* Minneapolis, MN: Augsburg Publishing House.

Shenk, W. R. (1996). The culture of modernity as a missionary challenge. In G. R. Hunsberger & C. Van Gelder (Eds.), *The church between gospel and culture: The emerging mission in North America* (pp. 69-78). Grand Rapids, MI: Wm. B. Eerdmans.

Skillen, J. W. (2001). Foreword. In B. Goudzwaard, *Globalization and the kingdom of God* (pp. 8-9). Grand Rapids, MI: Baker.

Taylor, W. D. (Ed.). (2000). *Global missiology for the 21st century: The Iguassu dialogue.* Grand Rapids, MI: Baker Academic.

Verstraelen, F. J. (Gen. Ed.). (1995). *Missiology: An ecumenical introduction: texts and contexts of global Christianity.* Grand Rapids, MI: Wm. B. Eerdmans.

Webster, W. (1976). In A. F. Glasser et al. (Eds.), *Crucial dimensions in world evangelization* (pp. 257-272). Pasadena, CA: William Carey Library.

Wind, A. (1995). The Protestant missionary movement from 1789 to 1963. In F. J. Verstraelen (Gen. Ed.), *Missiology: An ecumenical introduction: texts and contexts of global Christianity* (pp. 251-252). Grand Rapids, MI: Wm. B. Eerdmans.

Winter, R. D. (1999). The kingdom strikes back: Ten epochs of redemptive history. In R. D. Winter & S. C. Hawthorne (Eds.), *Perspectives on the world Christian movement: A reader* (pp. 200-210). Pasadena, CA: William Carey Library.

David Tai-Woong Lee serves as the chairman of the board of directors of Global Missionary Fellowship, as the director of the Global Missionary Training Center, and as a member of the Global Leadership Team of the World Evangelical Alliance Missions Commission. His wife, Hun-Bock (Song) Lee, teaches Family Life at GMTC, and they have two sons, Young-Min and Kyoung-Min. David has received both M.Div. and D.Miss. degrees from Trinity International University in Deerfield, Illionis. He has authored **Korean Missions: Theory and Practice** *and* **Training Disciples This Way**. *He has also written numerous articles that have been published both nationally and internationally. Email: dtwlee@kornet.net.*

Steve Moon *completed a Ph.D. in intercultural studies at Trinity Evangelical Divinity School. He and his wife, Mary, have served with Korea Research Institute for Missions in Seoul, South Korea, since 1990 (as executive director since 1998). Steve also teaches missions at Hapdong Theological Seminary in Suwon, South Korea. Steve and Mary are parents of two teenagers, Lottie and Chris. Email: ssmoon@hananet.net.*

Index